STUDIES IN CHRISTIAN HISTORY AND THOUGHT

Eschatology and Pain in St. Gregory the Great

The Christological Synthesis of Gregory's
Morals on the Book of Job

STUDIES IN CHRISTIAN HISTORY AND THOUGHT

Eschatology and Pain in St. Gregory the Great

The Christological Synthesis of Gregory's *Morals on the Book of Job*

Kevin L. Hester

Paternoster:
thinking faith

Copyright © Kevin L. Hester 2007

First published 2007 by Paternoster

Paternoster is an imprint of Authentic Media
9 Holdom Avenue, Bletchley, Milton Keynes, MK1 1QR, UK
and
P.O. Box 1047, Waynesboro, GA 30830–2047, USA

13 12 11 10 09 08 07 7 6 5 4 3 2 1

British Library Cataloguing in Publication Data
A catalogue record for this book is available from the British Library

ISBN 978–1–84227–437–8

Typeset by the Author
Printed and bound in Great Britain
for Paternoster
by Nottingham Alpha Graphics

Series Preface

This series complements the specialist series of *Studies in Evangelical History and Thought* and *Studies in Baptist History and Thought* for which Paternoster is becoming increasingly well known by offering works that cover the wider field of Christian history and thought. It encompasses accounts of Christian witness at various periods, studies of individual Christians and movements, and works which concern the relations of church and society through history, and the history of Christian thought.

The series includes monographs, revised dissertations and theses, and collections of papers by individuals and groups. As well as 'free standing' volumes, works on particular running themes are being commissioned; authors will be engaged for these from around the world and from a variety of Christian traditions.

A high academic standard combined with lively writing will commend the volumes in this series both to scholars and to a wider readership.

Series Editors

To Leslie, whose indefatigable efforts and immeasurable sacrifice have taught me the true meaning of love and friendship.

Contents

PREFACE

Two major themes of Gregory the Great's *Moralia in Iob* are eschatology and the experience of pain. These themes are connected, related and reconciled in Gregory's Christology, especially through his image of Christ as judge. The goal of this work, after identifying and illustrating Gregory's theological understanding of eschatology and suffering as found in and limited by the text of the *Moralia*, is to show how the underlying principle supporting both these themes is his Christology.

It was Gregory's conviction that the world was coming swiftly to its end. Gregory uses his eschatology as a motivational factor in spiritual advancement. The coming judgment at the end of the world is the focal point of Gregory's eschatology and Christ stands at the center as the judge. The final judgment is the completion of the mercy and judgment of God begun in election, manifested in the incarnation and fulfilled in the last judgment. The end will be terrible for the world but it will prove to be a triumph for the Church when it joins him to judge the world.

The book of Job is the *locus classicus* of any discussion of theodicy. In the Moralia, Job becomes an important example of the experience of pain and the way in which pain could be used by God and by those experiencing it to promote their ascent to God. The pain experienced in this world participates in the final judgment because God only judges once. If Christians will contemplate the reason for their pain and inflict the pain of penance upon themselves they will forego the punishment of the judge on the last day.

Gregory's Christology provides the link between his themes of eschatology and pain because he understood pain as judgment and the pain of judgment has its roots in Christ who judged himself so that humanity might not be judged. Sin brought pain but this pain has been turned into redemption. Christ came and died to show humanity the Father. The Church, as his body, suffers to show the Father to the world. Its pain drives it ever deeper in the knowledge of the judge and ever higher in its contemplation of God.

Gregory's spirituality is that of a contemplative looking for Christ and finding him in the pain of this world. The coming judge who punishes is also the God who saves and he does so often through the very pain of human existence. Gregory's emphases of the experience of pain and eschatology found in his *Moralia in Iob* find their connection in his Christology. Gregory's Christ is always the suffering servant and always the just judge of the final reckoning; dealing out both mercy and justice throughout the course of salvation history. The threat of his return brings fear and joy, terror and exultation but the pain of this life will find its final solace in the contemplative union of the self-judged sinner and the inner judge of salvation. In this contemplative union with Christ the pain of this life will make sense and in the last judgment the great mystery of God's divine purpose will be revealed.

Acknowledgements

The author would like to express his thanks to so many family, friends, professors and colleagues without whose guidance and support this work would never have been completed. He is especially indebted to the following: to his parents Gilbert L. Hester, Patricia Colburn, his step-father Jim Colburn and his sister Amy Myers for having taught him that he could think for himself; to Professor F. Leroy Forlines who is responsible for his love of theology; to Fr. Kenneth Steinhauser whose service as his mentor has placed him in a debt greater than he can ever repay; to Fr. Wayne Hellmann and Fr. Frederick McLeod whose contributions sharpened his thought and focused his arguments; to his friends Dr. Chris Crain and Dr. Matthew Heckel for their prayers, support, jokes and gibes; to Dr. Anthony R. Cross for his publication and editorial assistance; and to Dr. Robin Parry, Mr. Jeremy Mudditt and Paternoster, for their decision to publish this little volume on Gregory. *Soli Deo Gloria.*

Kevin L. Hester
Free Will Baptist College
Nashville, Tennessee
August 2006

Abbreviations

CCSL   *Corpus Christianorum series Latina*

CSEL   *Corpus scriptorum ecclesiasticorum Latinorum*

MGH   *Monumenta Germaniae Historica*

NASB   *Holy Bible, New American Standard Translation*

PL   J. P. Migne, ed. *Patrologia cursus completus.* Series Latina

SC   *Sources chrétiennes*

CHAPTER 1

Introduction

Thesis Statement

Two major themes of Gregory the Great's *Moralia in Iob* are eschatology and the experience of pain. No study has yet identified the relationship between these themes. How are they connected? These themes are connected, related and reconciled in Gregory's Christology, especially through his image of Christ as judge. This image of the judge has both an eschatological exteriority and a contemplative interiority. As Christians wait for the imminent return of the judge in power and glory they must prepare themselves on the interior. The judge that will come on the last day is already presiding in the heart of each individual. The judge is active in their present lives through the pedagogical exercise of pain. Through this pain, Christ the judge drives them to interior contemplation and by divine flagellation he spurs them ever upward in the ascent of the soul. The goal of this work, after identifying and illustrating Gregory's theological understanding of eschatology and suffering as found in and limited by the text of the *Moralia*, is to show how the underlying principle supporting both these themes is his Christology. This will lead to a demonstration of not only how rich but also how pervasive is Gregory's operative Christology.

Eschatology is not the first theological concept that modern exegetes or theologians raise when they come to the text of the book of Job. Why and how is it that it is so prevalent in the mind of Gregory? It was Gregory's conviction, following Augustine, that Scripture held within its texts a seed of interpretation that would be manifested to later readers. This concept allowed Scripture to speak to individuals in all cultural, social and temporal contexts. Gregory's context was nothing, if not oppressive. Surrounded on all sides by death, disease, and the sword and stricken with his own peculiar illnesses, Gregory readily applied apocalyptic concepts of the eschaton to the passages he interpreted. When this exegetical formula was coupled with the older philosophical concept of the *senectus mundi* that had long since been appropriated by the Christian tradition in the West a rich expectation of the end was sure to result.

Gregory clearly believed that he was living in the last age and that Christ's return to judge the world was imminent. He understood that the signs of the end found in the Olivet Discourse had been fulfilled and were continuing to be fulfilled during his lifetime. This expectancy, focusing upon the image of the judge, became for Gregory a primary motivational factor in the spiritual life. Spiritual progression began with the fear of the terrible judge but it did not end there. This earthly life was for Gregory merely prolegomena for the eternal state. As Christians sojourned here they awaited not the end but the actual beginning of their true spiritual existence. The contemplation of God, for which humans were created, had been upset in the fall of humanity but it would once again become their chief focus in that eschatological moment of *apokatastasis* when Christ would reorder all creation and consummate his reign. At that time the mutability and pain of this earthly existence will give way to immutability, corruption will put on incorruption, and the pain of this earthly existence will be forgotten as Christ wipes the tears from the eyes of the faithful.

The emphasis placed upon the experience of pain in Gregory's work on the book of Job is much easier to understand. The book of Job is the *locus classicus* for any biblical discussion of theodicy. Pain was and continues to be a common enough experience. Job becomes an important example of not only the experience of pain itself but the way in which pain could be used by God and by the one experiencing it to promote the ascent to God. As Christians contemplate the reason for their pain they are struck by the sinfulness of their lives and the holiness of the coming judge. But as they recognize that the coming judge is also the giver of mercy they are drawn to him in greater love.

Pain is not a good in itself. It was not created by God but exists as a punishment for the fall. All pain is ultimately the product of sin, but God has chosen to convert the punishment of humanity into its cure. Pain is meant to be redemptive and to drive the sinner away from this world into the spiritual regions of the heart. It convicts sinners for sin and wipes out their transgressions if they return to God in repentance. It is also prohibitive in that the fear of the pain of judgment preserves the penitents in their contrition promoting the virtue of humility and eradicating the vice of pride. Finally, pain is revelatory because it allows the manifold graces of God to shine forth from the lives of the elect. Pain becomes for Gregory a divine pedagogical tool that promotes contemplation and the ascent of the soul to God.

Gregory interprets Job's suffering allegorically as prototypical of the suffering of Christ. Sin had entered the world through the first Adam and death and pain had come with it. In the death and pain of the God-man Jesus Christ death could no longer be victorious. Pain and death were still inescapable parts of this life but under the sovereignty of God, they could be used to further the kingdom. In fact, the Church, as the body of Christ, could expect nothing less than to experience the same sufferings as its Lord. In the imitation of Christ, the Church "fills up that which is lacking in the suffering of Christ".[1] Through its pain the Church becomes Christ in and Christ to the world.

The text of the *Moralia* is replete with references to interiority and exteriority. Gregory uses these concepts to outline the redemption of Christ and the application of this redemption in salvation. The ultimate interiority is God but he has been exteriorized in the incarnation of Christ. This movement calls for an inverse reaction in humanity. As Christ moved from the interior to the exterior in the incarnation, humans must move from the exterior to the interior in conversion. Both the experience of pain and the fear of the coming judge provoke this move toward interiority at conversion. As the converted begin to contemplate the interior, they enter into the presence of Christ the inner judge. They then set themselves up as judges to try, convict and sentence themselves in the inner recesses of their hearts. The judgment of the elect is linked to the judgment of Christ because in order to forego the pain of the last judgment, the elect inflict the pain of penitence upon themselves during this life.

In the following work I will seek to demonstrate that the underlying principles guiding and informing Gregory's theology of suffering and eschatology as found in his *Moralia in Iob* are rooted in his Christology and both of these are best understood in a Christological context. It is only by focusing in contemplation upon the image of Christ the judge and allowing the pain of this life to drive them to conversion and the spiritual ascent to God that Christians will find themselves prepared to meet the judge on the last day and find in him not an executor but a redeemer.

Gregory's Historical Context

The themes of pain and an anxious expectation of the return of Christ are more easily understood when one grasps the perilous nature of the times in which Gregory lived. The seeds for the theological thought underlying the *Moralia* were being sown even before Gregory's birth (c. 540 CE) and were nurtured to full health in the midst of political oppression and plague. In Gregory's own physical and emotional suffering the fruit ripened. His life was full of difficulty piled upon difficulty until he could say that he was well qualified to speak on the book of Job noting that it was due to divine providence that one so stricken should expound the life of the stricken Job.[2]

The emperor Justinian (527-65) began his ambitious plan for the reconquest of barbarian held lands in 533. The Vandals were the first to be rooted out of North Africa. The Goths, however, who had occupied Italy for almost a

---

[1] Colossians 1:24.

[2] Gregory the Great, *Ad Leandrum*, 5.

century, were much more difficult to defeat. Fighting in Italy was sporadic but ongoing from 530 until around 550 when the main Gothic force was finally defeated. Justinian issued his *Pragmatic Sanction* in 554 which claimed victory over the Goths and established imperial rule once again over Italy.

The peace was not to last. Almost on the heels of Justinian's victory a new threat arose. In 568 King Alboin[3] together with his Lombard forces invaded Italy. He quickly took control of most of northern Italy including Milan, the imperial capital, and the Po Valley. King Alboin either died or was killed in 572 and the election of a king was disbanded after 574. Instead, the Lombards organized themselves under the traditional family clans into duchies in the occupied territories. The dukes of Spoleto and Benevento soon became powerful forces which served as the center for most of the ongoing military expeditions in Italy.

The Lombards first besieged Rome in 579 under Farwald the duke of Spoleto. Although they were not successful in taking the city, Rome was under constant threat. After Gregory's accession to the see of St. Peter, Rome was again besieged by the Lombards in 593 and in 595. The Lombards had returned to the policy of electing a king in 584 when Ariulf was chosen and it was he who orchestrated many of these later excursions in and around Rome. Each time they were bought off with funds provided by the pope. The skirmishes and raids continued until the dawn of the seventh century when the death of King Authari saw the beginning of an uneasy peace in Italy.

A nation at war is a nation in turmoil but the problems of war were further exacerbated by economic disaster and a general breakdown of the central government. Perhaps breakdown is too strong a word for the administration of Rome and of Italy had already fallen into ruin with the wars of reconquest. The schools had been disbanded. The Senate ceased to function and there is no mention of the office of the Prefect of Rome, the very position which Gregory himself had held before his monastic conversion, after 599.[4] Military personnel took over the role of the civil government and the prefecture gave way to the exarchate. Famine, the wars of reconquest, and the Lombards had worsened the problem of depopulation in the agricultural centers, affecting both the wealthy land owners and the tenant farmers. More and more refugees poured into the cities, including Rome, which only made overcrowding, inflation, and the scarcity of goods more problematic.[5] In addition to this, the emperor in Constantinople rarely seems to have opened the purse to have provided any

---

[3] Also spelled as Albion.

[4] R.A. Markus, *Gregory the Great and His World* (Cambridge 1997), 9.

[5] For an excellent discussion of the economic difficulties and population problems of this period see Michel Rouche, "Grégoire le Grand face à la situation économique de son temps", in Jacques Fontaine *et al.* (eds), *Grégoire le Grand*, (hereafter *Grégoire*) (Paris 1986), 41-58; and R. Krautheimer, *Rome: Profile of a City, 312-1308* (Princeton 1980), especially 59-87.

kind of relief for the people of Italy.

The plague was also a major factor in the tumult of the period.[6] It swept through Italy in 543 and seemed to return in waves between approximately 10 and 20 years with other outbreaks occurring in the middle of the 560s and the early part of the 570s. Flooding between 589-591 and an ensuing drought seem to have contributed to another outbreak of the plague in 590 which was most likely the cause of pope Pelagius' death. Once again in 599 the plague returned during Gregory's pontificate. The unburied bodies together with the congestion of Rome could only have heightened the effects of the pandemic. It is extremely difficult to imagine or even to gauge the full extent of the devastation of this plague but estimates of the death toll have reached as high as approximately one-third of the population.[7]

Gregory's life was full of sundry problems; economic, civil and ecclesial. Even during his tenure as pope between 590 until his death in 604, during which time he was revising his *Moralia*, he found no rest from his troubles. He was burdened with the task of overseeing all the papal patrimonies as well as providing for the indigent population of Rome. He continued to work for reunion with the schismatic Istrian bishops and attempted to squash what he saw as the last vestiges of Donatism in North Africa. He was constantly under threat from the Lombards, sometimes buying them off and sometimes entering into treaties with them, with or without imperial approval. His associations with the emperor and his representatives were not always pleasant.[8] He was at odds with the Exarch of Ravenna on more than one occasion and had at least one fairly serious altercation with the Emperor Maurice.[9]

The seriousness of this situation coupled with Gregory's own infirmity helps to explain why Gregory felt such a work was needed and why he came to express his spirituality with such an emphasis upon suffering. Turmoil often breeds apocalypticism and the social and political upheaval of Gregory's time also enlightens his anxiety over the coming end of the world. Theologically, he weds these two concepts through his Christology. Christ the judge punishes sin even now with pain but he makes of this pain a divine cure for sin. He is also coming soon to judge all humans openly. Unless Christians seek out the judge

---

[6] For an especially graphic description by an eye-witness of the plague in Constantinople and a presentation of the symptoms brought on by the plague including coma, delirium, swelling, skin lesions, and the vomiting of blood see; Procopius, *De bello Persico*, 2.22-23.

[7] J.B. Bury, *History of the Later Roman Empire* (London 1923), vol. 2, 62.

[8] Gregory often bemoans the Lombard threat in his letters. See *Epistulae* 5.36; 39; and 44.

[9] Emperor Maurice had called Gregory "simple-minded" in a letter which was critical of his ongoing peace negotiations with the Lombard Duke Agilulf. Gregory complained that the Emperor had called him "foolish" (*fatuus*) when all he had sought was the good of his land while the Emperor, in contrast, stood by doing nothing. Gregory, *Epistulae.* 5.36. See also 5. 37; 39; 40; 42; and 45.

of the interior and condemn themselves before him they will be condemned by him on the last day. Gregory demonstrates in his *Moralia* a Christology informed by both his experience of pain and a keen eschatological expectation. Both the fear of the coming judge and the experience of pain are pedagogical tools used by God to promote a life of spiritual interiority and inner contemplation of God.

Gregory's Spiritual Theology

Gregory has long been seen as perhaps the most important hinge figure between late antiquity and the early medieval period. He passes on a wealth of earlier theological and exegetical tradition to a new era. His contributions are outlined in many fine sources; the best of which are the biographies on his life by F. Homes Dudden and Claude Dagens and the works on Gregory's thought by R.A. Markus and Carole Straw.[10]

Dudden's work, though dated, still retains much of its value despite its age. In fact, his two volume tome is still the touchstone for Gregorian studies. He sees Gregory as a great man of action and the primary figure through whom the medieval period found its connection to the fathers. Dudden says that Gregory was no great theologian but his gift was in understanding and expressing earlier ideas. In this way, he argues, Gregory gave a certain "tone" to theology that highlighted many images and concepts that would become more important as the medieval period progressed.[11]

The exact nature of this "tone" has been the subject of a great deal of debate in Gregorian studies.[12] Carole Straw has argued that the tone offered by

---

[10] F. Homes Dudden, *Gregory the Great: His Place in History and Thought*, 2 vols. (London 1905). Claude Dagens, *Saint Grégoire le Grand: culture et expérience chrétiennes* (Paris 1977). R.A. Markus, *Gregory the Great and His World* (Cambridge 1997). Carole Straw, *Gregory the Great: Perfection in Imperfection* (Berkeley 1988).

[11] Dudden, *Gregory*, vol. 2, 286.

[12] Much of this debate has centered around what appears to be primarily a semantic argument over whether or not Gregory can be called a "theologian". Most of those who argue that he is not point to his lack of a critical method in exegesis, a lack of originality and a lack of theological speculation. See Dudden, *Gregory*, vol. 2, 286-292 and G.R. Evans, *The Thought of Gregory the Great* (Cambridge 1986), 152. Dudden was not the first nor perhaps the most important commentator on Gregory to have made this charge, see also Adolf von Harnack, *History of Dogma* (New York 1961), vol. 5, 62. Harnack argues that Gregory appealed to a declining civilization sunk in superstition and magic, and he created a crude work-religion. For a more nuanced opinion of Gregory on this topic see Pierre Boglioni, "Miracle et nature chez Grégoire le Grand," in *Cahiers d'études médiévales*, I: *Epopées, légendes et miracles* (Montréal 1974), 11-102. Jean Laporte has championed the cause of seeing Gregory as a theologian based upon his rich use of symbolism in exegesis and his thematic emphasis upon the nature of suffering in his works. He refuses to distinguish between Gregory's "spirituality" and his "theology". Jean Laporte, "Une théologie systématique chez Grégoire?" in Jacques

Gregory to theology is based in his systematic construction of an edifice upon which to organize his spiritual ideas.[13] Dagens' work *Grégoire le Grand* attempts to add nuance to the questions of Gregory's contribution. He seeks to examine the thought of Gregory through his writings and finds as a key to Gregory his distinctive monastic concept of the spiritual life. Gregory is said to have wed the theological thought of the fathers, especially that of Augustine, and the apologists with the ascetic movement's emphasis upon the spiritual life and contemplation. This advance in Gregory, according to Dagens, is not theological but spiritual. Gregory's spiritual direction as well as the theology which holds it, is multiform and multifaceted but one constant is the eschatological horizon of his spirituality. Dagens feels that Gregory's spirituality is driven by an "echo of a permanent anxiety, that of a world conscious of its own decline".[14] Gregory's work is not speculative but contemplative and his thought is monastic rather than systematic.[15]

Jean Laporte in his article "Une thélogie systématique chez Gregoire?" has argued that there are many different thematic and unitive factors in Gregory's theology. Laporte points out that Gregory's exegetical method enriches the symbolism of the text through developing and consistently presenting a theme in the *Moralia* which is also common to his other works; that of "suffering".[16] Suffering for Gregory becomes the basis for the knowledge of God. The images of suffering presented in the *Moralia* serve to develop his exegesis in ways which link Job to Christ, Job to the Church, and the Church to Christ. The unity of the common experience of pain is an outer indicator of the inner bond already present. This concept of "interiority", Laporte argues, is the "unifying principle par excellence".[17] Interiority is a concept which, in Gregory, drives all

---

Fontaine, Robert Gillet and Stan Pellistrandi (eds), *Grégoire le Grand* (Paris 1986), 235-254.

[13] Straw, *Gregory, Perfection* (Berkeley 1988), 6-7. She does agree however with Dudden's assertion that Gregory's thought is unoriginal.

[14] Dagens, *Grégoire*, 432. "L'écho d'une inquiétude permanente, qui est celle d'un monde conscient de son déclin."

[15] Dagens, *Grégoire*, 432. "Ce n'est pas l'intention spéculative: Grégoire n'a aucun goût pour les abstractions et il lui faut plutôt éclairer la foi des simples. Ce n'est pas davantage la polémique doctrinale: il n'a pas à combattre d'hérésies caractérisées et il se méfie des joutes oratoire."

[16] Jean Laporte, "Une théologie systématique?", 236. "Le thème de la souffrance prédomine, et, à partir des *Moralia*, semble rayonner sur toute l'oeuvre grégorienne et lui servir de base."

[17] Jean Laporte, "Une théologie systématique?", 236. "Il est une principe unificateur par excellence." Dagens refers to Gregory's concept of interiority as "un thème central de la doctrine spirituelle de Grégoire". Dagens, *Grégoire*, 136, esp. 135-204. See also on this concept, P. Aubin, "Intériorité et extériorité dans le *Moralia in Iob* de saint Grégoire le Grand," *Recherches de sciences religieuse* 62 (1974), 117-166; and Carole Straw, *Gregory, Perfection*, 28-65.

his further theology. Theological concepts are discussed from the basis of how they impact the spiritual life. In fact, this concept of interiority becomes the nexus from which Gregory expounds all his theological assertions. It is a wonderful example of a spiritually "lived theology". Dogma must be checked and rechecked; assimilated and evolved by constantly seeking out the spiritual ramifications of the doctrine to the spiritual life.

Gregory's role as pastor always manifests itself in a spirituality and a call for the people to a spirituality which is theologically developed in the images which Gregory uses in the work. Laporte seeks to establish the importance for the concept of interiority as a unitive force which links the theological concepts of theodicy, Christology, and the inner spirit of the human person.[18] Job becomes not just an image of the suffering person but of the suffering Christ. Christ's suffering becomes, anticipates, and participates in the suffering of his body the Church. The way in which these two images play back and forth serves to demonstrate that Gregory is working on both an allegorical and a moral exegetical principle at one and the same time.

Laporte argues that Gregory's theology is original not only in his development of several "themes" in his exegesis but also in the area of the problem of evil. Gregory builds an edifice whereby all the evil of the world may be seen as the *flagella Dei*. Although this concept is present in Clement of Alexandria, Origen, Chrysostom, Augustine, and Cassian Gregory adds to their understanding teachings on the spiritual value of evil.[19] The emphasis on interiority found in Gregory allows him to develop a "psychology" of pain which allows the sufferer to meditate upon the experience as an "act of love".[20]

The tone of Gregory's theology is his spirituality and it is a spirituality based upon the monastic tenet of contemplation. His exegesis, in the form of allegory allows him to make the identification between the suffering Job, the suffering Christ, and the suffering Church; and it is his insistence upon an "interior" reading that makes the evil of this life not something simply to be endured but something to be embraced. Gregory's spirituality calls all humans to see the *flagella Dei* not as punishment but as the love of a father scolding his children. "Let the elect be chastised with a passing affliction of the rod so that the strokes may reform them from their depravity, whom fatherly mercy keeps as an

---

[18] Laporte, "Une théologie systématique?", 236. "Le livre de Job fournit non seulement le thème de la souffrance purificatrice et expiatrice, et la christologie qui l'anime de l'intérieur, mais encore et tout d'abord, le cadre où cette théologie s'insère."

[19] For a discussion of these fathers of the Church and their contributions to Gregory's thought see, Jean Laporte, "Gregory the Great as a Theologian of Suffering," *The Patristic and Byzantine Review* 1 (1982), 22-29.

[20] Jean Laporte, "Une théologie systématique?", 239. "D'autres additions seront faites par la suite, que l'antiquité n'avait pas perçues, par exemple la valeur spirituelle de la souffrance dans son aspect psychologique, le sentir, comme acte d'amour."

inheritance."[21] In expounding the book of Job, Gregory finds a way to incorporate his own distinctiveness and to combine and connect two of his favorite themes of eschatology and suffering in his Christology; and his Christology is driven by his monastic understanding of contemplation which combines these themes in the interior of the human person before the inner judge.

A Brief Introduction to the *Moralia*

Sometime between 578-579 Gregory was called by either Pope Benedict I or Pope Pelagius II to serve the Roman church. He was ordained a regionary deacon and then sent by Pelagius II to Constantinople as *apokrisarius* or papal legate to the emperor in Constantinople. His purpose in this enterprise was to represent the pope before the emperor but especially to seek aid for Rome against the Lombard invaders; a task which, for the most part, proved unsuccessful. Gregory served in this capacity under the emperors Tiberius II and Maurice. While in Constantinople Gregory met and befriended Leander of Seville, John the Faster, patriarch of Constantinople, and Anastasius, ex-patriarch of Antioch.[22] It was also here in Constantinople that Gregory began the work that would become his *Moralia in Iob* as a series of sermons or lectures on the spiritual life which he delivered to a group of monks whom he had brought with him from his monastery dedicated to St. Andrew on the Coelian Hill at Rome.

This dates the beginning of the work to, during or shortly after 579. The work was however not completed until at least 595 when Gregory sent an early copy to his friend Leander of Seville, whom he had met in Constantinople.[23] The work must have been revised after this time because the final edition of 35 books in six volumes mentions the Augustinian mission to England.[24] Since this mission was not begun until 596 the date of completion for the final edition

---

[21] Gregory the Great, *Moralia*, 21.4.8. "Transitorio autem verbere affligantur electi, ut a pravitate flagella corrigant quos paterna pietas ad hereditatem servat."

[22] For more on the personal associations of Gregory in Constantinople see R.A. Markus, *Gregory the Great and His World* (Cambridge 1997), 11-12.

[23] Gregory the Great, *Ad Leandrum*, 2. Gregory details some of his editorial work on the *Moralia* in his dedicatory epistle to Leander. He tells us that the first parts of the book were written down as he expounded the work while the latter parts, owing to the fact that he had more time, were dictated. He then revised the earlier orally delivered portions and added to them. He mentions that he strove in the later dictated portion to maintain the style of the original oral material.

[24] P. Meyvaert has demonstrated the existence of some fragments from what appears to be an earlier version of the *Moralia*. P. Meyvaert, "Uncovering a Lost Work of Gregory the Great: Fragments of the Commentary on Job," *Traditio* 50 (1995), 55-74.

must necessarily fall sometime between 597 and Gregory's death in 604.[25]

Gregory the Great's *Moralia in Iob* takes the form of a commentary on the book of Job.[26] We would err however if we seek to find in the *Moralia* a "commentary" in any modern sense of the word. Perhaps we could best describe the work as a group of religious reflections surrounding the book of Job. We must always bear in mind the audience of the *Moralia*. Gregory himself comments on the importance of always keeping in mind the spiritual benefit of the hearers.

> But yet whosoever is speaking concerning God, must be careful to search out thoroughly whatsoever furnishes moral instruction to his hearers; and should account that to be the right method of ordering his discourse, if, when opportunity for edification requires it he turn aside for a useful purpose from what he had begun to speak of; for he that treats of sacred writ should follow the way of a river, for if a river, as it flows along its channel meets with open valleys on its side, into these it immediately turns the course of its current, and when they are copiously supplied, presently it pours itself back into its bed. Thus unquestionably, should it be with every one that treats of the divine Word, that if, in discussing any subject, he chance to find at hand any occasion of seasonable edification, he should, as it were, force the streams of discourse towards the adjacent valley, and, when he has poured forth enough upon its level of instruction, fall back into the channel of discourse which he had proposed.[27]

Gregory does not appear to have been overly interested in either technical questions of exegesis or a critical evaluation of the text of the book of Job. Although he does spend a bit of time discussing the authorship of the work, this is as abstract as he gets and everything else serves as a spiritual reflection on

---

[25] For the dating of the *Moralia* see Carole Straw, *Gregory the Great*, vol. 4, *Authors of the Middle Ages*, ed. Patrick J. Geary, no. 12 (Brookfield 1996), 49-50.

[26] For a good introduction to the text of the *Moralia* see Robert Gillet, "Introduction," in *Grégoire le grand: Morales sur Job*, Sources Chrétiennes no. 32 (Paris 1975), 1-113.

[27] Gregory the Great, *Ad Leandrum*, 2. "Sed tamen quisquis de Deo loquitur, curet necesse est, ut quicquid audientium mores instruit rimetur, et hunc rectum loquendi ordinem deputet, si, cum opportunitas aedificationis exigit, ab eo se, quod loqui coeperat, utiliter derivet. Sacri enim tractator eloquii morem fluminis debet imitari. Fluvius quippe dum per alveum defluit, si valles concavas ex latere contingit, in eas protinus sui impetus cursum divertit, cumque illas sufficienter impleverit, repente sese in alveum refundit. Sic nimirum, sic divini verbi esse tractator debet, ut, cum de qualibet re disserit, si fortasse iuxta positam occasionem congruae aedificationis invenerit, quasi ad vicinam vallem linguae undas intorqueat et, cum subiunctae instructionis campum sufficienter infuderit, ad sermonis propositi alveum recurrat." All English translations of the *Moralia* and of its dedicatory epistle to Leander (*Ad Leandrum*) are taken from *Morals on the Book of Job, by S. Gregory the Great*, vols. 18, 21, 23, *A Library of Fathers of the Holy Catholic Church*, 46 vols., translated by Members of the English Church (Oxford 1838-85). The Latin text is taken from Marci Adriaen, ed. *S. Gregorii Magni: Moralia in Iob*, vols. 143, 143A, 143B, *CCSL* (Turnhout 1979-85).

the text itself. His exegesis has no real literary analysis or systematic exposition.[28] Instead, we find a "psychological" reflection on the spiritual life and Gregory gets from the text to his moral exposition through allegorical exegesis. It is to this that we now turn.

Gregory's Exegesis in the *Moralia*

Gregory's respect for the Scriptures has no bounds. He sees them as the source of all knowledge and truth. The discovery of this truth is greater than all other knowledge and is meant not only for the advanced but also for the simple. Scripture is like a river that is "both shallow and deep, wherein both the lamb may find a footing, and the elephant float at large".[29] As it was written with all sorts of people in mind it naturally bears more than one meaning and can exercise both the simple in its historical sense and the advanced by its allegorical and moral senses. Holy Scripture is:

> superior to every form of knowledge and science. It preaches the truth and calls us to the heavenly fatherland; it turns the heart of the reader from earthly to heavenly desires; it exercises the strong by its obscurer sayings and attracts the little ones by its simple language; it is neither so closed to view as to inspire fear, nor so open as to be despised, but familiarity with it removes distaste for it, and the more it is studied the more it is loved; it helps the reader's mind by simple words and raises it by heavenly meanings; it grows, if one may so speak, with its readers, for the ignorant find therein what they already know, and the learned find therein something always new. I say nothing of this however. I do not dwell on the importance of the subject matter. But I do say that Holy Scripture is superior to every form of knowledge and science even in the very manner of its speech. For with one and the same word it at once narrates a fact and sets forth a mystery. It can speak of the past, and, in so doing, predict the future. And, without any change of language, it can both describe what has been done, and in the selfsame words declare what is to be done.[30]

---

[28] R. Gillet, "Introduction," 11-13.

[29] Gregory the Great, *Ad Leandrum*, 4. "...planus et altus, in quo et agnus ambulet et elephas natet."

[30] Gregory the Great, *Moralia*, 20.1.1. "Quamvis omnem scientiam atque doctrinam scriptura sacra sine aliqua comparatione transcendat, ut taceam quod vera praedicat, quod ad caelestem patriam vocat; quod a terrenis desideriis ad superna amplectenda cor legentis immutat; quod dictis obscurioribus exercet fortes et parvulis humili sermone blanditur, quod nec sic clause est ut pavesci debeat, nec sic patet ut vilescat, quod usu fastidium tollit, et tanto amplius diligitur quanto amplius meditatur; quod legentis animum humilibus verbis adiuvat, sublimibus sensibus levat, quod aliquo modo cum legentibus crescit, quod a rudibus lectoribus quasi recognoscitur, et tamen doctis semper nova reperitur; ut ergo de rerum pondere taceam, scientias tamen omnes atque doctrinas ipso etiam locutionis suae more transcendit, quia uno eodemque sermone dum narrat textum, prodit mysterium, et sic scit praeterita dicer, ut eo ipso noverit futura praedicare,

Gregory declares that he will expound the text on three levels: the historical, the allegorical, and the moral.[31] He explains that each of the verses will not be expounded in this way. Some will be examined only as to the historical sense, others in the allegorical and others in the moral; whereas some would be treated in more than one fashion and some even in all three.[32] In the first part of the work he is more consistent in actually discussing all three of the meanings but this quickly fades into the background and more and more we see that the moral exegesis of the text is actually what will become the primary aspect of the work.

The audience of the *Moralia* gives us an understanding as to why the work proceeds in this way. The monks were interested above all in the advance of the soul to God and this is what they demanded from Gregory; that he would "investigate the allegorical sense not only through the literal word but to also incline the allegorical sense immediately in the exercise of morality and also (another grave burden) to strengthen the various meanings with texts, and that these texts, if they seemed complicated, to unravel through additional explanation".[33] The monks were desirous of this meaning above all and Gregory, with his pastoral heart could only oblige them.

Grover A. Zinn has spoken of this pastoral emphasis of Gregory as the "setting" for the jewels of his exegesis.[34] Certainly there is a dynamic quality to Gregory's textual interpretation. The focus of the work as a whole helps us to understand why and how Gregory proceeds in his exegesis as he does. Questions about the legitimacy of his interpretive method are softened, or perhaps at least better understood, when we hold the interpretation of a given passage in tension with the purpose of Gregory in writing. Zinn notes that Gregory's exegesis is performed in service of the spiritual quest for God.[35] Gregory seeks these jewels under the guidance of the Holy Spirit and then shares his bounty with his hearers. The uniqueness of the jewel is formed against reference points of the contemplation of God and the needs of the hearers but most of all by the field in which the jewel is found. This field is of

---

et non immutato dicendi ordine, eisdem ipsis sermonibus novit et acta describere, et agenda nuntiare..."

[31] Gregory the Great, *Ad Leandrum*, 1.

[32] Gregory the Great, *Ad Leandrum*, 1.

[33] Gregory the Great, *Ad Leandrum*, 1. "Qui hoc quoque mihi in onere suae petitionis addiderunt, ut non solum verba historiae per allegoriarum sensus excuterem, sed allegoriarum sensus protinus in exercitium moralitatis inclinarem, adhuc aliquid gravius adiungentes, ut intellecta quaeque testimoniis cingerem et prolata testimonia, si implicita fortasse viderentur interpositione superadditae expositionis enodarem." Translation mine.

[34] Grover A. Zinn, Jr., "Exegesis and Spirituality in the Writings of Gregory the Great," in John C. Cavadini (ed.), Notre Dame Studies in Theology Series (Notre Dame 1995), 169.

[35] Zinn, "Exegesis and Spirituality", 168.

course, the whole of Scripture. In the *Moralia*, Gregory provides page after page of "witnesses". These witnesses are other snippets of Scripture used to illustrate, inform, and explain Gregory's particular interpretation of a given passage. Often Gregory will survey the various ways in which a word or group of words in Scripture has been interpreted. He will then choose one, or in some cases more, of the interpretations and apply it/them to the text at hand. The use of the whole of Scripture at once binds Gregory as an exegete to the whole of the inspired text and to the apostolic tradition of interpreting it. This practice in fact, far from providing a free reign for the exegete, actually restricts the potential domain of interpretations just as it colors them in light of the preceding textual tradition.

Although Gregory sees the importance of the historical meaning and sometimes seems to insist upon its primacy, he certainly feels that the allegorical interpretation and the moral interpretation are the deeper meanings.[36] In fact, in words reminiscent of Origen he claims that the literal meaning of the text is sometimes contradictory, either to good sense or to good theology, and this is an indicator that the reader or expositor should "look for something else in them".[37]

The significance of the various meanings is found in the illustration of a house or building which Gregory uses to discuss the different exegetical senses. He says, "now first we lay the foundation of the historical meaning, next we lift up the fabric of the mind in the citadel of faith by the signification of types and finally through the gift of the moral sense we decorate the building with added color".[38] Gregory then, at least as a concept, held to a three-fold interpretation of Scripture. The historical meaning dealt with the literal text and its meaning was, for the most part, apparent. The allegorical or typical meaning had reference to and was fulfilled primarily in the person and work of Christ. The moral meaning, which is often, in Gregory, difficult to disentangle from the allegorical, has reference either to the Church or to individuals within the Church. It is in this way that Job can serve as a "type of Christ, and, because of Christ, therefore also of the Church, the body of Christ, and of every individual Christian".[39] This concept as it applies to Job is based upon the observation that Gregory saw Christ as the subject of all Scripture and emphasized the mystical union of Christ and the Church.[40] Markus argues that in practice Gregory actually employs only a two-fold exegetical process which holds to a historical

---

[36] Gregory the Great, *Ad Leandrum*, esp. 4; and *Moralia*, 1.37.56; 20.27.56.

[37] Gregory the Great, *Ad Leandrum*, 3. "...aliud in se aliquid quod quaeratur ostendunt."

[38] Gregory the Great, *Ad Leandrum*, 3. "Nam primum quidem fundamenta historiae ponimus; deinde per significationem typicam in arcem fidei fabricam mentis erigimus; ad extremum quoque per moralitatis gratiam, quasi superducto aedificium colore vestimus." Translation mine.

[39] Dudden, *Gregory*, vol. 2, 306.

[40] Dudden, *Gregory*, vol. 2, 306.

and an allegorical meaning wherein the allegorical meaning could be applied typically to Christ or morally to the Church.[41] The distinction then is one in word only. The "allegorical" meanings are differentiated not in accordance to method, which is almost always identical, but according to the subject matter or application. The real dichotomy lay in the exterior and the interior meaning of Scripture; the exterior being the historical sense and the interior the allegorical.[42]

This allegorical exegesis allowed Gregory to move easily across time and salvation history from the suffering of Job to the suffering of Christ in redemption to the suffering of the Church in the days leading up to the second coming of Christ in judgment. By employing this exegetical methodology, Gregory was able to read the events of his own time in those of Job and this led him to a firm belief that he was living in the last days before the end of the world. From such exegesis Gregory developed a "lived eschatology" that was rooted in a contemplative spirituality. It is to his eschatology that we now turn.

---

[41] Markus, *Gregory*, 46. See also R. Manselli, "Gregorio Magno e la Bibbia" *Settimane* 10 (1963), 67-101.

[42] Markus, *Gregory*, 46.

CHAPTER 2

The Eschatology of the *Moralia*

Evangelical Eschatology Before Gregory

And as He was sitting on the Mount of Olives, the disciples came to Him privately, saying, "Tell us, when will these things be, and what will be the sign of Your coming, and of the end of the age?" And Jesus answered and said to them, "See to it that no one misleads you. For many will come in my name, saying 'I am the Christ,' and will mislead many. And you will be hearing of wars and rumors of wars; see that you are not frightened, for those things must take place, but that is not yet the end. For nation will rise against nation, and kingdom against kingdom, and in various places there will be famines and earthquakes. But all these things are merely the beginning of birth pangs. Then they will deliver you to tribulation, and will kill you, and you will be hated by all nations on account of my name. And at that time many will fall away and will deliver up one another and hate one another. And many false prophets will arise, and will mislead many. And because lawlessness is increased, most people's love will grow cold. But the one who endures to the end, he shall be saved. And this gospel of the kingdom shall be preached in the whole world for a witness to all nations, and then the end shall come.....But immediately after the tribulation of those days the sun will be darkened, and the moon will not give its light, and the stars will fall from the sky, and the powers of heaven will be shaken, and then the sign of the Son of Man will appear in the sky, and then all the tribes of the earth will mourn, and they will see the Son of Man coming on the clouds of the sky with power and great glory. And He will send forth His angels with a great trumpet and they will gather together His elect from the four winds, from one end of the sky to the other. Now learn the parable from the fig tree; when its branch has already become tender, and puts forth its leaves, you know that summer is near; even so you too, when you see all these things, recognize that He is near, right at the door. Truly I say to you, this generation will not pass away until all these things take place. Heaven and earth will pass away, but my words shall not pass away. But of that day and hour no one knows, not even the angels of heaven, nor the Son, but the Father alone. For the coming of the Son of Man will be just like the days of Noah. For as in those days which were before the flood they were eating and drinking, they were marrying and giving in marriage, until the day that Noah entered the ark, and they did not understand until the flood came and took them all away, so shall the coming of the Son of Man be."[1]

Gregory clearly believed that the end of the world was close at hand. This awareness fills his homilies, his letters and his writings. His ideas regarding the end must not be taken out of the context in which they developed. Gregory develops earlier Christian ideas of the end as well as rehearses older theological themes in his own eschatology. The eschatological themes of apocalypse and the triumph of the Church had arisen much earlier. Based largely upon the above selection known as the Olivet Discourse and found in the Gospels, the evangelical authors and early exegetes set a precedent for reading the events around them as signs of the coming end of the world. Gregory is doing nothing new by interpreting the events of his milieu as "signs of the end". What makes Gregory's contribution so unique is the way in which his eschatology became a lived reality which called for a spiritual response from him and the people. Such applications were in line with the tradition of his forebearers but Gregory goes beyond them in his spiritual reflection upon such texts.[2] In order to fully understand Gregory's context we must look more closely at evangelical eschatology before his time.

Eschatology, and specifically the timing of the end, was a topic that had engaged Christians since the beginning. Certainly the early Christians expected Christ's return in power and glory to be imminent. Such is the witness of the Olivet Discourse in the synoptic Gospels (Matthew 24-25, Mark 13 and Luke 21). This discourse, placed in the mouth of Jesus, outlines the way in which the apostolic church understood the impending, second advent of Christ.

This second advent was read in the light of the apocalyptic pronouncements

---

[1] Matthew 24:3-14; 24:29-39. This and all other biblical passages, unless otherwise noted, are taken from the *New American Standard Translation* (La Habra 1960).

[2] The most useful monograph on the eschatology of the early church for my purposes in this project was the work by Brian E. Daley, *The Hope of the Early Church: A Handbook of Patristic Eschatology* (Cambridge 1991). Daley specifically discusses Gregory's eschatology on pages 211-215. See also his "Eschatologie in der Schrift und Patristik" *Handbuch der Dogmengeschichte* IV/7a (1986), 245-248 "Gregor der Grosse". For Gregory's dependence upon earlier authors such as Origen, Tyconius, Jerome and Augustine see Raoul Manselli, "L'escatologismo di Gregorio Magno," In *Atti del I Congresso internazionale di studi longobardi* (Spoleto 1952), 383-387; and H. Wasselynck "La voix dún Père de l'Église. L'orientation eschatologique de la vie chrétienne d'apres S. Grégoire le Grand," in *Assemblées du Seigneur*, vol. 2, Series I (Bruges 1962), 66-80.

found in the book of Daniel especially chapters 9-12. The "abomination of desolation" was largely interpreted as the destruction of the Jewish temple by Titus in AD 70. The discourse also injects into the Christian psyche the concepts of the "signs of the end". Before the end there would be, "wars and rumors of wars...nation will rise against nation, and kingdom against kingdom, and in various places there will be famines and earthquakes...but all these things are the beginning of birth pangs".[3] The statement in verse 34 that "this generation will not pass away until all these things take place" certainly demonstrates a belief in the imminence of the return of Christ. It also promoted the application of these and other prophetic announcements of the end to actual events in the life of the Church and its members.

This apocalypticism, together with pastoral concern, is also manifested in 2 Peter which seeks to answer the question of the delayed *parousia* and again in the Apocalypse of John which treats the "signs of the end" and expands upon the notion of this period of great tribulation.[4] Nevertheless, the interpretation of passages like the Olivet Discourse was not monolithic. Whereas, the author of the *Epistle of Barnabas* emphasizes a strong eschatological expectation defined in apocalyptic terms, authors such as Clement in *1 Clement* and Ignatius of Antioch place eschatological tension into the background seeking only to affirm the imminent return of Christ and the judgment. Ignatius is also perhaps the first author to posit a "realized eschatology" which seeks to understand the kingdom of God as existing in the Church of the present and not the world of the future.[5]

Both of these positions found adherents in the ensuing centuries. The various pressures placed upon Christian communities, especially those in Asia Minor, contributed to their more apocalyptic interpretations and the rise of millennialism which posited an earthly reign of Christ after the second coming.[6] This position seems to have been later appropriated in the West by Tertullian and probably also by Hippolytus in his *Commentary on Daniel*.[7] But there were

---

[3] Matthew 24:6-8.

[4] See 2 Peter 3:3-13. The apocalyptic imagery of a coming "tribulation" in the book of Revelation includes: the four horsemen of the apocalypse, chapter 6; the seven trumpets announcing destruction, chapters 8-9 and 11; and the seven vials, chapter 16.

[5] Daley, *The Hope of the Early Church*, 12-13.

[6] This concept of a millennium is based on a very literal reading of Revelation 20. The millennium was said to be an earthly reign of Christ together with his followers after the tribulation of the Church before the last judgment and the consummation of the eternal state.

[7] I am assuming here that the *Commentary on Daniel* is an authentic writing of Hippolytus, as is common. This work is no doubt quite apocalyptic in tone and promotes a millenial kingdom of Christ. Other fragments however, if they are genuine, seem to indicate an understanding more in line with a realized eschatological position. No matter how the fragments are decided the *Commentary on Daniel* certainly serves as an important source for Western apocalypticism during the period. This debate has been

also influential authors who felt that such a millennial understanding was too fleshly and too Jewish. Origen was one of these authors. Although Origen does not shrink from applying the "signs of the times" to actual persons and events of his own lifetime he was quite dutifully opposed to a literal interpretation of the millennium preferring an allegorical application of the concept to growth in the spiritual life.[8]

The eschatology of Bishop Ambrose of Milan was, as was Gregory's after him, driven by his pastoral concern. Scattered as his comments on the last days are throughout his writings and his homilies, Ambrose cannot be said to have developed any truly systematic eschatological position. He is however, important for Gregory in two important ways. First of all, he was zealous of making pointed observations of the "signs of the end" to events and persons in his own day.[9] Second, he emphasized, for the purpose of his homilies, the judgment of Christ on the last day. He draws out the courtroom imagery of this judgment in order to make practical applications to his hearers in the performing of good works and their own spiritual purity. He warns them saying, "All things are manifest to the Lord, and before his judgment-seat neither can good things be hidden, nor those that are full of offense be covered".[10]

The early Jerome was reticent to interpret the apocalyptic images allegorically and to apply them to the Christian life. Instead, he understood such passages of tribulation and trial to have primary reference to spiritual warfare in the face of a coming death.[11] But for all his years in Palestine, Jerome could not overcome feelings of dismay at the troubles of Rome. He was quick to point to the barbarians descending upon Rome as the scourge of God for the city's sins but the unsettled nature of the times seemed to incline him toward a more literal interpretation of apocalyptic literature.[12] Even though Jerome refuses to acquiesce toward any kind of millennialism, in his *Commentary on Daniel*, he teaches that the coming Antichrist will be a real

---

intense over the last fifty years. A good description of the literature can be found in R. Butterworth, *Hippolytus of Rome: Contra Noetum* (London 1977), 21-33. See also V. Loi, "La problema storico-letteraria su Ippolito di Roma," *Richerche su Ippolito: Studi Ephemeridis 'Augustinianum'* 13 (1977), 9-16; "L'identità letteraria di Ippolito di Roma," *Studi Ephemeridis 'Augustinianum'* 13 (1977), 67-88; See also M. Simonetti, A modo di conclusione: una ipotesi di lavoro," *Studi Ephemeridis 'Augustinianum'* 13 (1977), 151-156.

[8] Origen, *De principiis*, 2.11.2 and *Commentariorum in Matthaeum*, 17.35.

[9] Ambrose, *Expositiones in Luc*, 10.10 and 10.14.

[10] Ambrose, *Epistulae*, 2.14.

[11] Jerome, *In Sophiam*, 1.14.

[12] Jerome discusses the barbarians as a scourge in *Epistulae*, 17; and in his *In Isaiam*, 7.22. For an excellent discussion of Jerome's life and writings during this period of his life see J.N.D. Kelly, *Jerome: His Life, Writings and Controversies* (Peabody 1975), Chapter 25, "Gathering Gloom".

person from the people of the Jews.[13] As Jerome was working on his *Commentary on Ezekiel* he heard of Alaric's sack of Rome. Beset by despondency, Jerome found himself unable to work and almost unable to remember his own name.[14] His *romanitas* was revealed in his statement that, "when the brightest light of the world was extinguished, when the very head of the Roman Empire was revered, the entire world perished in a single city".[15] If Rome, the conqueror of the world had been defeated how long could it be until the usurper took power presaging the coming end not simply of the city or of the empire but of the entire world?

The barbarian invasions unsettled the church right along with the rest of Roman society. The period became one of intense eschatological scrutiny with writers looking sheepishly for the coming Antichrist and the consummate trials of the church. Daley describes the period in this way.

> During the last decade of the fourth century...the constant pressure on the Roman Empire of barbarian invasions began to cast a pall of anxiety over many Christian writers, particularly in the Latin West. This dark mood was to continue through most of the fifth century, in sharp contrast to the historical optimism of Eusebius and the political engagement of Ambrose. As the institutions of Roman civilization seemed to verge on extinction, Christians became more and more convinced that the end of human history was at hand. Popular interest in apocalyptic speculation grew, and natural disasters and military defeats came more and more to be taken as signs of the imminent coming of Christ. Millenarian hopes – which, since Origen, had always been entertained more seriously in the West than in the East – again took a prominent place in the works of a present world into a world of stability and peace. It was in the midst of this eschatological ferment that Augustine developed his own, relentlessly theological interpretation of the prospects of human history.[16]

Augustine's picture of the world was two-fold. In his *City of God*, he outlines the ends of the city of God and the earthly city. The apocalypticism of other writers is absorbed into his concept of the aging world nearing its fiery end. The city of God however was marked by progress.[17] The last age had dawned with the first advent of Christ and would be consummated in his second advent. The Church was in a period of anxious waiting, longing in expectation for the fulfillment of its hope. Christians were therefore called to seek the kingdom of God and to amend their lives accordingly. The earthly city together with its trappings and values was to be ignored. It was, after all,

---

[13] Jerome, *Commentariorum in Danielem prophetam libri*, 2.7.7f.; 2.7.11; 4.11.21.

[14] Jerome, *Epistulae*, 126.2.

[15] Jerome, *Commentariorum in Hiezekielem*, prologue.

[16] Daley, *The Hope of the Early Church*, 124.

[17] See T.E. Mommsen, "St. Augustine and the Christian Idea of Progress: The Background to the *City of God*," in Dorothy Donnely (ed), *City of God: A Collection of Critical Essays* (New York 1995), 353-373.

doomed to a swiftly approaching end. God's providence was working for the triumph of the Church even as the earthly city decayed and was thrown down in destruction. We see therefore in Augustine a mixture of sentiments. He can decry the loss of Rome but the pain of the loss was a promise that even though the end of the temporal existence was drawing near, the eternal day was beginning to dawn. His apocalypticism is tempered by his triumphalism regarding God's providential guidance of the Church.

Although Augustine believed that Christians were living in the last age of the world and that many of the signs of the end were present he was hesitant to specify exactly how close the end was. He took the texts of Acts 1:7 and Matthew 24:36, which both speak of the impossibility of knowing the "day and hour" of the end, very literally preferring to remain an agnostic on the issue. He said that Christians ought to be gladly ignorant of the end because God meant for them to be ignorant.[18] The dangers for being wrong were too great. Either one could predict it to be too soon and be wrong thus risking damage to the faith or to believe it will be late and possibly be unprepared.[19] Augustine's personal choice was to "hope for the one...(be) resigned to the other, and...(be) wrong in neither of them".[20]

Augustine identifies the millennium with the kingdom of God inaugurated in Christ. Thus, the Church is the kingdom of God on earth. Individual Christians are even now reigning with Christ.[21] Of importance is his concept that the first resurrection was actually the initial spiritual awakening of individuals taking place in the liturgical act of baptism.[22] This follows in the spiritualized eschatology tradition of Jerome and Ambrose with their tendency to interiorize the millennium of God. What actually happens in such cases is that the millennium and thus the reign of God is manifested in the transformation of individuals within the Church. Eschatology becomes a lived spiritual experience as opposed to a future event. This link allows us to see the spiritual importance of eschatological teachings in the time leading up to Gregory.

Also of importance for the purpose of reading Gregory's theology is the tradition of emphasizing the judgment of God. We have already noticed this in the pastoral concern of Ambrose. In the *City of God*, Augustine stresses the absolute need for God's judgment on the world. In the present life some evil deeds go unpunished. God's holiness demands retribution and this retribution is made in the last judgment.[23] This judgment is also important in that it allows individual Christians who still have not met the full requirements of penance for their post-baptismal sins to be purged. In the final conflagration what

---

[18] Augustine, *Enarrationes in Psalmorum*, 6.2.

[19] Augustine, *Epistulae*, 199.54.

[20] Augustine, *Epistulae*, 199.54.

[21] Augustine, *De civitate Dei*, 20.7-9.

[22] Augustine, *De civitate Dei*, 20.9.

[23] Augustine, *De civitate Dei*, 20.2.

remains corruptible is made incorruptible.[24]

Signs of the End in Gregory

The "signs of the end" as found in the Olivet Discourse form the tone and tenor of Gregory's understanding of what sorts of things could be expected leading up to the second advent of Christ. There are, however, other interesting elements which are brought into his expression of what will come before the end. Some of these include older philosophical concepts that earlier Christians had argued were in line with the Christian understanding of the end and had thus become part of the Christian tradition since the time of the early apologists. The Christian concept of the last days had sometimes been expressed in extremely apocalyptic pictures while at other times the progress of the Church up to the conclusion of time had been presented in evolutionary, almost triumphant, terms. Gregory does his best to make use of both traditions.

The apparent conflict between apocalyptic and triumphant visions of the end may have more to do with the modern reader than it did with older Christian writers. It is after all, merely a subjective distinction. Once the Church was able to separate itself from the world, the ends of both could be reconciled within one world view. This concept of opposition is inherent in the New Testament and is even placed in the mouth of Jesus himself. This disparity is the reason for Jesus' teaching in parables; he says, "to you has been given the mystery of the kingdom of God; but those who are outside get everything in parables, in order that seeing, they may see and not perceive; and while hearing, they may hear and not understand".[25] Perhaps the most important expression of this dichotomy is found in Matthew 16:18 which reads, "and I also say to you that you are Peter, and upon this rock I will build My Church; and the gates of Hades shall not overpower it".[26] Although, the Olivet Discourse paints the end in apocalyptic terms this promise made to Peter and placed on the lips of Christ betrays a commitment to a concept of the Church as a special group blessed by God which, although it may be tried, will pass the test of the tribulation and move on to greater glory in Christ.

The instability of the Roman world of the late fifth and early sixth centuries did much to strengthen the apocalyptic flavor of Christianity which had been seemingly suppressed since the time of Augustine. Eschatology had only at times surfaced as a major component of theology. Augustine himself never seems to have been completely comfortable with it.[27] Nevertheless, his

---

[24] Augustine, *De civitate Dei*, 20.2.

[25] Mark 4:11-12. See also Matthew 13:11 and Luke 8:10.

[26] Matthew 16:18.

[27] This is apparent by his changing and sometimes waffling on various interpretations of the millennium and the events of the last day. See Daley, *The Hope of the Early Church*, 133-136.

enshrinement of the two cities in his *City of God* expressed the old dichotomy of the New Testament in a way that would become normative for later Christianity. His erection of these cities provided the basis needed for a new wedding of apocalypticism and triumphalism in eschatology.

During this period of barbarian invasions, plague, natural disasters, and economic upheaval, eschatology came to take a central place in theology.[28] Gregory, great theological synthesizer that he was, could not help picking up on this renewed undercurrent of apocalyptic thought. Daley explains Gregory's approach to the end in the following way.

> By the end of the sixth century, however, the atmosphere of Christian expectation had darkened considerably: mainly because of the strong sense of eschatological crisis that penetrated the writings of the Western Church's most prominent and eloquent spokesman of the age, Pope Gregory the Great. Although a man of considerable learning, Gregory had little interest in the secular sciences and philosophy, and characteristically explained the events of history and the phenomena of the world around him less in terms of natural causes than as signs of God's providential care for creation, and of God's struggle against the forces of evil. As a result, while Augustine remained cautious about reading in the disasters of his day signs that the end was near, Gregory did so without hesitation. Living in an Italy that was economically and socially ravaged by the Lombard invasions, and personally overwhelmed by a sense of Rome's political decline, the former *praefectus urbi* was convinced that the Parousia and judgment were not far off, and considered it one of his chief pastoral responsibilities, as Bishop of Rome, to communicate this sense of impending crisis to his hearers and to the wider Christian world.[29]

Daley does point out that even as graphic as Gregory's apocalyptic imagery is, not all his portraits of the end are quite as "bleak".[30] But Claude Dagens has gone further.[31] He has posited the presence of two distinct and possibly irreconcilable eschatological positions in Gregory's corpus. He notes that there is the "coexistence, in the spirit of Gregory, of these two, apparently different, visions of the Church; one which is dark, with the picture of apocalypse, and the other which is confident and sometimes expressed in terms of triumphalism".[32] In fact, Dagens sees the *Moralia* as presenting the more triumphant image of the Church whereas he sees Gregory's other writings as

---

[28] Daley, *The Hope of the Early Church*, 204.

[29] Daley, *The Hope of the Early Church*, 211.

[30] Daley, *The Hope of the Early Church*, 212.

[31] Claude Dagens, "La fin des temps et l'église selon saint Grégoire le Grand" *Recherches de Science Religieuse* 58 (1970), 273-288.

[32] Dagens, "La fin des temps", 275. "C'est la coexistence dans l'esprit de Grégoire de ces deux visions, apparement différentes, de l'Église, l'une qui est sombre, avec des tableaux d'apocalypse, et l'autre qui est confiante et confine parfois au triomphalisme."

expressing more of an apocalyptic focus on the coming cataclysm.[33] He argues that this disparity may not be explained by simple recourse to literary genre[34] nor is it simply the result of circumstance or rhetorical embellishment.[35] Gregory is a preacher, it is true, and his horrific pictures of the end, serve a rhetorical purpose but the dichotomy runs deeper. Dagens argues that the question really becomes not "why are there two eschatologies in Gregory" but "what is the connection between his eschatology and his ecclesiology".[36]

The answer to this question lies not simply in the rhetorical embellishment of a preacher but in the pastoral care of the pope. Gregory does separate the two images of the Church. Nevertheless, the one is the impetus for and the means to the other. "The situation of the world is more dramatic than that of the Church" but it serves to drive the Church to repentance for sins and preaching the Gospel.[37] The cataclysms of the imminent end of the world and the return of Christ become a pastoral focus on the interior, spiritual benefits that may be accrued through these difficult times of persecution. We can see then how an apocalyptic focus can eventually work itself out into a triumphalist picture of the Church. The Church will be victorious not in spite of these things but precisely because of them.[38]

Dagens concludes by categorizing Gregory as a prophet from the Jewish Scriptures. He stands in time at the brink of the end always warning others and hoping for their reclamation but secure that God will not fail the Church even in the midst of the most trying times. In fact, the Church, already made one with Christ in faith, will experience the reign of God more fully in the period to come. Gregory seems to have felt that it was his task to point out both of these aspects of the end and to embody them in his own ministry not as contradictory assertions but as symbiotic truths.[39]

---

[33] Dagens, "La fin des temps", 285. "Mais les *Moralia* évoquent généralement la fin des temps d'une façon moins dramatique..."

[34] Dagens, "La fin des temps", 274. "Il ne suffit pas de remarquer la différence de genre littéraire."

[35] Dagens, "La fin des temps", 275. "Il ne s'agit pas d'un thème de circonstance, ni d'une amplification rhétorique."

[36] Dagens, "La fin des temps", 275 "Autrement dit, quelle relation peut-on établir entre son eschatologie et son ecclesiologie?"

[37] Dagens, "La fin des temps", 278. "...la situation du monde est plus dramatique que celle de l'Église."

[38] Dagens, "La fin des temps", 286-288. Dagens calls the trials and the temptations of the end of this world, as they serve the benefit of the spiritual life, a "pédogogie divine" which betrays a wonderful grasp of not only Gregory's eschatology but also his basic program of the benefits of adversity in the Christian life.

[39] Dagens, "La fin des temps", 287-288. "Ce moine est enfin un mystique: et il espère de toute son âme l'avènement du Royaume de Dieu, par-delà les tristesses de ce monde. Ces éléments, si divers soient-ils, ne sont pas contradictoires: l'eschatologisme grégorien est à cosidérer dans son ensemble et, tel qu'il est, tantôt serein et très

Gregory's work does not express a rigorously defined eschatology but is simply the "expression of spontaneous sentiments in relation to the perspective of the return of Christ and the coming of his kingdom".[40] We must be careful to distinguish between the "eschatological orientation" of his apocalyptic understanding of the events occurring around him and the "eschatological orientation of the Christian life and of the Church" as demonstrated in his triumphalism.[41]

Dagens does an excellent job of pointing out the character of the two eschatological tendencies in Gregory. His presentation shows a wonderful, almost intuitive, grasp of the spiritual character and desire of the man. His conclusion is a good synthesis of both Gregorian trends and posits the most plausible reason for their coexistence. Dagens is at his best in demonstrating the pastoral concern Gregory has in the expression of his eschatological position to see the events of the exterior trials and tribulations as an avenue to inner contemplation. Nevertheless, there are a few refinements which could be made.

First, although Dagens does not explicitly state that all of the more triumphant passages occur in Gregory's *Moralia* this is the only source which he uses for this purpose. He also seems to imply that for some reason the *Moralia*, perhaps because of its more spiritual bent (being addressed to monks), does not make use of the more apocalyptic images. This is not the case. Although, the *Moralia* is more triumphant in tone it does not fail to contain apocalyptic imagery nor does it omit discussions of the several "signs" of the coming end of all things. Consider the following example wherein Gregory seeks to liken the signs of the coming end to a storm at sea.

> When a storm arises, first slight waves and afterwards greater billows are stirred up, finally the waves lift themselves up on high, and by their very height overturn all of them that are at sea. Thus, surely does that last tempest of souls hasten that it may overwhelm the whole world. For now it shows its beginnings by wars and havocs as by a kind of wave, and in proportion as we are daily made nearer to the end, we see heavier billows of tribulation rushing in upon us. But at the last all the elements being in commotion, the Judge from above when he comes brings the

---

spiritualisé, tantôt angoissé et influencé par les tribulations du moment, il a pénétré toute son oeuvre et profondément marqué la mentalité des chrétiens du Haut Moyen Age."

[40] Dagens, "La fin des temps", 288. "Il ne faut pas chercher chez Grégoire une réflexion méthodique sur l'eschatologie, une théologie des fins dernières, mais simplement l'expresssion de ses sentiments spontanés par rapport à la perspective du retour du Christ et de l'avènement de son Royaume."

[41] Dagens, "La fin des temps", 288. "Il est utile de distinguer chez lui entre la conscience eschatologique et l'orientation eschatologique de la vie chrétienne et de l'Église."

end of all things...and by these tribulations, which strike the world, they forecast what things may follow.[42]

The larger issue with Dagens is the way in which he seems to conflate the apocalyptic character of warnings in Gregory's writings for individual Christians as an impetus for spiritual conversion and growth with the more triumphalistic passages dealing with the Church. While focusing upon Gregory's triumphant bent as the delight of a monk/mystic waiting for God's kingdom to come, he seems to interpret these triumphant passages in a manner that is inconsistent with Gregory's pastoral emphasis upon the Church as the body of Christ. Dagens is correct in arguing for an ecclesiological connection but the connection must be made broader. It is not simply the individual within the Church who can rest in the coming victory of the Church but the Church as a body can be given comfort in the trials which it endures because of its coming glory in the kingdom of God.[43] To be sure, this is a fine distinction but to argue for any application of the triumphant character of Gregory's thought on any level lower than the corporate body of believers in the Church is to misunderstand the global character of the Roman pontiff. We should see an individualistic focus in the apocalyptic portions of Gregory's work, contained as they are in his homilies and letters delivered with a specific intent; his triumphant tone, however, must be understood in the words of Augustine as the victory of the city of God over the city of this world and not that of individuals within the city over their own fears.

Gregory believed that the end of the world was imminent and that Christ could return at any time. He pointed to various signs all around him that he read as heralds of Christ's swiftly approaching return to judge the world. These signs could be divided into those which had already appeared and heralded the proximity of the end and those that were yet to appear just prior to the coming of the Antichrist and the end.

One of these signs which was already announcing the nearness of the coming end of all things was the general decay of society. Gregory points out the numerous natural disasters, military invasions, and political destruction as indicative of the natural process of entropy upon the world. He likens the situation of the world to an elderly person. The earth had lived its course and

---

[42] Gregory the Great, *Moralia*, 21.22.36. "Tempestas quippe cum oritur, prius lenes undae et postmodum volumina maiora concitantur; ad extremum fluctus se in alta erigunt, et navigantes quosque ipsa sua altitudine subvertunt. Sic sic nimirum extrema illa properat, quae universum mundum subruat tempestas animarum. Nunc enim bellis et cladibus quasi quibusdam undis sua nobis exordia ostendit; et quanto ad finem cotidie propinquiores efficimur, tanto graviora irruere tribulationum volumina videmus. Ad extremum vero commotis omnibus elementis, supernus iudex veniens finem omnium apportat, quia videlicet tunc tempestas fluctus in caelum levat...atque ex his tribulationibus quae mundum feriunt praevident quae sequantur."

[43] Gregory the Great, *Moralia*, 7.32.47.

was now in its old age. It was exhausted and waiting only for the approach of death. His description of the earth as once "green in its physical health" and "lusty in begetting offspring" now being "weighed down with its old age" and beset by increasing troubles it is "oppressed...by the proximity of its demise" is repeated also in his *Moralia*.[44] The increasing evil in the world and multiplying of tribulations were marks of the world's decrepitude and swiftly coming death.[45]

This concept of the *senectus mundi* goes back through earlier Christian tradition all the way to the Stoic philosophers. Secular authors such as Lucretius, Sallust, Seneca the Elder and Florus furnished the background for this idea.[46] This concept had entered the Christian understanding of the end of time as early as the middle of the third century when Cyprian spoke of the old age of the world being demonstrated by a depletion in natural resources.[47] This same theme was repeated in Origen and Lactantius.[48] Perhaps the earliest Western author in the Christian tradition to make use of this concept is Ambrose. Ambrose looks at the tumultuous nature of his times wrought with war and natural disasters as signs of the coming end.[49] The world has "grown old" and lost its earlier vigor.[50] Jerome, although active in the East for the latter portion of his career is still considered a major contributor to this idea in the West. Owing no doubt to his wide reading of Stoic and other earlier philosophers and rhetoricians, namely Cicero, and his reading of earlier church fathers such as Origen, Jerome asserts that the world is "growing old" faced as it is with tribulations on every side.[51] Augustine, perhaps the most important

---

[44] Hurst, *Forty Gospel Homilies*, 18-19. This is a translation of Gregory's homily 1 in Migne, *XL homiliarum in Evangelia libri duo. PL* 1077.

[45] Gregory the Great, *Moralia*, 34.1.1. See also his *Homiliae in evangelium*, 1.1.1; and *Homiliae in Ezekiel*, 2.6.22ff.

[46] The general decline of the city of Rome in Cicero and in his opponent Sallust is universalized in Lucretius and Seneca. Lucretius specifically notes the failure of the land to produce crops while Seneca identifies the old age of the empire with that of the world. The decadence and therefore the decline of Rome becomes connected to the general decline of the world's natural resources. We can see that the concept of *romanitas* is active in all these authors as it will be again in Augustine and Gregory. For the ideas of the decadence and old age of Rome and the world see, Santo Mazzarino, *The End of the Ancient World*, trans. George Holmes (New York 1966), 21-43. See also, Hartke, *Römische Kinderkaiser* (Berlin 1950), 393 and following; P. Zancan, *Floro e Livio* (Padua 1942), 13-20; and M. Spanneut, *Le Stoïcisme des Pères de l'église* (Paris 1957), 258.

[47] Cyprian, *Ad Demetrianum*, 3-8. For Cyprian's appropriation of Stoicism and especially his debt to Seneca see H. Koch, *Cyprianische Untersuchungen* (Bonn 1926), 286-313.

[48] Origen, *Commentariorum in Matthaeum*, 36-7. Lactantius, *Institutiones*, 7.14.

[49] Ambrose, *Expositiones in Luc*, 7.7.

[50] Ambrose, *De bono mortis*, 10.46.

[51] Jerome, *In Isaiam*, 14.51.6.

source for Gregory, not only picks up this theme but expands it to include a particular spiritual application. He argues that even though the world has grown old and breathless, the youth of the Church and individual Christians will be restored like that of the eagle.[52] Christians should therefore take no thought about the world or their place in the world but concern themselves only with their spiritual relationship to the kingdom of God that will never grow old.

This concept also seems to be closely tied with Augustine's use of an older classical tradition of time being made up of a "week of ages" to be followed by a golden period of renewal.[53] In one work, Augustine sets the precedent followed by Gregory of picturing the ages of the world as the ages of human life. He speaks of infancy, childhood, adolescence, young adulthood, adulthood, and old age and argues that the world in which he lived was in old age awaiting the end of its life and the beginning of the next.[54] Later, he expresses the six ages of the world in light of the six ages of creation.[55] The six ages of humanity would of course be followed by a Sabbath of rest in God the creator.

Gregory also makes use of these ages of the world although it appears that the exact number of the ages of the world depends upon the text with which Gregory is working. It may be five as in his *Homilies on the Gospel* where Gregory is outlining the parable of the tenants or it may be the more traditional, or at least more Augustinian, six as in his discussion of the six men in the book of Ezekiel which he discusses in the *Moralia*.[56] Gregory is aware of the Christian tradition of the ages of the world and makes use of the concept in arguing that the wars and unsettled nature of the times coupled with the poverty of the people and the infertility of the earth were signs of the last age preceding the coming of the judge.

---

[52] Augustine, *Sermones*, 81.8. Other authors who may have influenced Gregory after Augustine in the concept of the *senectus mundi* are Orosius, *Historiarum*, 2.6.14; Orientius, *Commonitorium*, 2.185 and 2.210; and Peter Chrysologus, *Sermones*, 167.3.

[53] For classical and Christian usage of the "week" of ages see K.H. Schwarte, *Die Vorgeschichte der augustinischen Weltalterlehre* (Bonn 1966); O. Rousseau, "La Typologie augustinienne de l'Hexaemeron et la théologie du temps", in E. Iserloh and P. Manns (eds), *Festgabe Joseph Lortz* (Baden-Baden 1958), 47-58; and A. Luneau, *L'Histoire du salut chez le Pères de l'église. La Doctrine des âges du monde* (Paris 1964), 285-356.

[54] Augustine, *De genesi contra Manichaeos*, 1.35-41.

[55] Augustine, *De catechizandis rudibus*, 22.39; *Contra Faustum*, 12.8; *De trinitate*, 4.4.7; *Enarrationes in Psalmorum*, 92.1; and *De civitate Dei*, 22.30.

[56] Gregory the Great, *XL homiliarum in Evangelia libri duo*, 19.1. Here Gregory outlines the five ages with the hours of the day listed in the parable as follows: morning = from Adam to Noah, third hour = from Noah to Abraham, sixth hour = from Abraham to Moses, ninth hour = from Moses to Christ, and the eleventh hour = coming of Christ to judge and inaugurate the new creation. Gregory discusses the six ages in his *Moralia*, 22.18.44.

Another sign that had already appeared but was still awaiting its climax was the persecution of the Church. Just like Arcturus, the constellation of the bear, the Church was waning as it suffered the present persecution which in itself was a mere foretaste of the great persecution that would follow.[57] For Gregory, the constellation of Arcturus is a perfect example of the Church because it does not set throughout the entire night. Although it rises and falls its light does not cease to shine. Likewise, the Church, though buffeted by tribulation will not succumb but will remain steadfast in its original condition of grace and continue to receive the blessings of God.

The nature of the present sufferings of the Church foreshadows the great tribulation that is coming. Even now the Church is beset on all sides by evil wishers. The calamities which fall on the Church arise from both the "left" and the "right". Calamities arising from the left have their source in evil doers outside of the Church. The goal of the persecutors, those "sons of perdition", is that they might "put out the light of faith and (silence) the voice of preaching" in the Church because God has rendered them incapable of seeing the good of the Church and they imagine that all evil is a result of the Church.[58] In this battle against the Church they strike out both in secret and in the open. In secret, they seek to entice the faithful through their words and their example to sin just as they do. But the reprobate members of the body of Satan also attack the body of Christ in the open through swords seeking to dispel from the Church by force those whom they were unable to snare by evil words and bad examples.[59]

This persecution of the Church by those outside the Church is used by God to try the Church. The persecution of "words" exercises "wisdom" and the persecution of the "sword" exercises "patience".[60] The Lord allows this persecution but is careful to "restrict the wrath" of this persecution by his judicial dispensation.[61] The day is of course coming in which Satan would be released from his bonds and permission given to him to try the Church in all his fierceness. But that time, according to Gregory, had not yet come. He knew that it was coming soon because open persecution was occurring but it had not always been so. Whenever the Church lacked such an oppressive persecution by open adversaries from without it was and continued to be tried by

---

[57] Gregory the Great, *Moralia*, 29.31.72. See also 9.11.13-14 and 29.31.67.

[58] Gregory the Great, *Moralia*, 20.29.59.

[59] Gregory the Great, *Moralia*, 18.2.3. It should be noted that whenever the word "reprobate" is used in this text it does not bear the same meaning it came to have in the 16th century. I use it in as close a sense to that of Gregory as possible. Gregory does use the word *reprobus* but only to describe the non-elect as those outside the Church. Reprobation is for him, as it is for Augustine, a passive category and not an active process.

[60] Gregory the Great, *Moralia*, 18.2.3.

[61] Gregory the Great, *Moralia*, 28.17.37.

persecutors from within.[62]

Those from the "right" who are persecuting the Church are those who appear to be believers but demonstrate by their actions that they are not part of the true Church.[63] These enemies from within the Church are twofold. First, there are the heretics which lead many of the faithful away through the teaching of false doctrine. The heretics are doubly dangerous because their words and deeds not only lead away members of the faithful but they scandalize those who are outside the Church and might yet be converted.[64] Still more, they seek out those in power who they might convert to heresy and stir them up in tribulation against the Church.[65] Scandal is also caused by the second group of interior enemies of the Church. This second group is made up of those who have professed faith but refuse to adapt their lives to the teachings of the Holy Church. These enemies cause those who might have been converted to stumble as well as wounding younger Christians who, seeing their example and thinking evil actions acceptable, are entrapped in sin once again.[66] These hypocrites do great damage to the Church and as they refuse to submit themselves to be chastened by the penitential system of the Church they will be judged at the second coming as "thieves" who have stolen away the hearts of many.[67]

Another sign of the end which was already beginning to appear was the cessation of miracles and miraculous gifts in the Church. Gregory understands miracles and other charismatic gifts to have been a very important aspect of the early preaching of Christianity.[68] Miracles provided a sense of authority for the gospel and its preachers. Gregory argued however that by his time, in most of the world, this function had been surpassed by the more exemplary attestation of merit and good works.[69] In some places however, miracles continued to be performed because the gospel was still being preached among those who had never heard it. These miracles were, however, limited to new areas of evangelism because miracles were necessary for unbelievers but not for the faithful.[70]

Gregory argues that this withdrawal of miracles performs a vital function in

---

[62] Gregory the Great, *Moralia*, 18.51.83.

[63] Gregory the Great, *Moralia*, 20.22.48.

[64] Gregory the Great, *Moralia*, Preface.6.15; 7.34.50; 16.45.57-50.63; and 16.60.74.

[65] Gregory the Great, *Moralia*, 16.54.67; 31.28.55.

[66] Gregory the Great, *Moralia*, 25.10.26-12.30. Gregory expounds in this place the evils of such hypocrites and their ways. He also points out that their sins are more grave than the external persecutors of the Church because the hypocrites have tasted the Gospel but rejected it. Having refused to live a holy life they soon lose their faith as well and take other believers with them. Gregory points out that their sin is a sin of "intention" rather than of "ignorance" and is therefore to be more harshly judged.

[67] Gregory the Great, *Moralia*, 8.47.77; 15.14.18.

[68] Gregory the Great, *Moralia*, 27.18.36.

[69] Gregory the Great, *Moralia*, 27.18.36.

[70] Gregory the Great, *Moralia*, 27.18.36.

the Church for it both tries and strengthens the faith of the elect and places more guilt upon those who oppress the Church because of this lack of miracles. The crisis of belief for the faithful at the end will come not simply because of the cessation of miracles in the Church but also because of the abundance of miracles being performed outside the Church by its enemies. This situation serves to display the faith of the Church and this faith in the face of an apparent lack of visible power leads to a growth in merit. The faltering of miracles also serves to embolden the Church's enemies yet their ensuing actions serve only to heighten the pain of their eventual judgment and mark more clearly their coming destruction.[71]

Another sign of the end that Gregory discusses as having been completed or being very near completion is the preaching of the gospel to the "ends of the earth". Gregory takes as the basis for this belief a verse from the Olivet Discourse which reads, "And this gospel of the kingdom shall be preached in the whole world for a witness to all the nations, and then the end shall come".[72] Gregory sees his mission to England as fulfillment of this prophecy. In triumphant language he points out that even in the face of manifold persecution the kingdom is marching inexorably toward universal representation so that the entire world will rejoice in the "Hebrew alleluia".[73] This concept is closely linked to Gregory's understanding that at the end of the world there would be a great outpouring of the Spirit and that many people would convert to Christianity.[74]

Gregory saw his missionary efforts as leading up to the very end when God would bring about a great efficacy of preaching.[75] Gregory sees this outpouring of grace and inpouring of persons into the Church as a reward from God for the faithfulness of the Church in facing persecution. The Church loses many members now because of the persecution which it is enduring but at the end the Church will receive a double portion of all those which were lost in persecution.[76]

Gregory depends on the text of Paul in Romans 11:25-26 for this concept of a final outpouring of grace on the Church. Crucial to this final effulgence is the conversion of the "full number of Gentiles" and of the "Jews". In an interesting parallel Gregory outlines the history of how the gospel came to the Gentiles and points to the role that persecution will play in the return of the Jewish people to the faith. He affirms that "Judea, which is now left desolate, shall be gathered

---

[71] Gregory the Great, *Moralia*, 34.3.7.

[72] Matthew 24:14. (NASB).

[73] Gregory the Great, *Moralia*, 27.11.21.

[74] Gregory the Great, *Moralia*, Preface.10.20 and 30.9.32.

[75] Gregory the Great, *Moralia*, 19.12.19.

[76] Gregory the Great, *Moralia*, Preface.10.21; 35.14.24; 35.16.41.

into the bosom of the faith at the end".[77] Gregory argues that by the will of the creator the rejection of the gospel by the Jews and their persecution of the early preachers of the Church allowed the gospel message to be proclaimed to the ends of the earth.[78] The Jewish people persecuted missionaries such as Peter and Paul even as the honor of these preachers was being recognized by the nations.[79] Yet soon after the Gentiles were being converted they themselves broke out in open persecution against the Church. As this persecution increases toward the end of time the Jewish people will see the honor of the preachers and of the gospel and will be converted.[80] Gregory here develops an outline of the progress of the Church in persecution. Although the Church always loses members while it experiences persecution, the persecution itself witnesses to the honor and truth of the gospel to those who either have not heard it or have heard and rejected it in the past.[81]

The last sign which is to come as a herald of the final tribulation of the Church just before the end is the appearance of the Antichrist. Even now the Church marks the appearance of the Antichrist because many of his preachers are already active. These forerunners are lifted up in pride and are hypocrites. Though they preach with sweet words their life bears little light for they are full of iniquity and seek to snare the faithful.[82] They participate in the spirit of the Antichrist and are members of Satan's body just as the faithful are members of the body of Christ.[83] But this has always been the case. There have been many such as Cain, Judas, and Simon as well as many towns like Pergamos and Thyatira which, although they did not know the time of the Antichrist, were members of his body and tools used by him to persecute the Church.[84]

Nevertheless, the evil machinations of these forerunners will pale in comparison to the coming seed of evil. Gregory speaks of the Antichrist as

---

[77] Gregory the Great, *Moralia*, 9.8.9. "Quod Iudaea quae nunc deseritur, ad sinum fidei in fine colligatur."

[78] Gregory the Great, *Moralia*, 9.8.9.

[79] Gregory the Great, *Moralia*, 9.9.10.

[80] Gregory the Great, *Moralia*, 9.9.10.

[81] The history of anti-semitism in the Church is unfortunately a fair assessment. However, the recognition of this fact should be moderated by Gregory's understanding of the divine will and God's use of persecution to further the gospel. We should also consider the way in which Gregory seeks to protect the Jews and their rights in his pastoral administrative praxis in distinction from his hermeneutical use of the Jews. For an excellent discussion of this topic see, Robert Markus, "The Jew as a Hermeneutic Device: The Inner Life of a Gregorian Topos", in John C. Cavadini (ed), *Gregory the Great: A Symposium* (Notre Dame 1995), 1-16. See also S. Katz, "Gregory the Great and the Jews", *Jewish Quarterly Review* 24 (1933-1934), 113-136.

[82] Gregory the Great, *Moralia*, 33.35.59-60.

[83] Gregory the Great, *Moralia*, 29.7.15.

[84] Gregory the Great, *Moralia*, 29.7.15. Gregory also calls the synagogue, by virtue of its persecution of the Church, the "limbs of Satan" in Moralia, 31.23.42.

"that damned man".[85] Before the last day Satan, "our old enemy", will enter into that man of perdition.[86] He will be lifted up in pride as the tail of the behemoth and will surpass the natural endowments of humanity in both honor and miracles of a false holiness, through which he will draw many away from the faith.[87] Although, he now, in his members, draws away an "innumerable quantity" in that day he will sway all the carnal members of humanity to himself.[88] To the powerful he will display his secular power and dominion while to the faithful his false miracles and pretended holiness. In this way he will gather an army against Christ and wage war upon the holy members of the Church.[89]

Imminence of the End and Practical Ramifications

Gregory's opinion that he was living in the last days of human existence was not simply a rhetorical statement to prod listless hearers toward repentance but it was a belief which underlay his theology and his spirituality. This has not only been brought up by many modern authors[90] but was well established as early as the 9th century when Gregory's biographer John the Deacon wrote the following words. "In all his words and acts Gregory considered the imminence of the final day of future retribution. The more carefully he considered all aspects of all human affairs, the more he persisted in (his belief in) the nearness of the end, having observed the progress of its ruin."[91]

This belief haunts almost all of his writings. In discussing the Lucan account of the Olivet Discourse (Luke 21:25-33) he expresses his belief in the nearness of the end.

> We see some of these things already coming to pass, and dread that the rest are soon to follow. We see nation rising against nation and the distress that follows on the earth, more now in our day that we have read about in books. You know how often we have heard from other parts of the world that earthquakes have destroyed countless cities; we have suffered pestilence without relief; we do not yet clearly see the signs in the sun and moon and stars, but from the change in the air now we gather that these too are not far off. Before Italy was handed over to be struck by

---

[85] Gregory the Great, *Moralia*, 15.58.69. "In illo damnato homine."

[86] Gregory the Great, *Moralia*, 15.61.72.

[87] Gregory the Great, *Moralia*, 32.15.22.

[88] Gregory the Great, *Moralia*, 15.61.72.

[89] Gregory the Great, *Moralia*, 32.15.24-25.

[90] See Dudden, *Gregory the Great*, vol. 2. 430; Markus, *Gregory*, 51 and Carol Straw, *Gregory, Perfection*, 14.

[91] John the Deacon, *Gregorii magni vita*, 6.65. *PL* 75.214A-215B. "In omnibus suis dictis vel operibus, Gregorius imminentem futurae retributionis diem ultimum perpendebat, tantoque cautius cuncta cunctorum negotia perpendebat quanto propinquius finem mundi insistere, ruinis eius crescentibus, advertebat."

the pagans' sword, we saw fiery flashes in the sky indicating the blood of the human race that was later shed. No new confusion of sea and waves has yet welled up but when many of the things foretold have come to pass, there is no doubt but that even the few that remain will follow. The accomplishment of things past is a clear indication of things to come.[92]

This is further confirmed in the *Dialogues* where he speaks of the end as already "breaking forth".[93] This same sentiment is expressed in his *Moralia*. In its dedicatory epistle addressed to Leander, Gregory tells us that the present evils of the world portend that the "end of the world is at hand".[94] The tribulations which the Church is enduring demonstrate that the judgment of God is impending.[95] If the judgment of God is already evident the great day of divine judgment which these punishments foreshadow must also be imminent.[96]

So what did this belief in the imminent end of the world mean for the lives of the Christians to whom Gregory ministered? It certainly did not mean ceasing all activity. In fact it was a call to renewed activity. But this activity must have the proper focus; it must be focused in the spiritual life. For Gregory "ascetica and eschata go together; the latter motivates the former while the former prepares for the latter".[97] The nearness of the end serves as a motivation for the cultivation of the spiritual life. "All Gregory's eschatologically purple passages serve this end: to proclaim an ascetic Christian morality of renunciation."[98] In fact it is exactly this loss of renunciation that Gregory mourns in his dedicatory epistle to Leander in the context of the above quote regarding the end of the world. It was exactly at the time that Gregory felt that he ought to be practicing contemplation that he was forced into an active role in the Church.

Life on earth was, for Gregory, a pilgrimage. It was merely the road to the eternal kingdom. Gregory understands the distinction between the sacred and the secular a bit differently than had Augustine. "The eschatological tension

---

[92] Gregory the Great, *XL Homiliarum in Evangelia*, 1. *PL*, 76.1077. This translation is taken from David Hurst, trans. *Gregory the Great: Forty Gospel Homilies* (Kalamazoo 1990), 15-16. In this text it is listed as homily 3. Hurst has organized the homilies into sequential order based upon the liturgical calendar of Gregory's time as far as it is known. He argues that this homily would have been delivered on one of the first Sundays of Advent.

[93] Gregory the Great, *Dialogi de vita et miraculis patrum Italicorum*, 3.38.3.

[94] Gregory the Great, *Ad Leandrum*, 1. *CCSL*, 143. "Quia enim mundi iam tempora malis crebrescentibus termino adpropinquante turbata sunt." See also a similar statement in *Moralia*, 9.11.15.

[95] Gregory the Great, *Moralia*, 21.22.36.

[96] Gregory the Great, *Moralia*, 31.27.54.

[97] Robert E. McNally, "Gregory the Great and His Declining World", *Archivum historiae pontificiae* 16 (1978), 14.

[98] Markus, *Gregory*, 59.

between Augustine's two cities interwoven in all secular society as well as the Church in its earthly existence is transformed into another tension in Gregory's mind, that between the inner and the outer, the contemplative and the active, the carnal and the spiritual."[99] In this sojourn in a visible world all pilgrims must constantly bear in mind that their goal is the vision of the invisible God. The things of this world are obstacles that must be overcome. The fact that many of them are enjoyable means that they are all the more dangerous. It is only through the promise of the end that Christians can reevaluate their priorities and seek out the higher good; not the temporal and the physical but the eternal and the spiritual. "Whoever still longs after visible things does not understand the misery of his pilgrimage and does not have the skill to see the evil which he is suffering."[100] In light of the coming return of Christ, Christians must disentangle themselves from the weights of this world so that they can more easily ascend to the heights of contemplation.

We must not draw this distinction too starkly however. Gregory's accent on eschatology as an impetus toward the spiritual life also includes elements of service. The *servus servorum Dei* emphasized the necessity of good works as well. In fact these good works were the demonstration of the Christian's growth in grace through contemplation. Good works are impossible on one's own and can only flow from a relationship with God because they are only made possible through grace.[101] The relationship between the active and contemplative lives in good works is illustrated by his imagery of good works as "divine sacrifices offered to the Judge of the interior on the altar of the heart".[102] Most importantly however, good works, although they were not to be trusted without reservation, did provide a certain amount of security for the believer facing persecutions now or the coming tribulation and judgment of the future for "those established in good works rejoice in a sure hope in God".[103]

The impetus for seriousness in one's relationship with God and for the pursuit of good works came directly from Gregory's belief that the world was coming quickly to an end and the judgment would soon be upon this world. This conviction gave his preaching and his pastoral work its "intensity and urgency".[104] Gregory made use of this urgency through a rich development of the Jewish, scriptural theme of the "fear of God". Gregory sees a line of cause

---

[99] Markus, Gregory, 58. This tension is discussed at length in Carole Straw, *Gregory, Perfection*, 128-46. See also P. Aubin, "Intériorité et extériorité dans le *Moralia in Job* de saint Grégoire le Grand", *Recherches de science religieuse* 62 (1974), 117-66.

[100] Gregory the Great, *Moralia*, 34.3.5. "Quisquis enim haec adhuc visibilia appetit, peregrinationis suae malum non intelligit, et hoc ipsum viderequod patitur nescit."

[101] Gregory the Great, *Moralia*, 12.34.39.

[102] Gregory the Great, *Moralia*, 8.47.79. "...hoc ad honorem intimi iudicis in ara cordis immolemus."

[103] Gregory the Great, *Moralia*, 6.16.26. "...qui in bonis actibus positi, spe in Deum firma gratulantur."

[104] Markus, *Gregory*, 205.

and effect in the ascent of the soul to God. The end was soon coming. When humans contemplate their works in light of the coming judgment they find themselves wanting. This want works fear and this fear should bring compulsion to repent of past sins, commit one's self to following God and his precepts, and continue in good works.

Fear was first of all a means of prevenient grace. It made the sinner open to the Gospel and willing to change his or her life. Commenting on Job 28:26-27 and God's making "a course for the thunderbolt", Gregory allegorically interprets these thunder strikes as the judgments experienced by humanity here and now which are heralding the storm of God's swiftly appearing final judgment.[105] Just as a child fears a thunderstorm, humanity should fear the coming judgment. In this way, God brings humanity into the mind-set of being willing to listen. He interprets the tempest again as the law and specifically the law as it was presented by the preachers. In words reminiscent of Paul, he speaks of the way the law brings an awareness of sin into the lives of individuals.[106] When Christians become aware of their sins and shortcomings regarding the law they are struck with a fear and dread of the coming judgment. Thus, God has "made entry to the hearts of a humanity stricken with dread of the judgment to come".[107]

The fear of God's coming judgment causes Christians to immediately turn inward and assess their spiritual condition and progress. Gregory says that those who consider the end of all things find themselves "fearing the sentence of God's judgments and examining [their] own sel[ves]".[108] This fear is the first stage of compunction and the beginning of penance which is, of course, a grace for the "Lord spares sin at the very hour when, the moment we yield tears he does away with the guilt of sin".[109] In this way, fear is a means of grace as it brings penitents to contrition and then leads them on to the contemplation of God. "Behold, the terror of the converted is turned into power because while they punish their sins by penance they ascend even to the exercise of judgment".[110]

Not only should Christians contemplate their inner hearts in light of the

---

[105] Gregory the Great, *Moralia*, 19.7.13.

[106] See Romans 3:20, Galatians 3:24, and 1 Timothy 1:8-10. Paul speaks of the law as the "knowledge of sin," a "schoolmaster" and a "good" as long as it is used for its purpose of convicting the hearts of humanity.

[107] Gregory the Great, *Moralia*, 19.7.13. "Viam autem procelis sonantibus posuit, cum praedicatoribus suis ad corda hominum terrore venturi iudicii perculsa auditum fecit."

[108] Gregory the Great, *Moralia*, 23.21.41. "...aut iudiciorum Dei sententiam metuens et secum quarens, cogitat ubi erit."

[109] Gregory the Great, *Moralia*, 9.40.83. "Ad horum Dominus peccatum parcit, cum reatum culpae concessis protinus fletibus diluit."

[110] Gregory the Great, *Moralia*, 27.17.34. "Ecce conversorum terror vertitur in petestatem, quia dum mala sua paenitendo puniunt, usque ad exercendum iudicium ascendunt."

coming judgment but they should also contemplate their actions. Gregory has a keen awareness that all actions will be judged by the Lord when he comes and he is always zealous to promote fear in this regard. He says, "Let the righteous look to themselves with discreet attention and in all their actions be in dread because they are seen by the Lord".[111] The fear of judgment however, does not only entail actions that have been committed, it is also a force which drives individuals to perform the service and good works that they ought to perform. In light of the coming judgment and the strict justice of the Lord each person ought "never to pass over anything that ought to be done".[112] The fear of God, like most concepts in Gregory, has both a passive and a negative aspect. Persons must always examine their actions to make sure that they are done in accordance with God's law. They must look into their hearts to determine whether or not their motives are pure. Finally, they must remember that to fear God is not only to keep the letter of the law in its prohibitions but also to follow the law of love in acts of service.

The fear of God is not however the goal of the coming return of Christ. The goal is instead love and it is through this fear that Christians learn to love the coming judge. The Christians' fear leads them on to love as they proceed in the spiritual life. The grace of the fear of God is changed into the power of correction in their lives. It moves them to penance and drives them from the fear of the judge to the love of the one who has redeemed them and has forgiven their past transgressions.[113]

The coming judgment is both a reason to fear and a reason to love. Gregory strives to point out a thin line running between the fear of God and the hope of his return. His return is anticipated by the elect who desire to see him coming in glory. Gregory's primary concern is however to moderate both this fear and this hope by maintaining a middle position between both being careful not to be frozen in fear before the coming judge or content to live a life of idleness feeling secure in a false hope. Gregory hopes through this via media to avoid the extremes of desperation and pride and to inculcate an attitude of humility so that Christians may stand accepted on the day of judgment.[114]

Another practical ramification of the coming end of the world involves the pastoral task of preaching which Gregory understood to be a global task. Gregory was zealous not only to promote preaching among his bishops but also to provide missionaries to what he considered to be areas that were underexposed to the gospel.

Although Gregory does not explicitly link either of these tasks to the end of

---

[111] Gregory the Great, *Moralia*, 21.4.8. "...iusti vero semetipsos sollerter inspiciant, et in cunctis actionibus suis a Domino se videri pertimescant."

[112] Gregory the Great, *Moralia*, 1.3.3. "Deum timere est nulla quae facienda sunt bona praeterire."

[113] Gregory the Great, *Moralia*, 22.20.48

[114] Gregory the Great, *Moralia*, 30.27.83.

the world the concept is clearly inherent in his understanding of the "ages of preaching". Gregory outlines four distinct phases of preaching in the Church in an elaborate allegory of the life of a matron.[115] He identifies the earliest age of the Church's preaching with the image of a young girl who is too immature to feed the Church with preaching.[116] Gregory does not explicitly explain this identification but it is apparent from the next phase that he clearly means that this period was the time before Pentecost and the granting of the Holy Spirit in power. Thus, the period could be applied to either: 1) the time before Christ's first advent, or 2) the time from Christ's earthly ministry up to Pentecost.

The second phase of the preaching of the Church is maturity. After the granting of the Holy Spirit, the Church was in full figure and capable of nurturing her children with milk from the word of God. In fact the Church is "married to the Word of God".[117] "By the office of preaching she is pregnant with the conception of children, with whom by exhorting she travails, whom by converting she brings forth."[118]

In the present phase however, the Church has grown old because of sin. It is beyond the age of child-bearing. Its efforts in preaching find little to no effect. The Church has become "weak and does not have the strength to bring forth children by preaching".[119] All that remains for the Church is for her to "remember" the days of her past fruitfulness.[120] It was then that she truly served the Lord.

But this weakness was not to last. In a miracle reminiscent of the aged Sarah bringing forth Isaac, the Church will once again bear great fruit. The last day is coming and the triumph of the Church will be made evident through the power of preaching. The promise of Romans 11:25-26[121] assures Gregory that, "after a

---

[115] Gregory the Great, *Moralia*, 19.12.19.

[116] Gregory the Great, *Moralia*, 19.12.19. Gregory first quotes a passage from the Song of Songs 8:8 and then makes this application to Holy Church. "Hinc enim de illa dicitur: Soror nostra parvula est et ubera non habet quia nimirum sancta Ecclesia priusquam proficeret per incrementa virtutis, infirmis quibusque auditoribus praebere non potuit ubera praedicationis."

[117] Gregory the Great, *Moralia*, 19.12.19. "Adulta vero Ecclesia dicitur, quando Dei verbo copulata." In using this gendered language in reference to the Church I am attempting to follow Gregory's usage which is reflective of the image of the Church as the bride of Christ.

[118] Gregory the Great, *Moralia*, 19.12.19. "...sancto repleta Spiritu, per praedicationis ministerium in filiorum conceptione fetatur, quos exhortando parturit, convertendo parit."

[119] Gregory the Great, *Moralia*, 19.12.19. "quasi quodam senio debilitata, per praedicationem filios parere non valet."

[120] Gregory the Great, *Moralia*, 19.12.19. "reminiscitur fecunditatis antiquae."

[121] Romans 11:25-26 reads, "For I do not want you, brethren, to be uninformed of this mystery, lest you be wise in your own estimation, that a partial hardening has happened to Israel, until the fullness of the Gentiles has come in. 26) And thus all Israel will be

while, toward the very end of times, she is empowered with a mighty efficacy of preaching".[122]

This eschatological concept has obvious practical ramifications for Gregory and helps to explain not only his emphasis upon preaching but also his insistence upon sending missionaries and working for the conversion of "pagans" in Christianized areas.[123] The Church must do its part. The nearer the end was, the more the Church should be careful to prepare for the coming of the judge. The great influx of coming believers was to be brought about by preaching and Gregory would not allow any slacking in this aspect of the ministerial office by his bishops. There was no better tool for rousing the hearts of the hearers than preaching.[124] Even in the midst of the coming tribulation preachers would be persecuted and preaching rare[125] but their activity would not cease because God would strengthen the voice of the preachers against their persecutions.[126] Preaching was the primary vehicle of the gospel and it would continue until the very end. Not until God was revealed personally in all his majesty would the message of the preachers cease.[127] Only then would the pastoral charge to preach be loosed because at that time there would be no further chance for repentance; and repentance, after all, was the primary goal of all preaching.[128]

The end of time would also bring the oppression of heretics. In the spirit of Antichrist they would raise, and to a great degree had already raised, themselves up in pride against the Church. Yet for all Gregory's harsh words about the heretics in the *Moralia* he still shows a keen desire that they would

---

saved; just as it is written, The Deliverer will come from Zion, He will remove ungodliness from Jacob."

[122] Gregory the Great, *Moralia*, 19.12.19. "Quamvis post eosdem dies quibus deprimitur, iam tamen circa ipsum finem temporum grandi praedicationis virtute roboretur."

[123] See Markus, *Gregory*, 76-79 (Jews); 80-82 (pagans within the Empire); 177-187 (the Franks and the English Church). On the English mission see Dudden, *Gregory*, vol. 2, 99-159. For general arguments on mission in Gregory the Great see R.A. Markus, "Gregory the Great and a Papal Missionary Strategy," in G.J. Cumming (ed), *Studies in Church History* (Cambridge 1970), vol. 6, 29-38; and P. Benkart, "Die Missionsidee Gregors des Grossen in Theorie und Praxis" Ph.D. diss. (Leipzig 1946).

[124] Gregory the Great, *Moralia*, 26.24.42.

[125] Gregory the Great, *Moralia*, 20.41.79.

[126] Gregory the Great, *Moralia*, 29.23.47.

[127] Gregory the Great, *Moralia*, 30.10.37.

[128] Gregory the Great, *Moralia*, 13.5.6-6.8. Here Gregory emphasizes that the goal of preaching is not simply rebuke but a rebuke that leads to repentance. He points to the fact that different persons must be dealt with in different ways. The weak cannot be so sternly rebuked that they shrink away in fear of ever recovering but the strong of this world must be harshly rebuked so that they will see the error of their way and be made ashamed of their actions. Preaching is therefore the "art" of bringing about repentance and the preacher must always discern the character of those receiving the message so that it may have the appropriate effect.

come back to the faith. He commands the Church to maintain prayer for the heretics that they would see the error of their way and repent. Not only does Gregory command the Church to pray for heretics but he also outlines a methodology of winning them back to Holy Church. In medical imagery Gregory refers to heretics as a cancer that must be cut out so that the healthy flesh may be restored. Interestingly enough, the heretics are both the cancer that is removed and the healthy flesh that will be restored. Similarly, he also employs an agrarian metaphor that likens the heretics to both briars that are uprooted and fresh seed upon their return. This restoration will however only result if the Church is faithful in heralding true theology, fighting against heresy, and disproving the false statements of enemies.[129]

Gregory's concern for the heretics is due in part to his belief that many of them were simply misguided having "purity of heart" but holding to corrupt teachings.[130] Gregory believes that these heretics, if they were loved and prayed for by the Church would return.[131] Gregory draws a parallel between the friends of Job and the heretics. Just as Job continued to love and pray for his friends, and in the end offered sacrifices for them, the Church must love those who now persecute it through false teaching. "God's faithful people must never cease to call back to the truth, with loving affection, the very persons whom they suffer as persecutors."[132] Gregory outlines the reclamation of the heretic as a battle wherein one must be armed with both the "shield of patience" and the "darts of love" so that through charity the church will conquer the impenitent.[133]

de novissimis

Gregory's doctrine of the last things is largely a bundle of theological teachings with the emphasis placed upon the spiritual character of the particular eschatological dogma under discussion. Gregory is no speculative theologian but he is a contemplative theologian. Thus, in his discussion of the millennium, the final tribulation, the last judgment and the eternal state he affirms the traditional teachings of the Church while often making new spiritual and pastoral applications of these truths. In the end, it is not specific dogma that is most important; it is the spiritual character of the doctrine that is foremost in his mind.

---

[129] Gregory the Great, *Moralia*, 8.5.6.
[130] Gregory the Great, *Moralia*, 16.5.7.
[131] Gregory the Great, *Moralia*, 16.5.7.
[132] Gregory the Great, *Moralia*, 8.1.1. "...quia fidelis Dei populus ipsos quoque quos persequentes tolerat amando non desinit ad veritatem vocare."
[133] Gregory the Great, *Moralia*, 8.1.1.

The "Millennium"

Gregory joins Augustine in arguing that the millennium should be spiritually interpreted. He is loath to allow a literal interpretation of a concept so attached to this world and its physicality. There is simply no room for such a physical interpretation in his spiritual program. He says that if the millennium were understood to be an actual physical kingdom it would not be appropriate for the saints, "because minds that are devoted to this world are disturbed by the cares and anxieties of the present life, and therefore are quite unable to enjoy the repose of that Wisdom".[134] The common literal understanding of the millennium as it was understood to be presented in Revelation 20 was that the saints would be with Christ in this kingdom.[135] Yet Gregory understood that the saints' primary task was to contemplate and enjoy the presence of Christ. Gregory could not reconcile this task with a physical ruling of the saints together with Christ in the millennium.

Gregory was likewise dismissive of a literal interpretation of the 1,000 years. Gregory is fond of the theological interpretation of numbers throughout the *Moralia* and this one is no different. Instead of a literal 1,000 years Gregory prefers to see this time period as indicative of the completeness of God's activity in the world through his Church. It related not to a period of time but to the catholic nature of the Church's rule over the earth. In discussing the 1,000 years of the millennium as presented in Revelation 20 he says, "by the number 1,000, he denoted not the quantity of time but the universality, with which the Church exercises dominion".[136]

To what then does the millennium have reference? Positively, it is the reign of the Church and should be identified with the present kingdom of God. God exercises his dominion in the hearts of the elect. The elect agree with his governance and submit themselves to his authority. The primary locus for the kingdom is in the Church. The Church by virtue of its association with Christ actually has dominion over the world and reigns together with him.[137] This dominion rests in the spiritual authority given by Christ to the Church. Even though temporal authority may hold sway over the Church externally, the Church owns the keys to the kingdom and exercises universal, spiritual control over the temporal powers of this world. "Holy Church...even now does not

---

[134] Gregory the Great, *Moralia*, 18.42.67. "Et quia huic mundo mentes deditae praesentis vitae curis et sollicitudinibus perturbantur et idcirco eius dem sapientiae tranquillitate perfrui nequaquam possunt..."

[135] For Gregory's understanding of this text see C. Nardi, "Gregorio Magno interprete di Apocolisse 20," in *Gregorio Magno e il suo tempo*, vol. 2, *Questioni letterarie e dottrinali* (Rome 1991), 267-83.

[136] Gregory the Great, *Moralia*, 18.42.67. "Millenario enim numero non quantitatem temporis, sed universitatem qua regnat Ecclesia, designavit."

[137] Gregory the Great, *Moralia*, 9.3.3.

cease to judge all that either act wickedly or think foolishly".[138]

Negatively, this means that the authority and power of Satan has been greatly curtailed. In several places Gregory speaks of Satan during the time of the Church as being bound and cast into the pit.[139] The binding of Satan means that he has no authority over the Church and is confined to the hearts of the reprobate. Satan's binding then, since he is still present in the hearts of the reprobate, does not preclude his animosity against the Church or the faithful but it does mean that his actions are greatly restricted by God.[140]

This binding of Satan would not last forever for he would be released to wreak havoc upon the Church and the world during the last tribulation just before the end of the world. This "loosing" of Satan would manifest itself in the open persecution of the Church.[141] Nevertheless, this tribulation does not mark the end of the reign of the Church but only a final trial. The actual consummation of the millennial reign is completed when the Lord returns double to the Church for the members it loses in this persecution and the full number of believers mentioned by the apostle Paul in Romans 8 is added to the Church.[142]

The Final Tribulation

Gregory understands that even now in the peace of the Church, the Church is undergoing various types of tribulation. These tribulations come from both within (heresy and hypocrisy) and from without (barbarian forces) but the pressure placed upon the Church at this time is scattered and hidden. Once Satan has appeared in the assumed man, this Antichrist will institute an open and universal persecution of the Church.[143] Satan will be agitated to move against the Church in the last day with more severe temptations because he is aware that his end is drawing near. Through the events of these last days Satan will enlarge his pride by demonstrating all his worldly powers in order to take with him to destruction as many as possible.[144]

Gregory is quick to affirm the sovereignty of God even during the last tribulation of the Church. The image of Job provides a wonderful parallel with the tribulation period because just as God allowed Job to be tried by Satan, he will grant permission for Satan to try the world during this last period. Satan

---

[138] Gregory the Great, *Moralia*, 11.22.33. "Sancta Ecclesia...nunc etiam de cunctis prave agentibus, vel stulte sentientibus iudicare non cessat."

[139] Gregory the Great, *Moralia*. See 4.9.16; 18.42.67; 19.9.15 and 32.15.22.

[140] Gregory the Great, *Moralia*, 32.15.22.

[141] Gregory the Great, *Moralia*, 18.42.67.

[142] Gregory the Great, *Moralia*, 9.3.3.

[143] Gregory the Great, *Moralia*, 13.10.12. For the "Antichrist" in Gregory the Great see Hervé Savon, "L'Antéchrist dans l'oeuvre de Grégoire le Grand," in Jacques Fontaine, Robert Gillet and Stan Pellistrandi (eds.), *Grégoire le Grand* (Paris 1986), 389-405.

[144] Gregory the Great, *Moralia*, 34.1.1.

becomes a tool of God and serves as God's servant even against his will.[145] God permits this tribulation either in mercy, as it applies to the elect, or in judgment, as it applies to the reprobate.[146]

When God permits this tribulation in mercy he is purifying the elect members of his Church. "The author of the sin of wickedness ... [becomes] ... the scourge of discipline".[147] The elect are beaten out on the anvil of Satan.[148] God has promised however to protect the souls of the elect so that they will not fall in this persecution. They will stand in the persecution by God's grace and their souls are safeguarded.[149] However, this serves only to heighten the anger of Satan who multiplies his afflictions upon their flesh as he sees that they have no effect upon the spirit.[150]

Of course this physical torment of the elect works for their benefit because it works to estrange them from the evil lure of this material world and lift their spirits in an awareness of the world to come.[151] Satan's power in persecuting during the final tribulation also works the judgment of God. Those who are not members of the elect are led away by his false miracles and demonstration of power.[152] The work of the Antichrist in the last day is to embolden the reprobate to strike out against God and God's Church. Secure in the temporal power of the enemy, they assail the Lord's body with him and perform boldly what they were afraid to do before his appearance. In this way, they heap up judgment against themselves and prove outright what they had always been inwardly.[153] In this way, the evil will of Satan who seeks to work damnation actually serves the just judgment of God.[154]

This final tribulation also serves to purify the visible Church. It brings about a time wherein those who are outwardly rather than inwardly attached to the Church will manifest their true colors. Just as fire purifies metal, the Church will be purified in this last tribulation. Gregory's most poignant image of the final persecution of the Church is however, the image of the winnowing of grain and chaff at the harvest. He argues that the elect are, "the more genuinely cleared of the chaff of sins, the more they are bruised with affliction".[155]

---

[145] Gregory the Great, *Moralia*, 33.14.29.

[146] Gregory the Great, *Moralia*, 33.14.28.

[147] Gregory the Great, *Moralia*, 33.8.15. "Qui auctor fuerat ad vitium nequitiae, ipse flagellum fieret disciplinae."

[148] Gregory the Great, *Moralia*, 34.6.11.

[149] Gregory the Great, *Moralia*, 15.58.69.

[150] Gregory the Great, *Moralia*, 34.11.22. "Et quia nil se contra eorum spiritum praevalere considerat, in eorum carne crudelitatis suae omnia argumenta consummat."

[151] Gregory the Great, *Moralia*, 16.28.48.

[152] Gregory the Great, *Moralia*, 33.6.13.

[153] Gregory the Great, *Moralia*, 34.3.7-4.9. See also, 33.3.6.

[154] Gregory the Great, *Moralia*, 2.10.17.

[155] Gregory the Great, *Moralia*, 19.9.16. "...ut grana caelestibus horreis recondenda tanto verius a peccatorum paleis exuantur, quanto arctius affliguntur."

In this persecution a multitude of the faithful will fall away from the Church and even though the Church feels the loss, this pruning purifies the Church because those who faithfully remain see the example of the fall of the weaker members and although they sorrow in compassion for them and their lot they are themselves strengthened against a similar fall by a great fear of following after their example.[156]

The Last Judgment

The last judgment holds a central place in Gregory's thinking in the *Moralia*. At least for the purposes of this text, Gregory focuses the motivation for living the Christian life in the fact that all will be judged. The day of Christ's second coming will be the apex of human history and will usher in the final state. In this last moment before timelessness Gregory finds the fulfilled promises of God. It is at this point that Christ will be fully recognized by all human persons as the Son of God and will receive worship.[157] Satan will be cast out and Christ will be victor.[158] Humanity will be changed forever. The Church will receive its reward as it enters the kingdom.[159] In fact, the judgment is the portal through which all humanity will enter into the eternal state; either bowing before Christ as Lord or cowering before him as the just and exacting judge.[160]

One of the reasons why Gregory finds the last judgment such a helpful tool in which to focus the Christian life is his belief that the judgment is imminent. We have already seen how Gregory believed that almost all of the signs mentioned in the Olivet Discourse had been fulfilled and that he felt as well that the few remaining signs were beginning to show themselves. This means that the judgment was soon to follow as the consummation of all things. He describes the coming judgment as swift and likens it to lightning.[161] "The day of divine judgment is imminent, the very face of his fear is already visible...the glory of his majesty is presently approaching".[162]

This concept of the majesty of the coming judge serves to further outline how humanity should respond. Christ, the coming judge, makes all persons aware of his coming in judgment by words and signs which reveal his true majesty.[163] Christ appeared in his first advent in humility to call the nations to him but he would burst forth in his second coming in his full majesty. His

---

[156] Gregory the Great, *Moralia*, 19.11.18.
[157] Gregory the Great, *Moralia*, 20.3.9.
[158] Gregory the Great, *Moralia*, 33.20.37.
[159] Gregory the Great, *Moralia*, 4.11.19.
[160] Gregory the Great, *Moralia*, 6.7.9.
[161] Gregory the Great, *Moralia*, 34.5.10.
[162] Gregory the Great, *Moralia*, 31.27.54 "Ecce enim quia divini iudicii dies imminet, quasi ipsa iam timoris eius facies apparet...gloria majestatis eius appropinquat."
[163] Gregory the Great, *Moralia*, 35.14.34.

divinity will no longer be hidden but Christ will display the "terrors of his highness" and "glow in the majesty of his power".[164]

The majesty and power of the coming judge, the swiftness of his appearance, and the exacting nature of the future inquest all provide a focus for the Christian life. More than anything else, Christians should meditate upon the coming judgment of God so that they might be prepared. Gregory wants wise instead of foolish virgins and continuous contemplation is all that will provide for perpetual preparedness.[165]

At the second coming all of the humility of the first advent will be replaced by Christ's glory and majesty. The awesome power and privileged position of Christ as the Son of God will be revealed at this time. In truth, Christ will be presented unveiled in all his divinity. It is in this way that a proclamation of his status and divinity is made in a veritable *apokatastasis* of all things under the authority of the judge. Those that doubted his divinity because of his appearance as a man will be faced with the truth of their error. Thus, the second coming is really for Gregory a coronation. Christ who is the king will then be recognized as such. In this way, the full circle of Christ's dealings with humanity will be reached. The alpha and omega will appear and with his coming the "Truth" will become evident.[166] Gregory sums up this manner of thinking in his description of Christ as a "despised lamp" who though initially ridiculed will at his coming "flash judgment from heaven".[167]

But Christ is not the only despised lamp that will be made manifest in glory in the day of judgment. The Church and all its saints who continuously suffered ill at the hands of its enemies from without and hypocrites and heretics from within will also be vindicated. Inasmuch as the Church was persecuted and despised on earth it will be glorified in the last judgment. Just as Christ will shine on the day of the last judgment the Church, also a despised lamp, will reveal its true glory in participation with him.[168]

---

[164] Gregory the Great, *Moralia*, 17.32.53. "eius celsitudinis terrorem"; "in potestatis suae majestate canduerit".

[165] The issue of contemplation and fear of the judge will be more fully discussed in chapter 4 where we shall examine the Christological focus of the spiritual life in connection to the image of Christ as judge and the way that Christians are called to perform the work of the judge in themselves so as not to be judged by Christ.

[166] In the text of the *Moralia* the only term used to refer to Christ that is more numerous than "judge" is "truth." This of course has roots in the concept of Christ being the *logos* of God but can and should also be understood in the context of Christ's person being a form of revelation. Gregory, in line with the authors of Scripture, sees Christ as the express image of God the Father (Collosians 1:15, Hebrews 1:3) and argues that he will be established as the "true" God at his second coming in judgment where all will recognize his authority and divinity. This is the primary point in his comparison of the two advents of Christ in 17.32.53-17.34.54.

[167] Gregory the Great, *Moralia*, 10.31.54. "de caelo iudicium coruscat".

[168] Gregory the Great, *Moralia*, 10.31.52.

The glory of Christ in the second coming is passed on to the Church and to individual saints within the Church based upon their union with Christ. The Church as the body of Christ is bound to him in suffering in this world. As Christ suffered in his earthly life, the Church now suffers. Gregory speaks of Christ suffering even now in his body which is the Church.[169] This union is also a union of labor for the Church is presently busy doing Christ's work and will join Christ also in his work of judgment.[170]

So what is the work which Christ is accomplishing in the judgment? Christ comes not only to manifest the truth of his divinity and his glory but to judge humanity for sin. This judgment has been given to the Son from the Father because of the merits of his incarnation.[171] The judgment will be exacting.[172] Christ will judge sins that were actually committed as well as sins of omission.[173] It will extend not only to the actual works and deeds of humanity but to the inner desires and temptations of the heart.[174] All that has been done against God in secret will be made manifest for Christ will make a "public inquiry" and expose all misdeeds so that there will be none who can doubt the justness of the judgment.[175]

The judgment of Christ in the last day is a day of purification. Even the reprobate will be "sanctified" in this last day.[176] Of course, what Gregory means by this statement is that the reprobate will be "cleansed" in that they will realize how greatly they have failed to live up to the requirements set by Christ and by the continuous process of purgation which they will begin and continually undergo in hell just after the final judgment. This last day of judgment is the last separation wherein the visible Church will become identical with the invisible Church for all the chaff will be consumed in the fire of judgment leaving only the pure wheat.[177]

In this judgment the elect will be revealed. Many will be lost and only a small number will be saved.[178] The final aspect of Christ's role as judge in the last judgment is his service as the gatekeeper.[179] The last judgment is the

---

[169] Gregory the Great, *Moralia*, 3.13.25; 3.19.35 and 35.14.27.

[170] The Church judges the world now just as Christ judges the world. This act is an act of union wherein the Church participates in the divine role of Christ. Gregory points out that this is primarily accomplished through Church discipline. See *Moralia*, 11.22.33.

[171] Gregory the Great, *Moralia*, 28.1.5.

[172] Gregory the Great, *Moralia*, 8.34.57.

[173] Gregory the Great, *Moralia*, 15.19.23.

[174] Gregory the Great, *Moralia*, 4.14.26.

[175] Gregory the Great, *Moralia*, 25.8.19.

[176] Gregory the Great, *Moralia*, 27.23.45.

[177] Gregory the Great, *Moralia*, 34.5.10.

[178] Gregory the Great, *Moralia*, 20.28.56.

[179] This image is most likely based on the Johanine imagery of Christ as the "door" in John 7:9; and the image of the good shepherd sleeping in the door of the sheep-pen so that none will remove his sheep, John 10:7-18. The image of the gate as judgment is also

fulfillment of the kingdom of God.[180] At this judgment individuals will either enter into the kingdom by the gate which is Christ or they will be crushed in the gate as they attempt to enter falsely.

> For as the entrance of a city is called the gate, so is the day of judgment the gate of the kingdom, since all the elect go in thereby to the glory of their heavenly country...For the redeemer of mankind is the husband of holy Church, who shows himself renowned in the gates. Who first came to sight in degradation and in mockings, but shall appear on high at the entering of his kingdom...Holy Church then receives of the fruit of her hands when the recompensing of her labors lifts her up to the entertainment of heavenly blessings, for her works then praise her in the gates, when the words are spoken to her members in the very entrance to the kingdom; for I was hungry and you gave me to eat; I was thirsty and you gave me to drink; I was a stranger and you took me in; naked and you clothed me. The children then of this foolish man are lifted up before the gate but in the gate they will be crushed; in that the followers of this world carry themselves proudly in the present life, but in the very entrance of the kingdom they are struck with an everlasting visitation.[181]

Gregory argues that though Christ is established as the judge of all humanity he will not actually judge all persons. Gregory sets up four different groups of people within two classes; two of the groups will be judged and two of the groups will not be judged.[182] Gregory outlines the presence of two classes of the elect and two classes of the reprobate. The two divisions within these classes are based on whether or not the group will actually be judged by Christ at the last judgment.

The reprobate will of course perish, being cast into eternal fire but only a certain portion of these will actually be judged by Christ. Those who will not be judged are those who either never believed or failed to continue in their belief.

---

biblical and is suggested in Gregory's narrative when he comes to Job 5:4, which reads, "His sons are far from safety, they are even oppressed in the gate, neither is there a deliverer." (NASB)

[180] Gregory the Great, *Moralia*, 4.11.19.

[181] Gregory the Great, *Moralia*, 6.7.9. "Nam sicut urbis aditus porta dicitur, ita est dies iudicii porta regni quia per eum ab electis omnibus ad caelestis patriae gloriam intratur...Vir quippe est Ecclesiae human generis redemptor qui in portis se nobilem ostendit, qui despectus prius in contumeliis exstitit, sed in ingressu regni sublimis apparebit...Tunc quippe sancta Ecclesia de fructu manuum suarum accipit, cum eam ad percipienda caelestia laboris sui retributio attollit. Tunc eam sua opera in portis laudant, quando eius membris in ipso regni aditu dicitur: Esurivi et dedistis mihi manducare; sitiui et dedistis mihi bibere; hospes eram et collegistis me; nudus et cooperuistis me, et cetera. Filii igitur huius stulti ante porta elati sunt sed in porta conterentur, quia amatores huius saeculi in praesenti vita superbiunt, sed in ipso regni aditu aeterna animadversione feriuntur."

[182] Gregory outlines this division most fully in *Moralia*, 26.27.49-51.

Gregory understands that their judgment is unnecessary because they are condemned for their unbelief in themselves. Their conscience which refused to yield to the law in unbelief will now accuse them before the judge and their own sentence of condemnation will simply be ratified by Christ.[183] Their judgment has actually already been made when, because of their persistence in unbelief, God withdraws the light of wisdom and leaves them blinded in the errors of their own wickedness.[184] Gregory argues that they do not deserve to be openly condemned by Christ because they openly despised him in their lives.[185]

All the reprobate will be raised to life again in the second coming to meet their end but only those who maintain their profession of faith will be judged by Christ at that time. Those who have maintained in "words" their faith will at least hear their condemnation in the "words" of the judge.[186] These are condemned not because they did not assent to faith with their mouths but because they did not follow their faith with good works. They are the ones who saw the Lord hungry and gave him no food; thirsty and gave him no drink.[187] Because they had assented to the law by their words of faith and received the sacraments they will be judged by the law whereas those outside the Church will be judged of themselves without the law.[188]

The elect are likewise categorized in regards to whether or not they will be judged by Christ at the last judgment. All the reprobate will perish but all the elect will reign together with Christ. Those that are judged are those who repent of their evil and are the ones "who wipe away the stain of their life with their tears...atoning for their former misdeeds by their subsequent conduct (and) conceal whatever unlawful deed they might have committed from the eyes of the judge with the cloak of good works".[189] In this way we see that all individuals participate in the judgment of Christ by judging themselves. Their penance performed in this life works the judgment and permits them to pay their debt so that Christ will find nothing left in them to judge at the final inquest. Works are however not the covering of sin. They merely prove the penance which is ultimately the result of the mercy of the judge. "We have nothing to make the strict judge gracious toward us, but while we are unable to present our works as worthy of his regard, it remains (for us) to offer to him his

---

[183] Gregory the Great, *Moralia*, 27.15.47-48.

[184] Gregory the Great, *Moralia*, 27.26.49.

[185] Gregory the Great, *Moralia*, 26.27.50.

[186] Gregory the Great, *Moralia*, 26.27.50.

[187] Gregory the Great, *Moralia*, 26.27.50. Gregory uses this text of Matthew 25:42-43 in several places to demonstrate the importance of good works in the Christian life. See also 15.19.23.

[188] Gregory the Great, *Moralia*, 26.27.50.

[189] Gregory the Great, *Moralia*, 26.27.51. "Qui vitae maculas lacrimis tergunt, qui mala praecedentia factis sequentibus redimentes, quicquid illicitum aliquando fecerunt ab oculis iudicis eleemosynarum superductione cooperiunt."

own work for the propitiation of his favor."[190] Thus, the mercy of Christ in judging is the provision of his active as well as his passive obedience. As Christians recognize their own culpability and work in repentance for their sins Christ grants them his own merits so that as long as they judge themselves they will not be judged by him.

There are also those members of the elect who will not be judged but will reign. These are the perfect who have surpassed all the requirements of the law. This group is made up of the true saints who move on to a higher mode of life. They are not content with the general precepts of the law but "with surpassing eagerness desire to perfection more than they would learn from general precepts".[191] Because they have met and surpassed the general requirements of the law in their perfection they are beyond being judged by the law in the last judgment. There is nothing in them to condemn them under the law. All that is left for them is to reign together with God. As they learned to reign as judges in their own lives they have won the right to come with him as judges at the last judgment.

This last point brings up the interesting fact that the elect are said to reign and judge with Christ. Based upon the judgment of their own flesh and their dominion over it, the saints have won the right to sit together with Christ as his judges. The authority with which they ruled their bodies is transferred to the "power of retribution" because "they are placed forever on the throne of the kingdom of eternal elevation; and they there receive the power of justly judging others, just as they are here unskilled in unjustly judging themselves".[192] The role of the Elect as judges and rulers in the future, eternal kingdom is connected to their judgment of themselves in this present life. The humility of judging oneself brings glory in judging others. The present life is connected to the latter only by the role of judge. The object of the judging will however change. With this change will come also a change in situation. Here, Christians suffer as they afflict themselves in judgment but there they will be lifted up. "They then, who are journeying to their eternal home, now despise themselves in the place of affliction for a time, that they may then be truly exalted in the place of joy".[193]

---

[190] Gregory the Great, *Moralia*, 9.48.73. "...districtus iudex unde nobis fiat placabilis, non habemus. Sed cum nostrum opus eius obtutibus dignum exhibere non possumus, restat ut ad placationem illius suum ei opus offeramus."

[191] Gregory the Great, *Moralia*, 26.27.51. "...sed praestantiori desiderio plus exhibere appetunt quam praeceptis generalibus audire potuerunt."

[192] Gregory the Great, *Moralia*, 26.28.53. "...potestatem retributionis...sed in regni erectionis internae solio in perpetuum collocantur; et eo illic accipiunt alios digne iudicare, quo hic nesciunt sibimetipsis nequiter parcere."

[193] Gregory the Great, *Moralia*, 26.28.54. "Qui ergo ad aeternam patriam tendunt, nunc emetipsos temporaliter in afflictionis loco despiciunt, ut tunc in loco gaudii veraciter sublimentur."

The Eternal State

The eternal state is divided into two kingdoms by Gregory each being under the dominion of God. Heaven, the inheritance of the elect; and hell, the inheritance of the reprobate are entered by each respective group following the last judgment. Although the last judgment serves as an entrance into either of these two destinations Gregory does not divide it in such a neatly temporal fashion. In describing God's existence outside of time he reminds us that God experiences all time in a universal present. Human persons however, existing as they do in time are already in this life moving toward one or the other of these two destinations. "We are not led to the eternal world at once, but by a progression of cases and of words as though by so many steps".[194] This statement by Gregory is revealing because it shows that he understands the present life to be causally and really linked to the life to come. The eschaton is, after a fashion, already here in the lives of each human person and they are either being judged or helped by grace at any given moment. Heaven or hell, as the case may be, is not simply a future occurrence but is already breaking forth into the lives of each and every individual.

Gregory is very restrained in his description of heaven.[195] He refuses to indulge the senses with images garnered from this life. His discussion maintains a certain theological aloofness from physicality while at the same time emphasizing the spiritual union of believers with God in contemplation during this present life as a foretaste of what is to come. Gregory emphasizes two aspects of heaven throughout the *Moralia*. The first of these is the contemplation of God. While now humanity is limited to the contemplation of Christ who has been revealed to bodily eyes, at that time the elect will contemplate the fullness of the trinity in the spiritual kingdom.[196] The second aspect of heaven that Gregory emphasizes is the categorization of heaven as a reward.[197] It is the place wherein all the trials of this life come to fruition. Heaven is the fulfillment of this present life as one sees and comes to understand the *telos* of all that is experienced on earth. In heaven, the mutability of this present existence will be ended as the blessed enter into the place of the elect; the eternal light of God where they shall be with the immutable author of creation and salvation in the contemplation of love.[198]

Hell was of course the other potential destination for souls in the eternal

---

[194] Gregory the Great, *Moralia*, 2.20.35. "Quia igitur non repente sed causaru verborumque incrementis, quasi quibusdam ad aeternitatem passibus ducimur."

[195] For a good discussion of "heaven" in the thought of Gregory the Great see J.P. McClain, *The Doctrine of Heaven in the Writings of Saint Gregory the Great*, vol. 95, Studies in Sacred Theology Series 2 (Washington D.C. 1956). See also Eileen Gardiner, *Visions of Heaven and Hell Before Dante* (New York 1989).

[196] Gregory the Great, *Moralia*, 35.15.42.

[197] Gregory the Great, *Moralia*, 35.15.42.

[198] Gregory the Great, *Moralia*, 4.33.67.

state.[199] The reticence which Gregory shows in discussing heaven is not an issue in his presentation of hell. The *Moralia* comes to life with horrendous pictures of suffering and torture in vivid scenes and detail. The physicality of this present life which lured the reprobate from pursuing a spiritual life will be horrifically present in hell as well.

Hell is created by the almighty to deal with sin.[200] It is axiomatic for Gregory that because God is holy, God must punish sin.[201] Since not all sins are punished in this life it must therefore follow that there is a place for punishment in the eternal state.[202] Hell is the reward of the reprobate who neglect to show sorrow for their sin.[203] In this context of damnation and eternal punishment Gregory is zealous to affirm the mercy of God. God does not desire the punishment of any in hell. He is longsuffering and strives through various ways to bring the reprobate to repentance. Yet, if they continually refuse to respond, God gives them over to the blindness of their condition and assigns them an everlasting place in hell. "He brings out severity the more rigorously the more mildly he now spreads low his patience in calling sinners for he that waits a long time for some to be converted, if they are not converted, torments them without revoke".[204] In hell they will never have another opportunity to repent because they have squandered so many opportunities in this present life.[205]

Gregory is zealous to affirm the eternal nature of the punishment to be experienced in hell. He labels the idea that punishment will only be temporary as an error of Origen and devotes a lengthy argument against its cessation.[206] Here he argues that Christ's own words bear witness to the eternal nature of hell.[207] He argues that even though the sins of the reprobate are limited by the span of their life their punishment should still not be limited because had they had the opportunity they would have continued in their sin indefinitely. He says

---

[199] On "hell" in Gregory the Great see I. Fonash, *The Doctrine of Eternal Punishment in the Writings of Saint Gregory the Great*, vol. 66, Studies in Sacred Theology Series 2 (Washington D.C. 1952); and Eileen Gardiner, *Visions of Heaven and Hell Before Dante* (New York 1989).

[200] Gregory the Great, *Moralia*, 15.29.35.

[201] Gregory the Great, *Moralia*, 10.11.21.

[202] Gregory the Great, *Moralia*, 25.5.7. Gregory also points out that the more God forebears in his punishment of sin now the greater will be the punishment in hell. In other places Gregory demonstrates the circular character of an argument of this sort by stating that if God punished everything now there would be nothing to punish in hell; see, *Moralia*, 5.18.35.

[203] Gregory the Great, *Moralia*, 9.63.95.

[204] Gregory the Great, *Moralia*, 10.31.54. "Et tanto tunc durius districtionem exerit, quanto nunc vocandis peccatoribus suam lenius patientiam sternit. Qui enim diu convertendos exspectat, non conversos sine retractatione cruciat."

[205] Gregory the Great, *Moralia*, 9.63.95.

[206] Gregory the Great, *Moralia*, 34.19.34-38.

[207] Gregory the Great, *Moralia*, 34.19.35.

that they sought to sin more than they sought to live and their eternal punishment fits the eternal nature of their rebellion against God.[208] It is only by God's grace that they are not allowed to live longer because they would then only be heaping up worse judgment upon themselves. God is not pleased with this punishment but his justice demands it and it also serves to allow the elect to measure the joy they experience against the punishments they have avoided through his grace.[209]

Punishment in hell is both physical and spiritual because human persons are made up of both body and spirit and actually sin in all elements of their being.[210] The fire of hell is a bodily fire.[211] It torments those in hell but does not consume them.[212] Yet the worst punishment of hell is inflicted upon the spirit of the reprobate. They are overwrought by confusion and despair.[213] This confusion comes from the nature of their punishment as an "eternal death".

> And these punishments both torture those that are plunged therein beyond their powers, and at the same time preserve them alive, extinguishing in them the forces of life, that the end may so afflict the life, that torment may ever live without end, in that it is both hastening after an end through torments, and failing holds on without end. Therefore, there is done upon the wretches death without death, an end without ending, failing without failing; in that both death lives, and the end is ever beginning, and the failing is unable to fail. Therefore whereas death at the same time slays and does not extinguish, pain torments but does not banish fear, the flame burns but does not dispel the darkness.[214]

But the greatest pain of hell is the separation of the soul from God. Physical death may separate the soul from the body but spiritual death is all the more tragic. The human person was created to enter into a relationship with God, "to contemplate his creator, that he might ever be seeking after his likeness, and dwell in the festival of his love".[215] In hell, however, this relationship is severed

---

[208] Gregory the Great, *Moralia*, 34.19.36.

[209] Gregory the Great, *Moralia*, 34.19.37.

[210] Gregory the Great, *Moralia*, 16.14.19.

[211] Gregory the Great, *Moralia*, 15.29.35.

[212] Gregory the Great, *Moralia*, 9.65.98.

[213] Gregory the Great, *Moralia*, 8.18.34.

[214] Gregory the Great, *Moralia*, 9.66.100. "Quae tamen supplicia in se demersos et ultra vires cruciant, et in eis vitae subsidium exstinguentes servant, ut sic vitam terminus puniat; quatenus semper sine termino cruciatus vivat quia et ad finem per tormenta properat, et sine fine deficiens durat. Fit ergo miseris mors sine morte, finis sine fine, defectus sine defectu, quia et mors vivit et finis semper incipit, et deficere defectus nescit. Quia igitur et mors perimit et non exstinguit; dolor cruciat, sed nullatenus pavorem fugat; flamma comburit, sed nequaquam tenebras discutit..."

[215] Gregory the Great, *Moralia*, 8.18.34. "Ad contemplandum quippe Creatorem homo conditus fuerat ut eius semper speciem quaereret, atque in sollemnitate illius amoris habitaret."

and the soul is consigned to an eternity of dark separation, always aware of its loss.[216]

Conclusion

The eschatology of Gregory plays an active role in his teaching on the spiritual life. He begins with the foundation that has been laid for him in the gospels. The Olivet Discourse provides the signs of the end as an impetus toward spiritual preparedness. The early exegetes repeat the same theme and set a precedent for applying these scriptural signs to the events of their own lives, especially after the destruction of the temple in Jerusalem by Titus in 70 CE. The Jewish apocalypticism reflected in Daniel 9-12 is taken up by many in the Christian Church. At the same time however, less flamboyant images of a "realized eschatology" appeared in Clement and Ignatius.

Gregory does his best to make use of both of these traditions. The *romanitas* of Jerome and Augustine's concept of the two cities provide the basis for his synthesis. His apocalypticism in reference to the city of the world is tempered by his triumphalism regarding the city of God. When Gregory couples this with the emphasis of both Ambrose and his pupil Augustine on the image of Christ as judge the synthesis is complete. The judgment of the world experienced by all becomes the means whereby the Church will triumph. Though the members of the Church may suffer, they are spiritually invigorated by the struggle and their advance in contemplation is assured. As the world falls the Church rises and the judge rules over all.

Gregory discusses the signs of the end in light of this apocalyptic and triumphant eschatological dichotomy. The signs that have already appeared serve to promote the readiness of the elect. Natural disasters, military invasions, and the natural entropy of the world show that the world is coming to an end and all that live here should look for a more sure foundation in the spiritual as opposed to the physical realm. The tribulation of the Church and the cessation of miracles serve to try and strengthen the faith of its members. The signs yet to appear are looked for by the Church in anticipation. Christ has promised a great outpouring of grace wherein the full number of Gentiles and the Jews will be converted. At the same time however, the coming of the Antichrist and the great and final tribulation of the Church are sources of fear and concern. Nevertheless, God will use this period to purify his Church and though it is oppressed it will still prevail.

The imminence of the coming end had many practical ramifications for individuals. It was not a call to cease activity but a cry for renewed vigor and activity focused in the spiritual life. The realization of the coming end calls all individuals to a consideration of the inner rather than the outer life. With the prospect of the end looming, one should be more concerned about spiritual

---

[216] Gregory the Great, *Moralia*, 9.63.95.

matters and should seek the contemplation of God. Christians should also look within themselves. Their works should be assessed and the intent of their hearts tried. The fact that the end was coming meant that the judgment was also drawing near. Gregory calls everyone to the Jewish tradition's emphasis on the "fear of God". This fear turns the soul inward and moves it toward contrition and the contemplation of God but it must not stop there. Fear must find its end in love. As Christians fear correction they are brought to correction which is followed by penance. Penance begins with the fear of the judge but ends in the love of the redeemer.

The Church must also be aware of the implications of the end for it. The nearness of the end meant that the ministry of the word must continue. Gregory wants to emphasize preaching and missionary efforts as the world draws to a close. The Church has grown old and is now beyond childbearing years. But it is called to hope for the future for just as Sarah in her old age brought forth Isaac, the Church is awaiting a final outpouring of grace. It must look to its glorious past and take hope in its future. The heresy that has arisen inside it must be no great cause for alarm. Instead, the Church must pity those of a good heart who are misguided and have fallen into error. It must strive daily through preaching and prayer to draw these poor ones back into its ranks.

Gregory's teachings on the last things also serve a practical purpose. He is very traditional in what he asserts as dogma but brings original spiritual and pastoral applications to these theological expressions. The millennium is already present in the kingdom of God inaugurated by Christ in the Church. In this kingdom the Church is to rule over all things and can be assured that Satan's power has been curtailed.

The open and universal persecution of the Church coming at the final tribulation is used as a forum for Gregory to discuss the sovereignty of God. Though Satan seeks to do evil to the Church, God will see to it that the experience serves to purify his Church. For the reprobate during the final persecution God begins, in his divine wisdom, to judge them with his strictness in all the adversities that will come upon them.

The last judgment is a central theme in the *Moralia*. The most important motivation for the Christian life is that all will one day be judged by Christ. At this time Christ will be fully recognized as the Son when he comes in the fullness of his majesty. All who refused to bow to him in their life will bow to him then. Satan will be cast out and the final victory will be won. Gregory emphasizes two implications of the judgment. The first of these is that all should fear the judgment of God. The second is that glory is coming upon Christ and the Church. The fear which Christians feel for the coming judgment is converted into glory. As they lived this life in abasement they will rule and reign with their Lord in the next. Just as Christians have participated in judging themselves in this life through penance, they will judge others at the last judgment. The present life is connected to the future state by the role of the judge.

The eternal states of heaven and hell are the two possible ends for all of humanity. Heaven is the contemplation of God and the reward for the elect. Hell is described in vivid detail as the place of punishment. Here the reprobate eternally suffer physical and spiritual pain in separation from God. What is most important for us to note regarding Gregory's discussion of the eternal state is its connection to the present. In this life each individual is already moving toward one or the other of these destinations. The present life is causally related to the next. Each person will either suffer or be blessed there for his or her words, thoughts, and deeds here in this life. For Gregory, the eschaton is already here in the lives of each person. Everyone is in this life already participating in the blessedness or the punishment that is to come.

What we find in all of Gregory's eschatological passages in the *Moralia* is a real expectancy, a motivation for the spiritual life, and an awareness that the kingdom is already present in the Church. The eschaton will not break into history; it has already begun. The incarnation of Christ in his first advent serves as the basis for and is intimately connected to the second advent. His coming in glory will be the consummation of the first coming just as it will be the consummation of the world. As Christians appropriate the presence of Christ through contemplation they feel the coming union already. As they judge themselves now they participate in the final judgment. As they turn from the distractions of this physical world they find the spiritual kingdom already present in the Church and in their lives. Christ is the figure who binds the kingdom to come with the kingdom of the present in the unity of his two advents. As the Church is united to Christ as his body it is already being drawn into the eternal present of his divine kingdom.

CHAPTER 3

Flagellantis Iudicium[1]

The Stricken Gregory and the Stricken Job

The issue of theodicy has concerned theologians throughout history. The question of why a good God would allow evil to happen in the world may very well be one of the inescapable questions of life. Gregory's purpose is not to write a theodicy in the *Moralia* but he is not afraid to confront the issue. In fact, Gregory tackles it head on. But he does so in a manner quite different from most theologians. Instead of trying to deny the pain of this existence or to explain it away, Gregory embraces the pain that all humans confront every day. He establishes strict paradigms that he uses to interpret all human events. God is good. God governs all things. Humans experience pain. If humans experience pain it must come from God. If it comes from God, pain must be good. Of course he goes to great lengths to argue that pain is not a good in itself. It is instead, neutral. What makes pain good or evil is a person's reaction to it. Pain is a direct result of the fall of the original parents and is therefore a punishment for their sin passed on to all humanity. But God has chosen to use this pain as a good, either to glorify himself by his just judgment in punishment or to turn sinners back to him.

Gregory begins his interpretation of Job with an awareness that all people suffer pain and loss. This is a constant for humanity after the fall. Gregory feels that he himself is no stranger to pain. He argues in his dedicatory letter to Leander of Seville that God has uniquely prepared him through the pain of his

---

[1] Gregory the Great, *Moralia*, 32.4.5. Gregory understands pain to be the flagellation of the judge. This term expresses the fact that pain is the result of sin and will be judged by God. As we shall see in this chapter it may be either retributive or redemptive in nature but is always a response to sin.

life to comment on the book of Job.

> When illness wears at the body, the mind is troubled and even the energy for
> speaking grows weak. Many years have now run their course while I have been
> troubled by frequent disorders of the stomach. I am bothered at all hours by
> weakness from the enfeebling of my digestion, and I struggle to draw breath in the
> midst of mild but constant fevers. In the midst of these troubles, I think with care
> of the words of scripture, "Every son found acceptable by God is scourged." The
> more I am weighed down by present troubles, the more confidently I breathe with
> hope of eternal comfort. And perhaps this was the divine plan, that in my trials I
> should tell of the trials of Job and that I would better understand the mind of one
> so scourged if I felt the lash myself.[2]

We learn two important things from this quotation. First, Gregory sees
himself in the suffering of Job. Job's suffering is not uncommon. Gregory has
experienced suffering as well and this suffering serves as a unitive force
between the two. Gregory is united to Job in shared suffering. Second, Gregory
understands that there must be a providential reason for his suffering. In this
case he explains it as a means to allow him to better grasp the meaning and
application of the text of Job.

Gregory interprets the name Job to mean "grieving" and argues that Job is a
type of holy Church in all the pain and tribulation that he experienced.[3] Job is
set out as an example for all of God's children to follow. He is one of the stars
set in the sky by God to guide them on their way.[4] Job's suffering served this
purpose as well as the purpose of demonstrating his merits. Job was a righteous
man before his suffering and a righteous man during his suffering but had he
not experienced all these calamities by God's permission no one would have
known of him or of his virtues.[5]

Job's suffering did not only serve to make him an example and to
demonstrate his merits but it also showed forth the glory of God. Job's merits
were not his own but were the result of grace and this grace was bound to the
suffering which he experienced. Thus, the stripes that fell upon him "rebound
to the praise of divine glory" because of his perseverance under them.[6]

---

[2] Gregory the Great, *Ad Leandrum*, 5. "Multa quippe annorum iam curricula
devoluuntur, quod crebris viscerum doloribus crucior, horis momentisque omnibus
fracta stomachi virtute lassesco, lentis quidem, sed tamen continuis febribus anhelo.
Interque haec dum sollicitus penso, quia scriptura teste: omnis filius, qui a Deo recipitur,
flagellatur, quo malis praesentibus durius deprimor, eo de aeterna certius praesumptione
respiro. Et fortasse hoc divinae providentiae consilium fuit, ut percussum Iob percussus
exponerem, et flagellati mentem melius per flagella sentirem."
[3] Gregory the Great, *Moralia*, Preface.7.16. See also Preface.6.13-4; 1.24.33; 14.25.29;
17.1.1; 27.33.63 and 32.3.4.
[4] Gregory the Great, *Moralia*, Preface.6.13-4.
[5] Gregory the Great, *Moralia*, Preface.2.6.
[6] Gregory the Great, *Moralia*, Preface.5.12. "divinae gloriae laus cresceret."

Gregory also sees Job as a prophet.[7] He is a man out of time and a man in time. He is a type of Christ in his suffering.[8] Just as Christ's suffering brought great benefit to the Church, so also Job's suffering, if understood correctly and applied to one's life will be an impetus to spiritual growth. Job's experiences and his words are linked to the experience of everyone who suffers and especially the members of Christ's body the Church.[9] His experiences foretell what the Church is experiencing in Gregory's day and what it will experience in the end.[10]

Gregory sees Job's prophetic vision as based on his contemplation of God. Through contemplating his tribulations, Job turns inward and discovers that the workings of God in his life are a form of revelation. The visible realities of this life are not the true realities at all. The spiritual breaks into the physical realm most easily when the physical world is upset. God is able to use bad experiences to force individuals to come to grips with the eternal instead of the temporal. There is a power in pain which is supernatural and this supernatural force is centered upon a God who seeks to reveal himself to humanity. Because of this, Gregory makes no strong distinction between the two worlds. God, as the creator has every right to enter into creation and does so without hesitation. Indeed, all of life is an instance of the "inbreaking" of God. The natural laws of cause and effect have no physical meaning outside the providential ordering of God. Carole Straw has noted this tendency in Gregory.

> In Gregory's world, invisible reality exists alongside the visible reality it sustains and determines. The other world is at one's very elbows, though often hidden to those of carnal minds. Yet those whose vision is restored, like the holy man and the good Christian, see invisible causes all the more clearly since they are, in fact, the more 'real.' Consequently, the familiar distinctions that once governed reality now become blurred. Natural causation is eclipsed by supernatural intervention. Natural disasters such as earthquakes, fires, or storms are expressions of God's

---

[7] Gregory the Great, *Moralia*, 19.9.15; 23.1.2.

[8] Gregory the Great, *Moralia*, Preface.6.14; 1.24.33; 7.1.1; 13.30.34; 14.25.29; 17.1.1; and 23.1.2, among others. Gregory makes this statement most often in reference to the suffering of Job but also sees in Job and his story a foreshadowing of other aspects of Christ's life and ministry including: the humility of the incarnation, the resurrection, and the glory of Christ at the second coming, just to name a few.

[9] Gregory the Great, *Moralia*, Preface.6.14; 1.24.33; 13.30.34; 14.25.29;27.38.63; 32.3.4. You will notice than many of Gregory's comments that designate him as a type of Christ designate him as a type of the Church in the same place. This is most likely owing to his use of Tyconius' rules of interpretation which point out the need for discerning the head and the body in scriptural images of Christ.

[10] Gregory the Great, *Moralia*, 17.1.1.

wrath, or his trial of man; a nun's indigestion is not caused by the cabbage, but by the devil lurking in its leaves.[11]

God's sovereignty rules over all that happens in the universe. All of the things that happen must therefore be providential. Gregory outlines God's sovereign care for humanity by his right as creator. He points out the continual maintenance of God of the created order and then remarks that this providence surely extends to humans who he created to exist in relationship with him.[12]

We can see then that pain is understood in the light of providence and therefore becomes an important pedagogical tool in Gregory's understanding because it can lead humanity away from what is exterior and provides for it an opportunity for the interior contemplation of God.[13] Pain for Gregory is a primary source of enlightenment and aids in the contemplation of God by the contemplation of humanity's own frailty.[14] Pain leads the oppressed to fear God which is the beginning of virtue. Dealing with pain measures the believer's progress in the Christian life pointing out weaknesses of character. It assures the awareness in those tried that they are nothing and have no virtue within themselves apart from the grace of God.[15]

The trial of Job is the perfect test case for this pedagogical understanding of pain in Gregory. He says that Job grew by the stroke and multiplied his virtues under them.[16] His spirit was magnified by the pain he endured.[17] His merit was increased.[18] Job's smiting was a sign of God's favor instead of his disfavor for the heavier he was chastised the higher he was raised.[19] This being the case, Gregory sets Job up as an example of how all people should deal with pain and tribulation in their own lives.[20]

It is this pedagogical purpose that answers the question of theodicy for Gregory. Humans are incapable of understanding all the things that happen to them in the course of their lives. Yet God's sovereignty should assure each one that God's purposes will be served in the world and in their lives. Even if their sufferings seem unjust Christians must trust in the nature of God for God

---

[11] Carole Straw, *Gregory, Perfection*, 10. The reference to the diabolical vegetable comes from Gregory's *Dialogues*, 1.4.7.

[12] Gregory the Great, *Moralia*, 24.20.46-21.47.

[13] The theme of God's pedagogy in Gregory is discussed most fully by Claude Dagens, *Saint Grégoire le Grand*, passim. See also Marc Doucet, "Pédagogie et théologie dans la *Vie de saint Benoît* par saint Grégoire le Grand," *Collectionae Cisterciensis* 38 (1976), 158-73.

[14] Gregory the Great, *Moralia*, 3.9.15.

[15] Gregory the Great, *Moralia*, 28.9.20.

[16] Gregory the Great, *Moralia*, 3.1.1.

[17] Gregory the Great, *Moralia*, 23.1.1.

[18] Gregory the Great, *Moralia*, 24.19.45.

[19] Gregory the Great, *Moralia*, 28.preface.1.

[20] Gregory the Great, *Moralia*, Preface.2.4. See also 3.3.3 and 23.1.1-2.

cannot be unjust.[21] Any affliction a person undergoes is rightly inflicted according to the secret judgment of God.[22] Because God is greater than humankind his judgment must be just regardless of our lack of understanding.[23]

In these trials humanity seeks for reasons because it knows that the understanding would bring a certain level of comfort; yet God has assured everyone in Scripture that his grace will be sufficient for them, they do not need a reason.[24] Even if they had a reason, they would most likely not be able to understand the purposes of God which are always linked to his purposes in election. God's providential decrees made outside of time are realized slowly in the exteriority of this world but couched as they are in the secret judgments of God the human person can scarcely trace God's hand.[25] Humans can never understand the judgments of God or the way he guides them through the pain and tribulation that they experience on earth. All that is left for them to do is to submit to the trials in patience, examining themselves for secret sin, and to worship God, venerating his judgment in silence.[26]

It was this patience of Job under the blows of judgment that Gregory wanted to call to the attention of his readers.[27] Job's actions in his trial demonstrate how every believer should respond. They are to love the judgments of God as they experience them just as Job did.[28] Everyone must welcome the sentence against them and believe that it is just.[29] In this way they will be released from their own unrighteousness as they trust in the rightness of God's providence. The righteous will of God should serve as their consolation because the justness of his justice can never be in doubt.[30]

Through his combat with Satan, Job becomes humanity's champion. As an athlete about to enter the arena Gregory describes his fitness for the battle that is to come.[31] And through this battle Gregory paints Job as the representative example of patience and virtue for all to follow. Even more, Job has become

---

[21] Gregory the Great, *Moralia*, God is just in allowing Satan's unjust will to serve the purpose of his just judgments, 2.10.17; He is the "Just Avenger," 9.65.69; we can not complain against the justness of his judgments because he has already judged the angels who possess a more "refined" nature, 15.54.61; and God rules over creation with the equity of a judge, 23.18.33.

[22] Gregory the Great, *Moralia*, 23.19.45.

[23] Gregory the Great, *Moralia*, 23.18.33.

[24] Gregory the Great, *Moralia*, 23.19.34. The verse to which Gregory is referring is 2 Corinthians 12:9 wherein the Apostle Paul examined the reason for his "thorn in the flesh" but was required to be content with this answer.

[25] Gregory the Great, *Moralia*, 29.18.33.

[26] Gregory the Great, *Moralia*, 23.18.33; 32.1.1.

[27] Gregory the Great, *Moralia*, 32.4.5.

[28] Gregory the Great, *Moralia*, 24.24.51.

[29] Gregory the Great, *Moralia*, 32.5.7.

[30] Gregory the Great, *Moralia*, 32.5.7.

[31] Gregory the Great, *Moralia*, 1.3.4.

God's champion. The trial of Job becomes the trial of God. Satan aimed to destroy Job through his temptations but God had taken upon himself the effort of the contest and the accusation of the debate (*intentionem certaminis*).[32] Neither did Job fail to prove victorious in the match for in the midst of all his sufferings he did not sin.[33] Had he sinned not only would he have been defeated but God would have been defeated as well.[34]

As God had fought for and pledged himself to Job, God fights with and pledges himself to all persons in their own trials. This ought to give comfort to Christians who are experiencing pain because God has also joined in their struggle with Satan. They can have peace knowing that God's will is accomplished through the painful experiences of their lives.

Gregory has set the stage for the understanding of pain in the *Moralia*. God may not be the immediate cause of all the pain that is experienced but he is certainly the ultimate cause. Since this is the case, human rationality must rest in the higher reasoning of a God who can according to nature do only those things that are just and right. His sovereignty over all that humanity experiences including pain means that God's goals are being accomplished through them. Pain becomes a pedagogical tool in the hand of God that leads his children away from the finite world and into the infinite contemplation of God. This explains how God uses pain but one question still remains. If God is good and he created the world good then where did pain come from? We have learned a bit about how it can be used but why does it exist? Why must it exist?

Pain as a Result of the Fall

Gregory develops a very traditional concept of the creation of humanity and the fall in his *Moralia*. He does however augment the tradition with some interesting thematic elements on the war between the body and the soul and the effect of the fall on the ability of humanity to contemplate God. This contemplation of God is established by Gregory as the reason for creation.[35] Humanity's sole purpose was to render glory and honor to God in worship and to continually maintain a spiritual relationship to him. It was at this point that the fall was most damaging.

If the human person was created to contemplate God, this required that humankind be made in the image and after the likeness of God.[36] This likeness was understood to consist in innocence or purity. Humanity was created with the "splendor of innate innocence" and "created for righteousness".[37] The

---

[32] Gregory the Great, *Moralia*, 23.1.1.
[33] See Job 1:22.
[34] Gregory the Great, *Moralia*, Preface.3.8.
[35] Gregory the Great, *Moralia*, 7.1.2.
[36] Gregory the Great, *Moralia*, 9.49.75.
[37] Gregory the Great, *Moralia*, 35.16.43. "Ingenitae innocentiae splendore." "Ad iustitiam condidit."

dignity of the human race was also important in demonstrating the way in which the creation of humanity existed on a higher plane.[38] The other creatures were created to serve humanity and humanity was created to rule over them. In this way the dominion of humanity over creation was for Gregory an important aspect of the image of God.[39] This ruling is tied closely to the image and likeness of humanity to God although Gregory is not as careful to distinguish between the image and likeness as others had before him.[40] The image of God for Gregory rested primarily in the mind.[41] Gregory, as most Christian theologians before him, had strict anti-anthropomorphite tendencies.

Although he saw the body as indifferent, it was not tied to the image of God in any way although it had been created "upright".[42] Gregory also seeks to establish that the life of humanity before the fall was characterized by peace, immortality and the grace of God.[43]

The fall of humanity into sin was ultimately the result of pride. This pride was in itself the first sin whereby humans sought to usurp God's authority as creator and to rule themselves without recourse to him and his commandments.[44] The ultimate problem was that humans sought to be like God not in his righteousness in which they were already participating but in his power which was not theirs to presume.[45] Gregory's discussion of original sin in his *Moralia* is replete with many such theological assessments. He does not however choose to go into explicit textual detail over original sin as it relates to the story recounted in Genesis 3. He is content merely to fill in the gaps of the narrative as they serve to aid his theological development of pain and its relationship to sin in the *Moralia*. The closest that Gregory comes in his *Moralia* to this is a theological expression of how Satan tempts each individual to sin as informed by the account of the fall.

---

[38] Gregory the Great, *Moralia*, 9.49.75.

[39] This concept of dominion as part of the image of God in humanity is especially strong in the Antiochene tradition including Diodore of Tarsus and Chrysostom. See Frederick G. McLeod, *The Image of God in the Antiochene Tradition* (Washington D.C. 1999).

[40] Origen, following the tradition of Philo Iudaeus and other Jewish exegetes distinguishes between the image and likeness of God. Although the repetition is most likely a Hebrew idiom used to strengthen the statement, a theological meaning was imported to the two separate pronouncements. Usually image referred most appropriately to mind and likeness to purity just as it is expressed here by Gregory. See Origen, *Homiliae in Genesim*, 1.13.

[41] Gregory the Great, *Moralia*, 22.16.36.

[42] Gregory the Great, *Moralia*, 8.6.8. If anything, the body was closely allied to sin for it was his flesh that Adam immediately covered after his sin. See, *Moralia*, 26.17.28. See also Carole Straw's assessment of the connection in *Gregory, Perfection*, 117-118.

[43] Gregory says that humanity enjoyed the blessings of salvation in their creation. *Moralia*, 35.17.44. See also, 8.10.19; 4.28.54; 19.1.2; and 34.3.5.

[44] Gregory the Great, *Moralia*, 24.4.7; 26.17.28; 29.8.18; and 29.10.21.

[45] Gregory the Great, *Moralia*, 29.8.18.

For the serpent tempted, Eve was pleased, Adam yielded consent, and even when called in question he refused in effrontery to confess his sin. The serpent tempted, in that the secret enemy silently suggests evil to man's heart. Eve was pleased, because the sense of the flesh, at the voice of the serpent, presently gives itself up to pleasure. And Adam, who was set above the woman, yielded consent, in that while the flesh is carried away in enjoyment, the spirit also being deprived of its strength gives in from its uprightness.[46]

Gregory makes the sins of the original parents a template for all sin.[47] He demonstrates through it that Satan tempts, the body (Eve) is entranced and the mind (Adam) yields its consent.[48] Pride is evident in the account via the fact that it is the authority of Adam (mind) over Eve (body) that is transcended. The original sin, indeed all sin, is the result of the body ruling over the mind. In the fall it is this betrayal of the right to rule within an established hierarchy that is emphasized. God's right to rule over humanity was ignored and humanity fell into sin.

For Gregory, what happened in the fall is the inversion of all things from what they were meant to be to what they are now. Humanity was created for God, to worship and contemplate him but it has now become the enemy of God.[49] Sin has set human nature against its creator because the original parents failed to meet his requirement of holiness. By sinning the original parents lost their innate innocence and thereby lost their likeness to God.[50] They forfeited their enjoyment of peace and inward joy replacing it with conflict and unrest.[51] Perhaps worst of all they lost the eyes of their mind; that spiritual organ that allowed them to be active in the contemplation of God.[52]

---

[46] Gregory the Great, *Moralia*, 4.27.49. "Nam serpens suasit, Eva delectata est, Adam consensit, qui etiam requisitus, confiteri culpam per audaciam noluit. Hoc vero in humano genere cotidie agitur quod actum in primo parente nostri generis non ignoratur. Serpens suasit quia occultus hostis mala cordibus hominum latenter suggerit. Eva delectata est quia carnalis sensus, ad verba serpentis mox se delectationi substernit. Assensum vero Adam mulieri praepositus praebuit quia dum caro in delectationem rapitur, etiam a sua rectidtudine spiritus infirmatus inclinatur."

[47] See Ferruccio Gastaldelli, "Prospettive sul peccato in san Gregorio Magno", *Salesianum* 28 (1966), 65-94.

[48] The understanding of "Eve" as sense perception or the body and that of "Adam" as the mind has a long history. It can be found in Philo, *Legum allegoriae*, 2.10.35; and *Quaestiones et solutiones in Genesin*, 1.25; and in Origen, *Homiliae in Genesin*, 1.15; among many others, being especially prominent in the Alexandrian school. A parallel with this passage and a sermon of Augustine (*de serm. dom.* 1.34.) in which he argues for a three-fold progression of sin has been argued by H. Suso Brechter, *Die Quellen zur Angelsachsenmission Gregors des Grossen* (Munich 1941), 108.

[49] Gregory the Great, *Moralia*, 8.32.52.

[50] Gregory the Great, *Moralia*, 29.10.21.

[51] Gregory the Great, *Moralia*, 4.28.54; 8.10.19; and 34.3.5.

[52] Gregory the Great, *Moralia*, 9.33.50. See also 8.30.49 and 9.13.20.

What Gregory calls "losing the eyes of the mind," is reminiscent of Augustine's teaching on concupiscence. Humanity, because of sin, lost its ability to respond to God and therefore was trapped in sin unless freed through God's grace. Gregory echoes this sentiment as well noting that even though humanity fell on its own it is unable to rise again from its own power and will.[53] This is of course due to the guilt and corruption that humanity contracted at the fall and its inheritance by all of humanity since that time. Humanity was created in a state of righteousness but because of sin every person is now born in a "time of guilt".[54] This sin has so affected humanity that it has lost not only its place before God but also its character. Humans can no longer contemplate God or live the life of righteousness and peace for which they were created. Instead, humanity has become the slave of sin and is now bound by corruption as a lion trapped in a cage.[55] This corruption is so pervasive and has so affected the bodies of each person that even after they have turned to God it is impossible for believers to live a life free from sin.[56]

Both guilt and corruption are inherited by humanity at birth together with the "ingrafted defect of frailty".[57] All are born already condemned sinners deserving death and stumbling about in the darkness of their own natural infirmity.[58] Although baptism may take away the guilt of original sin it cannot fully eradicate the corruption.[59] The reason for this is the connection of sin to the body. Just as humans have inherited physical characteristics from their parents they have also inherited a propensity to sin.

But this is not the only problem that has been brought upon the body because of sin. Humanity was created to be immortal but sin brought mortality together with mutability.[60] Death has become the debt owed by human nature.[61] But even the death of the flesh is not without a redemptive or pedagogical focus. Death serves to remind humanity of its fall and its original creation.[62] When humans contemplate that they are only dust, they are advised against pride thus rendering them more open to the grace of God.

But humanity has many other physical ailments that, although less decisive than death, at least at times appear to be more obtrusive. The physical aspect of the person's being no longer works as it was created to work. Its original state of immortality has given way to mutability and with this mutability comes a whole new host of physical infirmities and various annoyances. Gregory

---

[53] Gregory the Great, *Moralia*, 8.31.51.

[54] Gregory the Great, *Moralia*, 4.1.4.

[55] Gregory the Great, *Moralia*, 9.56.86.

[56] Gregory the Great, *Moralia*, 8.33.56 and 12.16.22.

[57] Gregory the Great, *Moralia*, 8.6.8. "inserto infirmitatis vitio nascimur."

[58] Gregory the Great, *Moralia*, 4.14.45.

[59] Gregory the Great, *Moralia*, 9.34.54 and 15.50.57.

[60] Gregory the Great, *Moralia*, 4.28.54. See also 9.10.19.

[61] Gregory the Great, *Moralia*, 24.11.32.

[62] Gregory the Great, *Moralia*, 29.10.21.

mentions the manifold problems associated with disease as part of this mutability but also argues that even the health of the body meets with continual, and often conflicting, efforts at maintaining this tenuous state.

> [The body] is liable to pains, gasps with fever; the very state of our body, which is called health, is straitened by its own sickness. For it wastes with idleness, it faints with work; failing with not eating, it is refreshed by food so as to hold up; going heavily with sustenance, it is relieved by abstinence, so as to be vigorous; it is bathed in water, not to be dry; it is wiped with towels, not by that very bathing to be too wet; it is enlivened by labor, that it may not be dulled by repose; it is refreshed by repose, that it faint not under the exertion of labor; worn with watching, it is recruited by sleep; oppressed with sleep, it is roused to activity by watching, lest it be worse wearied by its own rest; it is covered with clothing, lest it be pierced by the hardship of cold; fainting under the heat it sought, it is invigorated by the blowing of the air. And whereas it meets with annoyances from the very quarter whence it sought to shelter itself from annoyances, being badly wounded, so to say, it sickens by its own cure.[63]

The body also serves as the means through which everyone receives pain from the world around them. Just as their bodies no longer work correctly, the world which was created to serve humans now oppresses them. Sin brings about pain and the chastisements of God. God does not spare the stroke but engages the entire created order in the battle against his enemies. Humanity finds itself subject to all types of adversity from a world of insensible objects. This adversity does not come about by chance but serves a pedagogical purpose. It punishes individuals for the sins they have committed and strives to make them aware of their physical and spiritual depravity. Through creation, God attacks the body to reach the soul.[64]

The mutability which has fallen upon humanity has affected more than just the body and more than the world around it. It has also attached itself to the mind. The peace that humanity once had in its interior contemplation has been lost. All humans have a sense of not being at home; a sense of uneasiness. The peace and happiness that was once found in God has been replaced by a desire for the good that looks for its object in all the wrong places. Humans can never be happy in any situation for very long. They realize through the frailty of their minds and their own fickleness that they were made for a different kind of

---

[63] Gregory the Great, *Moralia*, 8.32.53. "Nam otio tabescit, opere deficit; inedia deficiens, cibo reficitur ut subsistat; refectione lassescens, abstinentia relevatur ut vigeat; aqua perfunditur ne arescat; linteis tergitur ne ipsa nimis perfusione liquefiat; labore vegetatur ne quiete torpeat; quiete refovetur ne laboris exercitatione succumbat; fatigata vigiliis, somno reparatur; oppressa somno, vigiliis excutitur ne sua peius quiete lassetur; vestibus tegitur ne frigoris adversitate penetretur; quaesito calore deficiens, aurarum flatu refovetur. Cumque inde molestias invenit unde vitare molestias quaesiuit, male sauciata, ut ita dixerim, de ipso suo medicamine languescit."

[64] Gregory the Great, *Moralia*, 6.12.14.

existence. Thus, through a life of unsettled searching, God hopes to sway his children from their intransigence against him.[65]

Since both the flesh and the mind have been corrupted it should not be surprising that the relationship between the two has been upset. In fact, the relationship between the flesh and the mind or the body and the spirit is the locus of Gregory's teaching on corruption.[66] The freedom of rule and the freedom of will (both closely linked) are lost in the fall. Humanity has become a slave to Satan and to sin.[67] In their attempt to gain what is only God's, humans lost not only God but themselves.[68] They sought to rule over God but now the body seeks to rule over the mind. The two are at war with one another and the order of God's good creation has been upset by the pride of the original parents. Gregory points out that this warfare means not that humans experience trials in their lives but that all of life is a trial and a war. This is due to the fact that it is not what is outside the person that is so threatening; it is the interior condition of *mutabilitas* that is capable of destroying the soul. The real battle rages not between the flesh and the world or between one person and another but between the body and the mind; the source of corruption and the portion of the individual that still bears traces of the image of its creator.[69]

Pain in Gregory serves a pedagogical purpose. God uses pain to drive humanity away from a focus on its temporal existence to the contemplation of its original creation. He uses it to show humankind what heights from which it has fallen and how grievous is its sin. The sin of the first parents has brought about the corruption of all that humanity experiences and its own sins merit the punishment it receives. All the hardships of the present life are God's tools which he uses to attempt to bring his creations back to him. Pain is not only punishment it is medicine.[70] In this sense, the divine doctor prescribes a cure from the same source as our sin. As humanity sinned in the body God punishes the body and by this punishment God seeks to turn the mind of humanity away from the flesh of its fallen nature to the mind of its spiritual nature.[71]

Gregory notes that Adam was created to contemplate God but after his sin fled from God's presence. The sin brought punishment. But after the punishment and by means of the punishment he realized the consequences of

---

[65] Gregory the Great, *Moralia*, 8.32.54. This passage also expresses Gregory's understanding of the need for humanity to continue to experience pain in this life so that it will continue to remember its present condition. The corruption of humanity has so greatly bound humankind in darkness that it needs continual tokens of remembrance.

[66] Straw, *Gregory, Perfection*, 107-27; especially 110-11 and 117-20.

[67] Gregory the Great, *Moralia*, 4.28.54.

[68] Gregory the Great, *Moralia*, 9.27.41.

[69] Gregory the Great, *Moralia*, 8.6.8. See also, 4.18.54; 9.10.19; and 9.36.57.

[70] Gregory delights in medical terminology and often refers to pain as a "medicine" and to God as a "doctor". For a few examples among many see *Moralia*, 6.25.42; 7.19.22; 8.32.53; and 24.1.1-2.2.

[71] Gregory the Great, *Moralia*, 24.4.7.

his betrayal and his mind was once again awakened to its right sense. In this newly regained vision he learned how he could flee from the darkness that was his since the fall and find his way back to God. Sin brought punishment but punishment brought love. It is in the light of this love, which is the punishment of God, that Adam found and all of humanity can find its road back home.[72]

Types of Pain

All types of pain are ultimately the result of the fall. Humanity's existence before the fall was full of peace and joy without pain. The pain that it now experiences comes upon it from all sides and from within and without. There are many ways in which humans experience pain and this pain is felt in both parts of a human's being. Since Gregory understands humans to be composite beings made up of a body and a soul, it follows that the pain they experience will impact the body as well as the soul. I will examine the types of pain that affect the human person under the headings of external or material pain (coming from outside the person and/or pertaining to the body), and internal or immaterial pain (coming from inside the person and affecting the soul or mind).

Many trials and much pain result from external forces. This is the type of pain most commonly recognized. It may come upon the individual either as the result of impersonal forces in the external world as a form of adversity or other persons can inflict pain or harm upon another in the form of oppression. We see both of these forces initially at work in the trial of Job. In the loss of his children and of his substance, Job immediately encounters pain in both of these ways.

First, Job experiences the pain of those oppressing him and Gregory interprets these oppressors as the reprobate who oppress the elect. The reprobate have been set against the elect so that they may purify them by their strokes and relieve them from their love of this world. Even if they are slow in advancing toward the heavenly rewards on their own the oppressors help to spur them on in godly fear.[73] The reprobate oppress the elect with two goals in mind; the removal of their temporal goods and the spoiling of their treasure of virtues. These oppressors come upon Christians from without and they strive through their machinations to spoil both outward goods and inner treasures.[74]

Humanity's external oppressors do not only come from the body of reprobate humanity. Persons are also assailed by malevolent spirits and, like Job, by Satan himself.[75] Gregory interprets the Sabeans who spoiled Job's

---

[72] Gregory the Great, *Moralia*, 11.43.59.

[73] Gregory the Great, *Moralia*, 26.13.21.

[74] Gregory the Great, *Moralia*, 26.14.22.

[75] The struggle of the soul with demons has a rich monastic heritage which is found in Gregory's writings as well. It should be noted however that Gregory's appreciation of the role of demons, as expressed in his *Moralia* is tempered by Augustine's emphasis of the sovereignty of God which is a continual theme in the *Moralia*. For an excellent

livestock as the demons who "inflict terrible wounds" (*graviter vulnerant*) and hurl "darts of temptation" (*iaculis temptationis*) at unsuspecting children (*pueros*) in the faith.[76] The young who have not proceeded to the constancy of their faith are the most vulnerable to such attacks. These demons assail the proud leading them on from one sin to another. If perchance a person withstands one demon and his vice another soon rises with a new temptation based most often in their last success.[77]

Satan has no power over the elect but God sometimes allows him to exercise his malevolent will for the accomplishment of God's purposes.[78] But even then, he has no power over the spirits of the elect so he is forced to concentrate his power and cruelty upon their flesh.[79] Since he does not abide within, he must attack from without.[80] Satan's contrivances cause personal pain but accomplish God's will in forming the character of his saints for Satan is merely the anvil upon which the elect are fully formed.[81]

Job's property is taken by two separate groups of oppressors and his servants killed. This loss of prosperity is a powerful tool of God because the mind of the reprobate is often set upon present things alone, that is, temporal goods. When God removes such from the ownership of the elect he strikes the thing they love. In the context of the two greatest commandments (to love God and to love one's neighbor as one's self), Gregory argues that God uses affliction of this sort to drive the elect away from this corrupted love affair. God also seeks to provide an opportunity for his children to love their neighbors in such circumstances. Goods are given to them so that they might part with them in aiding others.[82]

Possessions are not simply a source of pain when they are taken away by others; they are a pain to humans when they have them.[83] The more possessions

---

article on the oppression of demons see Jean Rivière, "Rôle du démon au jugement particulier chez les Pères", *Revue des sciences religieuses* 4 (1924), 43-64. Also interesting in this light is the article by Savon which draws many of the same conclusions in reference to the Antichrist, Hervé Savon, "L'Antéchrist dans l'oeuvre de Grégoire le Grand", in Jacques Fontaine, Robert Gillet and Stan Pellistrandi (eds), *Grégoire le Grand* (Paris 1986), 389-408.

[76] Gregory the Great, *Moralia*, 2.30.49.

[77] Gregory the Great, *Moralia*, 33.2.4. An example of this would be if a person avoided the lust of the flesh he might be quickly afflicted by a demon tempting him to pride over his chastity.

[78] Gregory the Great, *Moralia*, 33.14.28.

[79] Gregory the Great, *Moralia*, 34.11.22.

[80] Gregory the Great, *Moralia*, 17.32.51.

[81] Gregory the Great, *Moralia*, 34.6.11.

[82] Gregory the Great, *Moralia*, 7.14.29-15.30.

[83] Carole Straw's work on the "structural motif of complementarity" in Gregory proves helpful at this point as well. She demonstrates how, for Gregory, adversity can be seen as a good in the same sense that prosperity is an evil. Carole Straw, "'*Adversitas*' *et*

they have the more care they are forced to take to maintain them. Many possessions bring many distractions and desires increase together with possessions.[84] Although they can be at times useful and occasionally pleasurable they are given as a grace and should be used as such to help others.[85] Instead, they are too often a means of pride.[86] Possessions lead to a sense of self sufficiency and a lack of dependence upon God. For this reason the holy look down upon possessions and do not seek to have them because their desire is not for the temporal but for the eternal and immaterial contemplation of God.[87] In fact, Gregory argues that the loss of goods is not a pain at all but a benefit which lightens those so relieved of a great and grievous burden.[88]

We also see the natural catastrophes that came upon Job as a source of his pain. A strong wind caused the house in which his children were feasting to collapse and kill them all and the sheep and their attendants were destroyed by a fire from heaven. Gregory is convinced that nothing occurs by chance. If there is a drought or a tempest at sea there must be a reason. God breaks into the material world through the use of his material creatures and insensate creation. There is nothing to blame in them because they, unlike humanity, always follow the will of the creator. They are animated against humans in order to correct them and it is because of humanity's own sins that God's creation harasses and troubles them.[89]

Material pain also arises from one's own external body. Since sin entered humanity through the body God punishes the body with pain so that the same element which caused humanity to fall may also be the means of its deliverance.[90] Pain is first felt in the mutability which has passed upon the body. There are seemingly interminable necessities that must be met so that the body can survive but even then there is no middle ground for the one thing which benefits the body, if used too frequently may injure it.[91] The body has

---

'*Prosperitas*': une illustration du motif structurel de la complémentarité", in Jacques Fontaine, Robert Gillet and Stan Pellistrandi (eds.), *Grégoire le Grand* (Paris 1986), 277-288.

[84] Gregory the Great, *Moralia*, 23.1.1.

[85] Gregory the Great, *Moralia*, 30.10.38. See also 7.15.30.

[86] Gregory the Great, *Moralia*, 23.1.1.

[87] Gregory the Great, *Moralia*, 15.47.53-15.48.54.

[88] Gregory the Great, *Moralia*, 31.13.22.

[89] Gregory the Great, *Moralia*, 6.10.12. This negative view of creation was not the only position taken by Gregory. He is also zealous to maintain the way in which creation can be used as a way to God. By contemplating the world around us we can be led back to God because the image of the Creator shines in it. God's creations demonstrate the beauty of the finger of God as well as the humility appropriate to a creature thus serving as a lesson to the mind. See 4.29.55 and especially 16.12.17-18.

[90] Gregory the Great, *Moralia*, 24.4.7.

[91] Gregory the Great, *Moralia*, 4.34.68

become frail through sin in its own nature. The care humans are forced to take for their bodies is a type of pain but the instruments they desire to use for the benefit of their bodies actually "pierces" them with pain because it is these means of pleasure and comfort that have become so burdensome in their procurement and so enslaving in their use that they bring more pain to the soul than they bring comfort to the body.[92]

Because humanity lost its immortality in the fall it is prone to sickness and even death. Gregory's picture of humanity's present estate is so dark that he describes the whole life of an individual as one long sickness. With each and every breath a person sickens and is in constant need of different medicines and cures. But even these medicines become a "sore" for they often inflict harm on another part of the body as they provide a service for one part.[93] This life of sickness ensures humanity that death, the punishment for sin, is swiftly approaching. "Every moment of every day that we live we are constantly passing away from life."[94] This death that all persons face, although pain and a punishment for sin, is the power of God's mercy for it destroys the pride of the human person.[95] Death of the flesh is the last temptation that all individuals undergo. For the elect, it is the final purging of the last remnants of pride and prepares them to enter humbly into the full contemplation of God.[96]

We are also troubled by another type of pain. Internal or immaterial pain arises from within the person and affects the soul or mind. This type of pain, though different from material pain, still arose from the fall and has its roots in our corruption. The first of these inner pains is the loss of the joy of the first estate. Humanity has been shut out from the inner joys that were meant for it in its contemplation of God. Sin has rendered it incapable of the relationship for which it was created. Although humanity's present blindness means that it can not fully comprehend this pain, the soul groans for the loss no matter how mild the conception of it may be in relationship to reality. But not only have humans lost sight of their creator they have lost sight of themselves. Humanity knew its role before the fall but since that time it cannot even determine its own course to say nothing of its destination. "For the human race being shut out from the interior joys, because of sin, lost the eyes of the mind; and it is unable to determine where it is going with the steps of its own rewards."[97]

We have already noted how the mind is at war with the body but the mind

---

[92] Gregory the Great, *Moralia*, 34.2.3.

[93] Gregory the Great, *Moralia*, 8.32.53.

[94] Gregory the Great, *Moralia*, 25.3.4. "Ut eo ipso cotidiano momento quo vivimus incessanter a vita transeamus."

[95] Gregory the Great, *Moralia*, 29.9.20.

[96] Gregory the Great, *Moralia*, 29.10.21.

[97] Gregory the Great, *Moralia*, 9.13.20. "Seclusam quippe ab internis gaudiis genus humanum, exigente culpa, mentis oculos perdidit, et quo meritorum suorum passibus graditur nescit."

also does battle with itself. Having absorbed the foreign germ of sin, the mind cannot reconcile its new corruption with the remnants of its originally innocent nature. In language that almost sounds bipolar Gregory describes the incessant waves of conflict that have ensued. At times humans catch a glimpse of the inner joy they have lost only to have the vision crushed by the continual propensity to sin which has implanted itself in their minds. The continuing presence of sin continues to prevent even Christians from enjoying the contemplation of God for more than a "hasty glance".[98]

Just as humans receive pain at the instigation of Satan and his demons in the temptation of the body, they find a source of temptation in their own minds.[99] Gregory describes the human mind as "rotten". Corruption has worked itself into the mind through the body. Because of this even the thoughts of the mind become a source of sin which pierces itself with the sting of temptation.[100]

Gregory divides the temptation of the mind into two types; one which comes upon even good persons suddenly with the hopes of ambush, another which slips in quietly by degrees to resist the soul through a slow corruption.[101] There are various types of temptation but the most common and most perverse temptation of the mind is the temptation to pride. Yet in God's mercy, it is this very temptation which causes the elect to see how weak they are in themselves and to realize a bit of the depth and breadth of the grace of God. Humans are so corrupt that their righteousness is nothing before the strict judge. As long as they stay anchored to this truth in humility or are led back to it by a temptation to pride they will find themselves more thankful for God's mercy and more open to the contemplation of God.[102]

Despite all this, Gregory's purpose is not to outline the various types of pain in his work. For the most part, he takes pain for granted. All that is needed to

---

[98] Gregory the Great, *Moralia*, 23.21.43.

[99] Even though these temptations arise in the mind of the human person Gregory still insists that Satan is ultimately responsible for them. Satan tempts humanity in two ways; outwardly by the pains of tribulation and inwardly by the pains of persuasion or temptation. See *Moralia*, 3.8.12 and 33.24.44. This provides an interesting if not irreconcilable sidebar to his statement in 11.48.64 that temptation arises from no other source than the human nature.

[100] Gregory the Great, *Moralia*, 11.48.64. It should be noted that even though Gregory is speaking in this place about temptations common to the mind he is either unwilling or unable to make a clear division between the flesh and the mind. Even as the human nature exists in two parts, these parts are fully united in one person and any separation would be artificial. Nevertheless, he continues to see the flesh as the primary seat of corruption in the human person. This connection of the interplay between the flesh and the mind in temptation is more fully outlined in 21.8.13. where he argues that temptation sometimes comes upon the mind through the flesh but sometimes the mind uses the flesh to fulfill the temptations that come upon it without the medium of the flesh.

[101] Gregory the Great, *Moralia*, 12.18.22.

[102] Gregory the Great, *Moralia*, 26.45.82.

know is that pain exists; that it is an inescapable aspect of human existence since the fall. It may come upon the oppressed from without or from within. But the important thing about pain is not how it is experienced but what is done with it. Pain is a tool to be used. It is the God-given medicine of the soul which if used according to the prescription will lead humanity from its corruptible state back to saving health.

Uses of Pain

Gregory's outline for the way in which God uses pain in the lives of individuals is divided into two very distinct classes. God's use of pain is established in Gregory's doctrine of election. He falls back upon the classes of the elect and the reprobate to distinguish the nature of pain. All people experience pain but the ultimate end of that pain rests in the eternal decrees of God. Gregory makes a pastoral application of the Augustinian doctrine. The world contains both classes and even the Church is mixed with both the elect and the reprobate while in its season of pilgrimage. Gregory likens God's decree of election to the measuring of a geographical area with lines or ropes. Those that are enclosed become members of the elect but those left outside the lines are left in their sin.[103]

Gregory is zealous to affirm that the decrees of God are just even if they are not understood by humanity.[104] It is this sense of justice which drives Gregory to understand the experience of pain, both in the life of the believer and in the life of the reprobate, as he does. The election of certain individuals to salvation does not depend at all upon the works or efforts of a given individual before God.[105] Election depends solely upon the mercy of God and this mercy is manifested in the bestowal of prevenient grace.[106] Yet the mercy of God cannot exist without the justice of God. These two are for Gregory two sides of the same coin. Just as mercy is shed upon the elect justice will be served upon the

---

[103] Gregory the Great, *Moralia*, 28.7.18. Gregory, like Augustine, prefers to emphasize God's activity in electing some to salvation and the justness of leaving the reprobate in damnation.

[104] Gregory the Great, *Moralia*, 28.7.18. See also 25.14.32.

[105] Gregory the Great, *Moralia*, 28.4.7 and 33.21.38-40. The first of these references is very interesting seeing as how it seeks to answer the question of infants dying without baptism. Gregory seems to be convinced that death without the sacrament assures one of the individual's reprobation but is unwilling to argue that the person would have lived an unholy life should he or she have lived. Although he notes this response he does so with the intent of arguing against it believing that if this were the case God would actually be punishing sins that were as yet uncommitted. This obviously does not correlate with Gregory's understanding of the justice of God or with his understanding of the role that pain as punishment (including death) plays in God's plan; as we shall soon see.

[106] Gregory the Great, *Moralia*, 33.21.39.40.

reprobate. At the same time, the mercy received by the elect is served by the pain of justice in this life. And this justice which brings pain in this present life actually contributes to the spiritual growth of the elect. In the same way, God sometimes withholds affliction from the reprobate now in order to increase the judgment necessary in the hereafter. In this way, God dispenses both mercy and justice to both classes of individuals. He dispenses justice to the elect now so that they will not be punished in the eschaton whereas he offers mercy to the reprobate now in order to more perfectly display his justice upon them in the afterlife. In this way, the elect can rejoice in coming mercy and the reprobate have no recourse to accuse God's justice.[107]

For the reprobate, pain in this life is always punitive. The retributive nature of pain for the reprobate is demonstrated by their lack of repentance. No matter how grievously they are afflicted by God they never amend their ways.[108] They are stricken by God and since they do not respond in humility they use their free will to reject God's means of bringing them to his mercy through his justice. Left without the grace of God they have been blinded by sin and have been enslaved by visible objects.[109] They no longer desire the contemplation of the creator for which they were created. Even though they receive punishment from God they refuse to allow their hearts to be softened by the affliction.[110] In an interesting use of imagery Gregory argues that the reprobate through setting their affections and desires on sensible things have become insensible to the affliction of their bodies which God has attempted to use to drive them to contemplation.[111]

But the reprobate are not always punished for their sins in this life. Questions about theodicy do not only revolve around why bad things happen to good people; they also involve why good things happen to bad people. Gregory asks this question himself. He says, "Who can understand what is the secret reason that a just man frequently returns from a trial, not only unavenged but even punished besides, and that his wicked adversary escapes, not only without punishment but even victorious?"[112] Gregory raises this question in this place in order to promote humility in all of those experiencing pain or tribulation. Humanity does not know and can not understand the mystery of the election of God which is attached to the experience of every individual in this life. Nevertheless, Gregory does have an answer.

Gregory believes that the reprobate are sometimes not punished in this world

---

[107] Gregory the Great, *Moralia*, 33.21.39.

[108] Gregory the Great, *Moralia*, 6.17.27.

[109] Gregory the Great, *Moralia*, 30.5.21.

[110] Gregory the Great, *Moralia*, 7.22.26.

[111] Gregory the Great, *Moralia*, 7.21.24.

[112] Gregory the Great, *Moralia*, 29.33.77. "Quis intellegat quae esse ratio secretorum potest, quod saepe vir iustus a iudicio non solum non vindicatus, sed etiam punitus redeat; et iniquus eius adversarius non solum non punitus, sed etiam victor abscedat?"

so that they might be punished more heavily in the judgment to come. Even though they sin now, they escape punishment for a time so that God can amass an ever-lengthening list of offences. The reprobate are wrong in feeling that temporal blessing here is a special sign of God's favor. When they find themselves in a position of ease and comfort they are fooled either into believing that they have been accepted and blessed by God or that God does not see and judge their actions.[113] But God does see their actions and will judge them. His forbearance is in itself a punishment because it means that what remains unpunished here will be more terribly punished at the judgment.[114]

Gregory spends most of his time in his discussion of pain in the *Moralia* on the uses of pain in the lives of the elect. Delivered to his audience of fellow monks in Constantinople during one of the most tumultuous periods of late antiquity, the *Moralia* is replete with discussions of how oppression, pain and disaster may be used in the spiritual life. The monastic focus of contemplation forms the heart of Gregory's reflection on the nature of pain.[115] He outlines his understanding of the uses of pain in the preface to the work. His understanding of grace implies that God scourges Christians for his purposes and the Christian's goal is to make himself or herself open to the message from God in the scourges.

> For of scourges there are sundry kinds; for there is the scourge whereby the sinner is stricken that he may suffer punishment without withdrawal, another whereby he is smitten that he may be corrected; another wherewith sometimes a man is smitten, not for the correction of past misdeeds, but for the prevention of future; another which is very often inflicted, whereby neither a past misdeed is corrected, nor a future one prevented, but which has this end, that when unexpected deliverance follows the stroke, the power of the deliverer being known may be the more ardently beloved, and that while the innocent person is bruised by the blow, his patience may serve to increase the gain of his merits.[116]

The first of this group is punitive and retributive serving only to punish the

---

[113] Gregory the Great, *Moralia*, 8.37.61. See also 25.4.5.

[114] Gregory the Great, *Moralia*, 25.5.6

[115] Jean Doignon shows how Gregory has appropriated and expanded this monastic and spiritual theme from the earlier fathers, especially Cyprian and Augustine. Jean Doignon, "'Blessure d'affliction' et 'blessure d'amour' (*Moralia*, 6,25,42): une jonction de thèmes de la spiritualité patristique de Cyprien à Augustin", in Jacques Fontaine, Robert Gillet and Stan Pellistrandi (eds.), *Grégoire le Grand* (Paris 1986), 298-314.

[116] Gregory the Great, *Moralia*, Preface.5.12. "Percussionum quippe diversa sunt genera. Alia namque est percussio, qua peccator percutitur ut sine retractione puniatur; alia qua peccator percutitur ut corrigatur; alia qua nonnunquam quisque percutitur, non ut praeterita corrigat, sed ne ventura committat; alia qua plerumque percutitur per quam nec praeterita culpa corrigitur nec futura prohibetur sed ut, dum inopinata salus percussionem sequitur, salvantis virtus cogitata ardentius ametur; cumque innoxius flagello atteritur ei per patientiam meritorum summa cumuletur."

individual without bringing them into a state of grace. As such, it most appropriately pertains only to the unrepentant or the reprobate, serving as a foretaste of the eternal pain and punishment to be experienced in hell. Gregory says of those scourged here because of sin who do not turn away from their sin before death that, "their smiting begun here is completed there, that so to the unreformed there should be one and the same scourge, which begins here in time but is consummated in eternal punishment, that to those that wholly refuse to be amended, the dealing of present scourges now should be the beginning of the torments to ensue".[117]

The rest of the punishments pertain to the elect. The first of these is punitive for the elect just as it is with the reprobate but instead of being merely retributive it is also redemptive. It is redemptive because it forces sufferers to come before the just judge in humility and by their penance behold the judge as the giver of mercy rather than the executor of wrath. The purpose for such punishment is to correct the one who is in sin. Weighed down as humanity is with this body of depravity, sin is an unavoidable evil. Since Christians cannot live a sinless life they must avail themselves of the next best thing which is repentance. Unfortunately, Gregory does not feel that Christians are too keen on this either. Because of this, God often punishes sinners to show them the error of their ways and to awaken in them a spirit of contrition. It is by God's gift that punishment follows transgressions so that repentance may be stimulated in the transgressor. In this way the pain of punishment itself becomes a means of enlightenment to the truth of the fallen human condition.[118]

The second purpose of pain in the life of the elect outlined by Gregory in his preface is to restrict the commission of future sins. Pain is not only punitive, it can also be prohibitive. Even those who will not listen to the commandments of God and obey them will often shy away from committing sin out of a fear of the possible consequences.[119] But this fear is not a bad thing because "the love of God, though it has its birth in fear, yet it is changed by growing into affection".[120] Gregory envisions sin to be a slippery slope wherein one sin soon leads to another sin, each sin growing in intensity and contemptuousness.[121]

Pain interrupts this normal course of events and, as punishment for sin, nips this sinful cycle in the bud before it can take root in the individual. But this pain need not be our own. Part of the reason God often punishes sinners in this

---

[117] Gregory the Great, *Moralia*, 18.22.35. "Quia eorum percussio hic coepta illic perficitur, ut incorrectis unum flagellum sit quod temporaliter incipit; sed in aeternis suppliciis consummatur, quatenus eis qui omnino corrigi renuunt iam praesentium flagellorum percussio sequentium sit initium tormentorum."

[118] Gregory the Great, *Moralia*, 6.23.40

[119] Gregory the Great, *Moralia*, 18.22.35.

[120] Gregory the Great, *Moralia*, 7.24.28. "Quae tamen divina dilectio per timorem nascitur, sed in affectum crescendo permutatur."

[121] Gregory the Great, *Moralia*, 10.11.21. See also 7.28.36.

world is to prohibit others from following them. Many times Christians are called to a holy fear by the destruction of others. Seeing their losses Christians are reminded that the punishment that they deserve is equally as terrible. When they realize this they are humbled before God and resolve by his grace not to do as they have seen others do.[122] Punishment brings the fear of God and this fear serves to suppress future sins.[123]

The final category of God's use of pain mentioned by Gregory in his preface touches upon that which is undeserved. It neither results as a punishment for sins nor does it effect the prevention of future ones. Instead, it serves the purpose of God by increasing the love of the individual for God the deliverer and providing an opportunity for merit. Thus, the undeserved evils which are experienced in this world allow Christians the opportunity for more growth and ascent in the spiritual life. Pain, like nothing else, draws humanity to seek the face of God for only in him can it find the consolation of its desire.[124] In an inexplicable interplay of the lover and the beloved, the soul loves its object more the more it is repelled. It is for this reason that God often withdraws himself from the life of the elect for a time and allows them to be tormented not only by outward oppression but also by the inner awareness of his absence.[125]

Undeserved pain also gives Christians the opportunity to increase their merits. This is certainly the case for Job.[126] Although he was just before the scourges he grew more just after them and the heavier he was chastised the higher his life was raised in the praise of God.[127] The same opportunity is offered to the elect when they are afflicted not on the account of sin. Even if there is nothing left to correct in a saint there is always some good which might be increased.[128] Patience is increased in suffering as the elect learn to wait on God.[129] Most importantly, pride is cast down and the humility which promotes the advance of virtues is strengthened.[130]

Pain and suffering are for the elect a means of grace. But these scourges from God do not always function in this way. It is not simply pain or suffering that is grace. The important factor in the determination is how those that are suffering use the pain with which they are afflicted. Suffering serves only as a means of grace to the believer who responds appropriately to it by a demonstration of humility based on a fear of the judge and a desire for mercy. Gregory explains the difference in the following quotation.

---

[122] Gregory the Great, *Moralia*, 18.23.37 and 7.31.44.

[123] Gregory the Great, *Moralia*, 29.15.28.

[124] Gregory the Great, *Moralia*, 16.26.32.

[125] Gregory the Great, *Moralia*, 20.24.51. See also 10.8.13.

[126] Gregory the Great, *Moralia*, 11.38.51; 13.30.34; 14.30.38; 24.19.45; and 26.10.15.

[127] Gregory the Great, *Moralia*, 28. Preface.1.

[128] Gregory the Great, *Moralia*, 31.53.107.

[129] Gregory the Great, *Moralia*, Preface.5.12.

[130] Gregory the Great, *Moralia*, 31.53.107.

It is plain that in this life, when he smites, if amendment follows the stroke, it is the discipline of a Father, not the wrath of a Judge, the love of one correcting, not the strictness of one punishing. And so by that very present scourge itself the eternal judgments ought to be weighed. For hence we ought with the greatest pains to reflect, how that anger may be borne that casts away, if the anger of his which purifies may scarcely now be borne.[131]

"All smiting from God is either a purifying of the present life in us, or a commencement of the punishment that follows."[132] It is for the elect to decide whether in their suffering they have a foretaste of hell or a means to heaven. If Christians respond correctly to their pain in this life it will bring joy in the next.

The Pain of Salvation: Justification, Sanctification and the Judgment

The person and work of Jesus Christ lie at the root of all theological reflection upon the nature of salvation. Gregory's operative soteriology is no different. Christ is the focus of his soteriological ruminations in the *Moralia*. What is different about his unique approach to the situation? In discussing soteriology in a reflection upon the book of Job, Gregory emphasizes the suffering of Christ as the backdrop for his soteriology. But in this work, Christ is more than just a suffering servant. He suffers for the Church not simply by following the will of the Father or simply through his passion but in every aspect of his becoming human.

Gregory emphasizes the incarnation as a unique soteriological moment. It is unique, however, not only because of Christ's becoming one in nature with humanity but in the union of his suffering with that of humanity. Christ's *kenosis* is his suffering. For Gregory, to be human is to suffer and Christ, in becoming human, took on this nature of suffering. "For his very incarnation is itself the offering for our purification, and while he shows himself as man, he is the intercession that washes out man's misdeeds, and in the mystery of his humanity he offers a perpetual sacrifice."[133] Even though Christ did not inherit the infection of sin from the incarnation he took upon himself the infirmity of the flesh by his own free will.[134] In fact, it is the infirmity of Christ's flesh which hid his divine nature and allowed him to win his victory over Satan

---

[131] Gregory the Great, *Moralia*, 21.22.36. "Constat autem quia in hac vita cum percutit, si percussionem correctio sequitur, disciplina patris est non ira iudicis; amor corrigentis est, non districtio punientis. Ex ipso ergo praesenti verbere iudicia aeterna pensanda sunt.Hinc etenim perpendere summopere debemus quomodo feratur illa quae reprobat, si ferri modo vix valet eius ira quae purgat."

[132] Gregory the Great, *Moralia*, 18.22.35. "Omnis ergo divina percussio, aut purgatio in nobis vitae praesentis est, aut initium poenae sequentis."

[133] Gregory the Great, *Moralia*, 1.24.32. "Ipsa quippe eius incarnatio nostrae emundationis oblatio est cumque se hominem ostendit delicta hominis interveniens diluit. Et humanitatis suae mysterio perenne sacrificium immolat..."

[134] Gregory the Great, *Moralia*, 2.22.41.

through this very weakness.[135] The weakness of the human nature that Christ took up was important not only in allowing his victory over Satan, it also set him up as an advocate for humanity and a revelation that could more easily be "read". The strength of Christ's divine nature was made visible to humanity only by the weakness of the assumed human nature.[136] The weakness of Christ's human nature made the divine nature available to all. As Christ suffered through the vicissitudes of human nature he offered the way to a renewed constancy through his weakness.

Christ also was at work redeeming humanity as he suffered in his flesh during his earthly life and ministry. Instead of seeking prosperity and glory in this life as humans do, he sought out adversity and affliction. He was persecuted for his words and for his manner of life. Suffering was his lot and he accepted it in humility. "The incarnate Lord came amongst them courting adversity, scorning prosperity, embracing insults, flying from glory."[137] All the pain of this earthly existence Christ endured of his own free will but more than that he actually foreknew and foreordained his own sufferings.[138]

The most poignant example of Christ's suffering for salvation is the passion of Christ. Gregory asserts this over and over again. Christ took upon himself frail human nature and even though he owed no penalty of corruption he paid humanity's debt as a mediator and through his death in the flesh freely serves as its propitiation.[139] His death and his willingness to undergo it demonstrate his great love for humanity and paint a picture of his mercy. Gregory argues that it was not necessary for Christ to have died to have redeemed humanity but his willingness to embrace the cross was a demonstration of his great love for us. His love was demonstrated in taking up the weaknesses of human nature and bearing this weakness to its final culmination in physical death.[140]

The pain that Christ experienced in his incarnation, ministry and death serves also as an example. Christians should embrace the adversity of this life just as Christ did.[141] Christians must reach out in compassion to those suffering around them with the same selfless love that Christ demonstrated in taking on the weakness of human nature.[142] If Christ ordained his own sufferings, Christians should not be upset with theirs but endure them patiently knowing

---

[135] Gregory the Great, *Moralia*, 2.22.41.
[136] Gregory the Great, *Moralia*, 16.30.37.
[137] Gregory the Great, *Moralia*, 30.24.69. "Venit inter eos incarnatus Dominus adversa appetens, prospera spernens, opprobria amplectens, gloriam fugiens."
[138] Gregory the Great, *Moralia*, 29.19.36.
[139] Gregory the Great, *Moralia*, 24.3.6.
[140] Gregory the Great, *Moralia*, 20.36.69. Gregory applies this concept pastorally to argue that all Christians should follow the example of Christ's love and compassion in the way that they experience pain for the benefit of others.
[141] Gregory the Great, *Moralia*, 30.24.69.
[142] Gregory the Great, *Moralia*, 20.36.68.

that God's will is being done through them.[143] Christians are admonished to drink the cup of Christ's passion so that they might find the way to humility and find recourse for salvation not in themselves but in the merits of Christ's incarnation, death and resurrection. Christ came to provide salvation for humanity through his own pain and humanity is drawn closer to him as it follows his example. "Accordingly, to this end the Lord appeared in the flesh, that the life of man he might by dealing admonitions arouse, by giving examples kindle, by suffering death redeem, by rising again renew."[144]

The pain and sorrow of this life is used by God specifically in three different times of natural life in preparation for three different parts or stages of salvation. Gregory outlines a movement from pain and sorrow to joy and security. Each stage begins with anxiety over the sinful condition of humanity which drives the Christian to embrace Christ and his merits. The end of this union is peace and joy. This movement plays itself out in salvation in three distinct time periods that Gregory labels conversion, temptation, and death.[145]

The first stage of salvation wherein the sorrow and anxiety of humanity's sinful position assail the mind is in conversion. Conversion must be identified with initial justification whereby Christians, enabled by God's prevenient grace, turn away from their life of sin and attach themselves to Christ. It is in conversion that the merits of Christ's active and passive obedience are applied to the Christian. Gregory likens the Christian's conversion to a seed that is first watered by the rain of God's grace and then disciplined by the Lord's secret dispensation so that it will not spring up too quickly.[146] God's grace enables Christians to see their bondage in the flesh and to bewail its hold over them. As the elect feel the sorrow of the frailty of the flesh through the afflictions of this earthly life they begin to feel the war in their own bodies between the good which they ought to do and the evil which they do. Thus in despair, they cry out to the one who is able to free them. Then, taking up the yoke of Christ, they rejoice in the afflictions of this life knowing that it is by them that their faith is put to the test and their repentance acknowledged as true.[147]

The second stage of salvation wherein Christians are tried by sorrow and affliction is in their sanctification. Gregory realizes that entire sanctification is unattainable in this life; nevertheless it is still the goal.[148] However, the elect are expected to grow in the grace of God and in the accumulation of merits. This is not possible, according to Gregory without the means of affliction and the

---

[143] Gregory the Great, *Moralia*, 29.19.36.

[144] Gregory the Great, *Moralia*, 21.6.11. "Ad hoc itaque Dominus apparuit in carne, ut humanam vitam admonendo excitaret, exempla praebendo accenderet, moriendo redimeret, resurgendo repararet."

[145] Gregory the Great, *Moralia*, 24.11.25.

[146] Gregory the Great, *Moralia*, 29.30.62.

[147] Gregory the Great, *Moralia*, 24.11.26. See also 24.10.23.

[148] On the impossibility of sinlessness in this life see *Moralia*, 8.33.56 and 12.16.22.

discipline of God. Conversion may produce security but security is the "parent of negligence". In order to spur his elect on to continued progress God assails them from without by hardship and allows them to be tempted from within.[149] The elect do not fear these trials and tribulations because they know that they "promote the interest of their righteousness" and lead them on in the holiness of sanctification.[150]

The trials and temptations that Christians face after their conversion lead them on to sanctification in several different ways. The most helpful thing that such trials promote in them is the contemplation of their redeemer. Pain turns the elect away from the outward physical life and toward inner, spiritual reflection. This tribulation opens the ears of the heart that sin had closed so that the elect can be moved by God.[151] Further, these tribulations open the eyes of Christians and give them a vision of their heavenly home.[152]

As the vision of the elect becomes clearer and the dross of sin is burned away their love is heightened. God inflicts his elect with wounds so that they might be inflamed by love for him. God wounds them so that they might be healed. The soul "on being struck with the darts of his love, it is wounded in its innermost parts with a feeling of pious affection (and) burns with the desire of contemplation".[153] The pain that repels the elect from the world drives them back to their source. As they contemplate the riches of the mercy of God who has taught them not to love the road (this present life) but the destination (God) they are enamored by his grace and infatuated by the one who has redeemed them from their debt and slavery to sin.[154]

The temptations that the elect face in this life after conversion aid their sanctification also by showing them their faults. As they see their own shortcomings in sin they realize first what they need to repent of and secondly how much they owe to the grace of God.[155] They come to realize that the virtues they felt they had with so much difficulty attained had never been their own. Thus, temptations and trials are a test of these virtues. "It is in tranquil rest that each man obtains the grace of the heavenly gift, but it is in trouble and adversity that he gives proof how much he has received."[156] The strength of the elect in virtues can never be known unless it is tried in adversity. But more than that, the virtues of the elect abound to others and serve as a witness to the

---

[149] Gregory the Great, *Moralia*, 24.11.27.

[150] Gregory the Great, *Moralia*, 8.10.21.

[151] Gregory the Great, *Moralia*, 26.35.64.

[152] Gregory the Great, *Moralia*, 24.6.11.

[153] Gregory the Great, *Moralia*, 6.25.42. "Percussa autem caritatis eius spiculis, vulneratur in intimis affectu pietatis, ardet desiderio contemplationis..."

[154] Gregory the Great, *Moralia*, 23.24.47 and 15.57.68.

[155] Gregory the Great, *Moralia*, 23.25.51.

[156] Gregory the Great, *Moralia*, 23.26.52. "Quia videlicet unusquisque superni doni gratiam in tranquillitate quietis percipit, sed quantum perceperit, in adversitate perturbationis ostendit."

power of God only when they are exercised in open battle. God's glory is magnified as the virtues of the elect shine out through adversity.[157]

Since these trials and temptations test the virtues of the elect and show them how much they lack in themselves they also serve to promote humility. The elect are often prone to pride as they increase in virtues and God uses such temptations to check their progress and to cause them to remember their infirmity.[158] In a wonderful use of language Gregory discusses the healing nature of sin in the elect.

> Behold! He who prides himself in virtue, through sin comes back to humility. But he who is puffed up by the virtues he has received, is wounded not with a sword, but, so to say, with a remedy. For what is virtue but a remedy, and what is vice but a wound? Because, therefore, we make a wound of our remedy, he makes a remedy of our wound; in order that we who are wounded by our virtue, may be healed by our sin. For we pervert the gifts of virtues to the practice of vice; he applies the allurements of vices to promote virtues, and wounds our healthy state in order to preserve it, and that we who fly from humility when we run, may cling to it at least when falling.[159]

Suffering under trials also serves to provide an opportunity for growth in sanctification through merit. First, the elect are taught to increase their patience through tribulation. Their patience is increased because their hope is tested. When they are assailed by misfortune they are to consider not the pain that they endure but the glory that is to come.[160] Merits are also increased because the suffering of the elect provides an opportunity for good works and charity. To contemn one who is smitten by God is to pass over an opportunity for virtue. Tribulation tests charity for it is only the true neighbor who loves in adversity as well as in prosperity.[161]

Gregory notes that the pain and sorrow of these three stages are followed by a joy that comes from God. The trials which promote the sanctification that we have been discussing are no different. As Christians advance in sanctification by the testing of their virtues and by the accumulation of merit they are brought to a realization of assurance before God. Although Gregory is very careful not

---

[157] Gregory the Great, *Moralia*, 23.26.52

[158] Gregory the Great, *Moralia*, 23.23.48.

[159] Gregory the Great, *Moralia*, 33.12.25. "Ecce qui de virtute se extollit per vitium ad humilitatem redit. Qui vero acceptis virtutibus extollitur, non gladio, sed ut ita dixerim, medicamento vulneratur. Quid est enim virtus, nisi medicamentum? Et quid est vitium, nisi vulnus? Quia ergo nos de medicamento vulnus facimus, facit ille de vulnere medicamentum, ut qui virtute percutimur, vitio curemur. Nos namque virtutum dona retorquemus in usum vitiorum, ille vitiorum illecebras assumit in arte virtutum; et salutis statum percutit ut servet, ut qui humilitatem currentes fugimus, ei saltim cadentes haereamus."

[160] Gregory the Great, *Moralia*, 11.34.47.

[161] Gregory the Great, *Moralia*, 7.24.29.

to posit an unequivocal assurance of salvation he is fond of quoting Hebrews 12:6 which reads "For those whom the LORD loves he disciplines, and he scourges every son whom he receives".[162] The persecution of the elect becomes for Gregory a sign of salvation and brings a tenuous joy of assurance. The wounds of the elect bring consolation in affliction because the oppressed are assured of God's good purposes in redeeming them and the trial therefore brings with it the hope of salvation and the promise of future health.[163]

The final stage of life that Gregory mentions as a sure place of sorrow and fear is death. The fear of death is linked to salvation because this fear is based on the dread of appearing at the last judgment. The Christian fears death not because of what it may do to the body but because they are aware that death will bring them before the strict judge.[164]

This fear of the judge is brought on primarily not by the evils which may be easily resisted and overthrown but by those which have escaped the notice of the elect.[165] The sins of the flesh may be beaten down but those of the mind are more difficult. They sneak upon the elect unaware and surprise them. The corruption brought upon humanity by its poor choice of free will has enslaved it and has become the source for all manner of evil thoughts. The elect, being aware of this, are thus afraid of the strict judgment of God because they know that if they are judged without mercy they will in no way be found clean.[166] But the fear and the sorrow which precede judgment are followed by joy. The mutability that passed upon humanity at the fall is changed to constancy at the sight of the merciful judge. Gregory offers consolation for the elect so weighed down with this fear by pointing out that the elect will be united with the judge. As the Christian enters into eternity and beholds the immutability of the divine nature he or she will slough off a robe of mortality and changeableness for an assumed nature like unto that of the judge.[167] The pain of earthly existence has finally given way to the eternal joy of the beatific vision.

We see then in Gregory how pain is a constant accompaniment to the spiritual life. Christ provides an example for the elect in the pain and sorrow of his incarnation, ministry and death. Pain makes the elect aware of their need for conversion by demonstrating their poverty. It drives them on in holiness by forcing them to inner contemplation. It provides an opportunity for growth in humility and patience while at the same time providing an opportunity for charity and good works. Finally, it brings them to continually reflect upon their life and to maintain an attitude of penance so that they can greet the coming

---

[162] Hebrews 12:6. (NASB) See Gregory the Great, *Moralia*, 9.45.68; 14.30.35; 15.33.39; 22.20.50 and 26.21.37 among others.
[163] Gregory the Great, *Moralia*, 7.18.22.
[164] Gregory the Great, *Moralia*, 24.11.32.
[165] Gregory the Great, *Moralia*, 24.11.32.
[166] Gregory the Great, *Moralia*, 24.11.32.
[167] Gregory the Great, *Moralia*, 24.11.34.

judge as redeemer instead of condemner. Pain is, for Gregory, the constant motivating force behind the entire salvation experience from conversion to sanctification to the final judgment.

Conclusion: Gregory's Pedagogy of Pain

> But that every elect soul may escape eternal woe, and the poor mount up to everlasting glory, he must be bruised here below with continual stripes, that he may be found purified in the judgment. For we are every day borne downwards by the mere weight of our infirmity, but that by the wonderful interposition of our maker we are relieved by succoring stripes.[168]

Gregory does not set out in his *Moralia* to answer a question of theodicy. He does not seek to defend God for the evil in the world. Far from it, he embraces the evil that exists in this world. He takes it as a given and then uses it as a basis for an intricate exposition of the pedagogical use of pain by God.

Gregory begins by asserting that God is sovereign over all his creation. All the events of one's life, be they good or ill, fall under the providence of God. Nothing exists externally to God which he did not create. Since God is good and his judgments are always just if one experiences pain it must come from him and it must be good. God may not be the direct cause of suffering but must remain the ultimate cause. Pain exists because it is part of the will of God. As such, it exists as a topic to be studied and Gregory could have found no better place to discuss the pedagogical purpose of pain than the book of Job.

Job, for Gregory, means "grieving" and his suffering serves as a type of the archetype who is Christ. Gregory speaks of Job as a prophet who foreshadows and foretells the coming and the suffering of Christ. In the same way, as the Church exists as the body of Christ, Job's suffering is a type of the trials of the Church and thereby each individual's suffering as well. What Gregory argues from the life of Job is that humanity does indeed suffer in this world but this suffering is bound to grace. Pain is one way that the spiritual world breaks into the physical world. The normal boundaries between the two are surmounted in the nexus of pain. In this nexus the body suffers so that the mind may be enlightened and the fear of God may turn to love. Pain is a sign of God's favor and an opportunity for growth. Even if the oppressed person feels forsaken, Gregory reminds them that God enters the contest with us just as he entered the contest with Job.

Pain has become a nexus between the spiritual and the physical worlds through the war that has begun in human nature between the body and the mind

---

[168] Gregory the Great, *Moralia*, 6.22.39. "Sed ut electus quisque aeterna supplicia evadat et ad perennem gloriam pauper ascendat, debet hic assiduis flagellis atteri quatenus in iudicio valeat purgatus inveniri. Ipso namque infirmitatis nostrae pondere deorsum cotidie ducimur, nisi mira manu artificis per subvenientia flagella relevemur."

because of the fall. When the original parents sinned all of God's order for humanity was upset. Humanity was created in the image and likeness of God but sinned in pride when it sought to be like God not in righteousness (which they already were by virtue of their having been created in God's image) but in power. Thus upsetting the order of dominion in creation, the mind lost its dominion over the flesh and became its servant. Though created to contemplate God, the heaviness of the flesh now in power in humanity weighs down the mind so that it has lost all power of rightly contemplating God and even itself.

The punishment for sin was more sin. The guilt and corruption which the original parents earned is now passed on to each generation of their progeny. They are enslaved to sin and owe the debt of death. In fact, all of life is a continual dying for humanity is constantly beset by its own mortality and mutability. It suffers hunger and thirst, hot and cold, sickness and death. Even the world which was created to serve humanity has turned against it and serves God in executing punishment for sin through floods, droughts, earthquakes, and tempests of the sea. But Gregory reminds his readers of these things in order to demonstrate that this punishment is not simply pain but medicine and even though not every prescription of the doctor is a joy to endure the doctor always desires the health of the patient.

This medicine is designed for both the body and the mind. Since humanity is bipartite, pain is experienced in this life in both the body and the mind. External or material pain attacks the body in many ways. The body, though created immortal, now suffers in mutability. It is born, it grows, it gets sick and it dies. The time of this passage is full of all manner of physical evils and natural disasters. To make matters worse, some individuals are oppressed by others. The injustice that faces humanity has been brought upon it by its own sin and corruption but God uses such injustices for his own purposes. For example, material wealth is often seen as a blessing and its theft as a form of oppression but Gregory seeks to explain to his reader how the possession of many temporal goods brings more ill than good because they only bring more care and concern about their growth and their preservation. When these have been removed, Gregory argues that the elect are better able to see the spiritual world and to grow in grace being unencumbered by material wealth. Humanity is also oppressed from without by the temptations of Satan and his demons. But even in these instances God is at work. Satan is still a servant of God and is used by him despite his intentions. God is capable of using Satan's temptations in the elect as a lesson in humility and an opportunity for growth.

Humans also experiences internal or immaterial pain that arises from within them. The corruption that each person has inherited brings pain. Humans sorrow that the joys of their first estate in creation have been lost because of sin. They grieve that they can no longer contemplate God. Instead, they spend their days seeking fulfillment outside of God in an impossible effort to find this lost joy. Because of depravity their faculties of contemplation have been turned to other things and humans can no longer seek God much less find him. Neither can they contemplate themselves. In their inability they find that their mind has been so affected by corruption that it wars with itself. The sin that is attached to the body has taken its seat in the mind and serves as a source for innumerable temptations and grief.

Pain, since the fall, has become an inescapable part of human existence yet God maintains his control and guidance over his creation. God's use of pain is tied to the mysteries of election. The class of the reprobate and the class of the elect experience pain in much the same way but with differing results. The elect experience pain for their purification and growth whereas the reprobate experience pain only as punishment. Gregory outlines the way in which God's mercy is always mixed with his justice in the human experience of pain. The elect are judged in God's justice with pain here so that they will not be judged at the last judgment without mercy. Sometimes the reprobate are punished by pain here in order to demonstrate God's justice in the present. At other times, they are not judged here but receive the mercy of God's longsuffering. When they fail to respond to God's patient call, however, God's justice is served in that while they experienced his mercy here they were heaping up judgment upon themselves that will be conveyed at the last judgment. The judgment and mercy experienced in this life are tied to the life to come.

Gregory outlines several different categories of pain. The first of these is punitive and punishes the reprobate without withdrawing them from their sin. This is the only category of pain that Gregory reserves for the reprobate. The second group is also punitive but it has a different end. God often uses the pain of this world to punish the elect so that they will repent of their sins and convert.

God also makes use of prohibitive pain for his elect. He punishes them not for sins that they have committed but for the sins they would have committed had they remained unpunished. When the elect are faced with trials they draw closer to God and fear that they may be lost. Thus occupied, they do not have the time or the desire to fall into sin seeing that they are already being judged by him. These last two types of pain are ultimately redemptive because of how they work in the lives of the elect but God also allows pain to fall upon them so that they might be able to increase their virtues and merits. This pain increases the love of the elect for God in that when God withdraws himself from them for a time they are inflamed to seek him more ardently. Even when the pain is not personally experienced by individuals, it is meritorious in allowing them an opportunity for good works in meeting the needs of others and demonstrating Christian love for the oppressed.

This type of love of neighbor is best typified in the incarnation of Christ. Christ loved humanity by condescending in the incarnation and taking upon himself a weak human nature. He became one with humanity so that he might suffer the debt that all humanity owed for sin (death). This image of the suffering Christ is at the heart of Gregory's Christology and the heart of his soteriology. The incarnation of Christ, understood as the Son taking up a weak human nature, serves as the basis for Gregory's soteriology. Christ became weak and susceptible to pain of his own free will so that he could be like his human creation and serve as its mediator before God. Christ is the revelation of the Father and his weak human nature is an accommodation that allows this revelation to be read. Christ also offers the elect an example of how they ought to endure pain and suffering in their own lives through the way he endured the same in his life and ministry. He was content when he faced calumny and was humble and patient when faced with adversity. But the greatest example of his weakness was displayed during his passion when he suffered for all the debt of death owed to sin. This death, made possible by his human nature, allowed him to defeat the bonds of Satan through human weakness.

Just as pain accompanied the work that Christ accomplished for humanity it accompanies the work that Christ is doing in his elect. The pain and sorrow that the elect experience in this life are linked to their salvation. This occurs in three distinct stages. First, the elect suffer pain during their conversion. They are shown the height of their fall and the bankruptcy of their nature. They realize that they are nothing in themselves and fear the judgment for the sins which they have committed. God uses this pain to move them away from a preoccupation with the external world to an inner life of contemplation. As his prevenient grace prepares their hearts and pain afflicts their bodies the control of the body over the mind is loosened so that they can see their need for God and begin to find a desire for him. Gregory outlines the way that God, after the elect have been established in their conversion and have begun to make headway on their advance to virtue, allows them to suffer grave temptations. Their sanctification is enhanced by these temptations. Although this sounds odd, Gregory reminds his readers that pride is the root of all evil and pride too often accompanies the elect in their initial growth in virtues. When they are assailed by temptation they remember that the virtues which they have exist by the grace of God and are not the result of their own efforts. They are humbled and taught to trust in him alone. Pain and even sin, in the lives of the elect serve this pedagogical purpose. The sorrow of sanctification also develops merit by providing opportunities for service and opportunities for proving the strength of the virtues that they have been given by God. But with all the sorrow of salvation God always imparts hope and joy. In conversion the elect received the joy of first contemplating God. In sanctification they find the joy of assurance realizing that God afflicts those he has chosen and disciplines them as sons and daughters.

The final stage of life that Gregory discusses in the context of pain is death. Death brings sorrow because of the aspect of salvation which it represents. The elect fear death because they realize that it ushers them in before the just judge. Even though they have made progress in virtues by God's grace and done away with much of their sin they are still mutable. Sins creep up from the temptation of the mind even when they are not performed. The elect know that without mercy they can never pass the strict judgment of God. They also fear for the sins of which they are unaware. They know that the sins for which they have repented have been purged but their vision has been so affected by depravity that they fear they might have overlooked some sin or attitude. Nevertheless, when they die and meet the face of the judge they see there not a judge but a savior. They rejoice that the pain of their life has worked for their perfection and in their contemplation of God after death their corruptibility puts on incorruption and they are renewed in the immutable nature which humanity initially received at creation.

Pain is the result of sin and human mutability but God has turned the sin and its pain into a medicine. The corruption brought upon humanity by the fall is being burned out. Christ's incarnation, life, and death show the elect how pain works for their benefit. As Christ suffered for their salvation they suffer to apply his merits to their lives. The pain of sin has become the refiner's fire.

> Gold in the furnace is advanced to the brightness of its nature, while it loses the dross. And so like gold that passes through the fire the souls of the righteous are tried, which by the burning of tribulation through and through, both have their defect removed, and their good points increased.[169]

---

[169] Gregory the Great, *Moralia*, 16.32.39. "Aurum in fornace ad naturae suae claritatem proficit dum sordes amittit. Quasi aurum ergo quod per ignem transit probatur anima iustorum quibus exustione tribulationis et subtrahuntur vitia et merita augentur."

CHAPTER 4

The Christological Synthesis

Gregory is always a pastor at heart and his contemplations upon the nature and role of pain in the Christian life often express his pastoral leanings. His emphasis upon eschatology as an impetus toward spiritual conversion and growth may be classified likewise. In his eschatology, he emphasizes the redemptive focus of pain. Yet underneath both of these themes there remains his Christology. Gregory is the herald of the emerging medieval image of Christ as the judge. Gregory's eschatological statements and his theological reflection upon the nature of pain as they appear in his *Moralia* are rooted in the experience of Christ during the incarnation, his role as mediator, his suffering in redemption, the application of his suffering to the Church, and his role at the last judgment. The themes of eschatology and the experience of pain in the *Moralia*, seemingly disconnected, are actually both grounded in Gregory's Christology which serves as the basis for his moral reflections and applications taken from the book of Job. It is only in light of his Christology that these themes can be more fully understood.

Links in the Advents of Christ

Jean Laporte has argued for the centrality of Gregory's understanding of the person and work of Christ especially in the context of the Christian's experience of pain.[1] As Christians experience pain they look to the one who experienced pain for them as their perfect example and archetype. Carole Straw advances her highly developed structural analysis of Gregory's theological thought and spirituality by saying that "structurally, Gregory's is a Christocentric spirituality, for the remedies and reversals of Christ are the archetypes of the larger paradoxical order Gregory sees throughout the

---

[1] Laporte, "Une théologie systématique?", 236.

universe".[2] Both of these authors have understood the weight which Gregory places upon the importance of reading all the events of this life in light of the original created goodness of this world and in the coming *apokatastasis* wherein Christ will restore the original order of a good creation. This work of Christ was begun in the incarnation and will be completed in the eschaton at the last judgment. But even now Christ is serving as mediator as well as judge. Christ's work is on-going. Gregory does not make a great distinction between the two advents of Christ. He sees Christ's suffering in the first advent and Christ's coming in the glory of judgment to be a garment woven in one piece. The work of the one flows logically and really into the other. They should not be separated but held in one broad and expansive view of the vista of salvation history. Christ came in his first advent to redeem humanity from the sin that had enslaved it.[3] Christ came assuming the weakness of human flesh and he became a man to help humanity.[4] He came to reveal God to the world, accommodating himself in human form while at the same time serving as the exact image of the Father.[5] He also showed humanity the way back to God.[6] He took upon himself the wounds of humanity's sin.[7] His suffering serves as an example to Christians as they are called to imitate his passion.[8] "Accordingly, to this end the Lord appeared in the flesh, that the life of man he might by dealing admonitions arouse, by giving examples kindle, by suffering death redeem, by rising again renew."[9]

Christ also came into the world to judge the world. The mercy attending his first advent was not without the justice of judgment. In fact, the role of Christ as judge is based in the incarnation. Christ's humility in becoming a man and his obedience in following the will of the Father merited his exaltation as the judge to exercise authority over those he came to redeem.[10]

Not only is the future judgment rooted in the humility and obedience of Christ in the first advent but Gregory demonstrates that Christ's first advent was itself not free from judgment. Christ came to redeem humanity but judgment was the logical corollary of his appearing as well. The incarnation serves as judgment in that all humans are now compared to the perfect example of Christ's life and in the fact that the future judgment is based upon whether or

---

[2] Straw, *Gregory, Perfection*, 148.

[3] For a discussion of the work of Christ in redemption see Straw, *Gregory, Perfection*, 150-155 and Dudden, *Gregory the Great*, vol. 2, 336-347.

[4] Gregory the Great, *Moralia*, 16.30.37 and 22.17.42.

[5] Gregory the Great, *Moralia*, 5.34.63-5.35.64.

[6] Gregory the Great, *Moralia*, 30.24.69.

[7] Gregory the Great, *Moralia*, 20.36.68-69.

[8] Gregory the Great, *Moralia*, 17.7.9. See also 29.30.65.

[9] Gregory the Great, *Moralia*, 21.6.11. "Ad hoc itaque Dominus apparvit in carne, ut humanam vitam admonendo excitaret, exempla praebendo accenderet, moriendo redimeret, resurgendo repararet."

[10] Gregory the Great, *Moralia*, 28.1.5.

not an individual accepts or rejects Christ in his divine capacity as mediator. Christ accepted all persons that came to him recognizing their own shortcomings and failures to keep the law but those who were lifted up in the pride of their own achievements received his judgment. His coming provided the event by which all were and would be judged. The acceptance or rejection of his incarnation brought blessing or judgment. The elect thus came to him in humility but the reprobate rejected his coming and merited his judgment.[11]

The judgment of Christ in the first advent was also mixed with mercy. Humanity has a difficult time understanding how justice ought to be mixed with mercy. Gregory argues that humans often either tend toward mercy and deny the full action of a strict justice or tend toward justice and are deficient in the offering of mercy. The line is a fine one and impossible for fallen humanity to tread. However, Christ in his earthly ministry always maintained a happy medium between justice and mercy holding in tension both "simplicity and uprightness". Gregory cites as an example the story from John 8 wherein the scribes and Pharisees brought before Jesus the woman who had been caught in adultery. In the test Jesus avoided both extremes for "he neither in showing mercy parted with the strictness of justice, nor again in the exactitude of justice did he part with the virtue of mercifulness".[12] At all times and in all his actions Christ provided both justice and mercy. Gregory made no strong distinction between the first advent being a visitation of mercy and the second a visitation of judgment. The truth was more complicated than that. Actually, Christ's accomplishment of his work whether in the first advent or in the second is a mixture of both judgment and mercy.

The culmination of the judgment that began at Christ's incarnation will take place at the consummation of all things as Christ appears in his second advent to judge all of humanity. In the last judgment Christ will complete the work of election. That which was made manifest to a few prophets in the Old Testament and was proclaimed to multitudes of the elect during his incarnation will be made manifest to all at his appearance at the last judgment. Christ is an active agent in the secret of divine election. The mercy of his first advent and the judgment of his second are linked in the causality of divine election. Christ will not only be a judge at the final retribution; he was not only a judge in his first advent but had already manifested his justice in judging before the creation of all things in the secret dispensation of his election.[13]

At the inquest of the final judgment, Christ will make public the wickedness of the reprobate and cast them into hell.[14] His judgment will fall upon humanity

---

[11] Gregory the Great, *Moralia*, 2.35.57.

[12] Gregory the Great, *Moralia*, 1.12.16. "...nec in mansuetudine districtionem iustitiae nec rursum in districtione iustitiae virtutem mansuetudinis amisit."

[13] Gregory the Great, *Moralia*, 29.2.4.

[14] Gregory the Great, *Moralia*, 25.8.19.

as lightning consuming all it strikes.[15] The mercy with which he suffered the reprobate to continue in their sin will give place to the swift and minute exaction of the judge's decree.[16] All the secret and evil deeds which they committed in thought and deed together with their sins of omission will be brought to light.[17]

Nevertheless, even as justice is not absent from Christ's first advent, neither is mercy absent from his second. Gregory seeks to make this point through the use of a curious phrase (the wrath of the dove) taken from Jeremiah 25:38. Gregory establishes from his use of this verse two primary points. First, the Judge (Christ), like a dove being a simple animal, is unmoved and remains immutable in his exercise of judgment upon the unrighteous. Second, in his treatment of the righteous he is perceived in the calm and loving image of a dove. Though the judge appears wrathful to the unrighteous because of their awareness of their guilt, to the righteous he will appear as a calm and loving father of mercy.[18] Gregory is fully aware that humanity can never escape its depravity. Even the good actions of holy individuals are mixed with the sins of pride and vainglory. Even the most praiseworthy life, if it is judged without mercy at the final judgment will be overwhelmed by the terrible appearance of the holy judge and will be found wanting in comparison to the perfect justice of the judge.[19] But the fear of this proposal will be mitigated in the righteous for they will hear the mild voice of the judge.[20] Christ will not judge the former lives of sinners who have come, even in the last days of their life, to a knowledge of him by a gift of divine grace.[21] Christ is merciful in the last judgment in that, "he doubtless never exacts retribution for guilt of sin from him, whom faith, hope, and charity hide beneath the shelter of his pardoning grace".[22]

Gregory outlines at least two modes of acting in the work of Christ.[23] The modes are related to the two advents of Christ. Gregory notes that the first advent of Christ was colored with gentleness and humility.[24] In the second advent however, his wrath will disturb those who encounter him as a tempest and a whirlwind.[25] Gregory does indeed seek to characterize the first advent of Christ as marked by grace and the second advent as marked by justice. This is

---

[15] Gregory the Great, *Moralia*, 34.5.10.

[16] Gregory the Great, *Moralia*, 8.16.32.

[17] Gregory the Great, *Moralia*, 21.10.16.

[18] Gregory the Great, *Moralia*, 32.7.9.

[19] Gregory the Great, *Moralia*, 29.18.34.

[20] Gregory the Great, *Moralia*, 6.30.48.

[21] Gregory the Great, *Moralia*, 27.18.38

[22] Gregory the Great, *Moralia*, 10.7.12. "...ab eo procul dubio vindictam de culpae reatu non expetit quem sub eius venia spes, fides et caritas abscondit."

[23] Gregory the Great, *Moralia*, 17.33.54.

[24] Gregory the Great, *Moralia*, 17.32.53.

[25] Gregory the Great, *Moralia*, 28.1.1.

however far from a separation. The whole point of the comparison is to make a pastoral charge to his hearers to prepare for the coming judgment.[26]

Judgment was present in the first advent of Christ and this judgment was couched within an overall tenor of mercy. How awful will his judgment be when it is unleashed in all its raw character? Gregory's whole argument for preparing for the second advent of Christ rests upon the inability of humanity to withstand the judgment that was already present in the first advent of Christ. If none could stand before him in the incarnation what will happen at the second coming? Though there may have been two modes of action which characterized the two advents of Christ these two modes were actually united in the one role of Christ as the divine mediator between God and humanity. In his role as mediator Christ demonstrates both the love and the judgment of the Father.

> At the center is Christ, joining flesh and spirit, God and man. Christ's sacrifice changes man's vision of God. If God is the terrifying judge, Christ's sacrifice reveals God to be merciful and gentle, for his Incarnation displays God's humility in becoming man and dying for man's sake. As man, he is the Redeemer who suffers in the flesh as only a human being can. Yet his life on Earth also teaches perfect righteousness, for Christ is guided by the divine logos. As God, Christ will visit man with fierce vengeance on judgment day, yet he will also serve as the Advocate for the sinners he redeemed, continually interceding for mercy on their behalf. Christ is both priest and sacrifice, reconciler and reconciled. Through sacrifice, directions change and a cosmic equilibrium is attained.[27]

Gregory's Christology is based in Christ's role as mediator to the extent that it is always relationally attached to his doctrines of God and humanity.[28] For Gregory, Christ stands as both God and human capable of revealing God to humanity and interceding for humanity before God as a full member of the human race. In his incarnation, Christ becomes the propitiation which restores the severed relationship between humanity and God by judging himself so that humanity might not be judged. In his resurrection, Christ becomes the intercessor who offers the pleas of the saints to God and returns the mercy of God to the saints.

Christ came to redeem humanity. He did this by first of all descending in humility and becoming one in nature with it. He took upon himself all that pertained to humanity with the exception of guilt. His conception by the Holy Spirit in a virgin prevented the corruption of original sin and his divine nature assured the absence of actual sin. Christ showed humanity the way back to the Father by showing them the Father. The corruption of original sin had so

---

[26] Gregory the Great, *Moralia*, 17.33.54.

[27] Straw, *Gregory, Perfection*, 259.

[28] Rodrigue Bélanger, "La dialectique Parole-Chair dans la christologie de Grégoire le Grand," in John C. Cavadini (ed.), *Gregory the Great: A Symposium* (Notre Dame 1995), 82.

encompassed human nature that its spiritual senses had been dulled. Humanity could no longer see God in the spirit so it must see God in the flesh and this is what Christ provided.[29]

The holiness of God required a sacrifice so that the breach which developed between him and humanity might be sealed. To do this Christ took humanity upon himself. Christ satisfied the righteous judgment of God by judging and he found the object of judgment in himself. In order to provide mercy for his children Christ took upon himself the punishment of their sins and paid the debt to death which every person owed.[30] Divine mercy is always mixed with judgment, in fact it demands judgment and this judgment was placed upon Christ as he suffered death for all.

Part of the work of Christ was also to judge humanity. He did this first of all by providing a perfect image of God. Weighed down with spiritual blindness humanity could not see God. Humans had no pattern after which to follow other than their own miserable examples of sin. Those that were sick needed a physician who could teach them how to fulfill the requirement of holiness demanded by God. But the first motion of amendment is judgment. In Christ's life he offered a counter-example that judged the inability of humanity and set forth a new course. The perfect humility and obedience of Christ set a new standard for humanity.[31] When Christians compared their lives to that of Christ, as the necessity of the coming, imminent judgment demanded, they were judged inwardly by their failure to meet the expectations of a holy and righteous God.

Second, Christ continues to judge humanity by virtue of his role as mediator. He was exalted to this position by the humility he demonstrated in the incarnation. All who refuse to humble themselves likewise but lift themselves up in pride not realizing the weakness of their corrupt state are judged because of their pride. It is only Christians who are willing to own their sin and weakness of nature who are able to break free from the consciousness of their guilt by the righteousness of their redeemer and thus escape eternal damnation.[32] Only those who realize their distance from the holiness of the redeemer receive his mercy. Those that have been deceived into thinking that they were united to him are judged for their sins and do not receive the merits of his death.[33]

Finally, the mediator will judge humanity in the last day. The redeemer who brought with him the grace of the Gospel and instituted the new covenant is

---

[29] Gregory the Great, *Moralia*, 22.17.42.

[30] Gregory the Great, *Moralia*, 24.2.3.

[31] Gregory the Great, *Moralia*, 24.2.2.

[32] Gregory the Great, *Moralia*, 24.3.5.

[33] Gregory the Great, *Moralia*, 24.3.5. This is the application Gregory provides for Christ's words of condemnation to the hypocrites in the Matthew 25:42-43; "I was hungry and you gave me nothing to eat." etc. See also 15.19.23; and 26.27.50.

also the author of the old covenant. The law has not been abrogated but is propagated in a different manner. Under Moses, it was commanded upon fear of death. Now the mediator bids humanity in meekness to accept and follow its precepts. Nevertheless, the punishment for ignoring the law is the same. When Christ comes in judgment he will exact in strict justice the punishment for failing to fulfill the law. He came to show fallen humans the law in his own person, fulfilling all its requirements but if they fail to see his example and listen to his admonition they will be judged apart from the grace they have scorned.[34]

Another focus of Gregory's reflection upon Christ's role as a mediator is his representation of humanity before God. As the second Adam, Christ became a representative of humanity without sin. In receiving the punishment for sin undeservedly, he mitigated the judgment of God by judging himself and thus won clemency for humanity. Christ not only judged himself for the crimes of humans and judges them for their failures but he also stands before God as the representative sacrifice of reconciliation. Gregory pictures the suffering of Christ as a rebuke of human sin and an infusion of righteousness that satisfied the justice of God. Christ serves as a mediator not only by taking upon himself the sin of humanity; thus satisfying God's righteousness, but also by offering his perfect life as a gift on the behalf of humanity; thus satisfying the requirements of God's holiness.[35]

Christ continues in his role as mediator to intercede before God for the Christian.[36] He gives voice to the prayers of the saints. His very act of intercession proves his like nature with humanity as well as his sinlessness. As he paid humanity's debt to death corporately he begs for forgiveness individually. Based upon the merits of his sinless life and sinless death he wins forgiveness from the Father for all who unite themselves to his model of humility offered in the incarnation.[37] This intercession is not merely the repetition of the prayers of the saints before the Father it is also the actual bestowal of grace and forgiveness. His intercession does not take the form of words but is the act of compassion that serves as a prelude to the grace of forgiveness.[38]

The graciousness of the mediator will likewise be found at the last judgment. Even the spiritually gifted are unable to withstand the exacting scrutiny and strict minuteness of the last judgment before Christ if they are judged without pity.[39] But the last judgment will bring pity for the elect. Even though the elect

---

[34] Gregory the Great, *Moralia*, 22.18.44.
[35] Gregory the Great, *Moralia*, 9.38.61.
[36] Gregory the Great, *Moralia*, 22.17.42. This is the quintessential passage from the *Moralia* regarding the continuing intercession of Christ on behalf of humanity.
[37] Gregory the Great, *Moralia*, 24.2.4-24.3.5.
[38] Gregory the Great, *Moralia*, 22.17.42.
[39] Gregory the Great, *Moralia*, 8.28.47.

feel the sting of the scourge now when the judge does come they will be hidden from the scourge.[40] Instead of the voice of doom they will hear the mild voice of the judge.[41] The judge will never exact retribution for the sins of the elect which have been covered by grace.[42] Instead of viewing the elect clouded by sin "in the eyes of the hidden judge he is bright with virtues and full of luster from the merits of his life".[43]

Gregory's Christology serves to link his themes of pain and eschatology in the *Moralia* through his unification of the two advents of Christ and his understanding of Christ's role as a mediator in these two advents. Mercy and judgment are always intertwined. As Christians look in dread toward the last judgment, their fear of the judge should lead them to contrition for their sin. But the prayers of their contrition will be heard by the mediator who will judge them with pity and not without grace. Just as Christ judged himself by paying the penalty of death through his suffering on the cross, Christians are enjoined to look at the example of Christ as a model. Their suffering here is a guarantee that they are being prepared not for but against the last judgment. At that time they will be hidden from the scourges that oppressed them in this life because of the very fact that they made a proper use of them here.

The Head and the Body

The whole of Gregory's discourse on the Christian's use of pain in the spiritual life is derived in consequence of Gregory's Christology and is applied in this text through the use of Job as a type of Christ. The pain that Job experienced both foretells the pain that Christ would experience and the pain that the Church would encounter. In all cases the pain was salvific. Job experienced pain to increase his merits. Christ experienced pain to gain humanity's salvation. The Church experiences pain to apply Christ's saving merits to itself and to proclaim the grace he has showered upon the lives of the elect.[44]

Gregory uses this Pauline image of the Church as the body of Christ to emphasize the character of the relationship between the Church and Christ.[45] Although he occasionally uses this image to discuss the nature of church order and authority within the church his primary emphasis is upon the complete and

---

[40] Gregory the Great, *Moralia*, 6.26.43.

[41] Gregory the Great, *Moralia*, 6.30.48.

[42] Gregory the Great, *Moralia*, 10.7.12.

[43] Gregory the Great, *Moralia*, 10.30.51. "Sed tamen ante occulti iudicis oculos virtutibus emicat, vitae meritis coruscat..."

[44] Gregory the Great, *Moralia*, 23.1.2

[45] See 1 Corinthians 12:27; Ephesians 1:22-3 and 4:15; and Colossians 1.24. For this image in the *Moralia* see Preface.6.14; 3.13.25; 4.11.18; 19.14.22; 20.3.8; 23.1.2; 28.10.23; and 35.14.24.

total union of purpose and will between Christ and the Church.[46] The union is so strong that it becomes almost organic to the extent that Christ "feels" the pain that his Church suffers in persecution.

It is because of this union that Job can serve as a dual type, signifying both Christ and the Church. Moving between the two figures, Gregory is able to more pointedly apply the suffering of Job to the redemption of Christ and the travail of the Church.[47] But this comparison is also eschatologically focused. The great suffering of Job led to his double blessing after his trial.[48] In the same way, the suffering of Christ led to the redemption of the elect. The Church also, at the end of time, when it has completed its trial will receive double for all it has suffered in the present life.[49] Gregory's application of this concept is first of all moral but extends to the teleological. The painful experiences of Job look forward to those of Christ and the Church but they also promise the benefit of the life hereafter following the present life of trial and tribulation.[50] This blessing is in large part due to the suffering the elect experience for it prepares them for a life of contemplation of God and the future beatific vision.[51]

Job serves as a type of Christ in several ways. Gregory seems to see Job acting as a "type" and his role as a prophet as part and parcel of the same thing. There is no distinction between the two for Gregory. They each portend what is to come in the person of Christ. Job's humility, suffering, and rejection proclaim what was to happen to the coming redeemer.[52]

In practice, Gregory applies the suffering of Job to the first advent and Christ's redemption of humanity but applies the reign of Christ over the Church and the second coming to the words of Job. In this way both the advents of Christ are linked in the figure and words of Job and a typological application is made which in a unique way melds allegory with anagogy in a teleological focus.

Job typifies Christ by foreshadowing his incarnation. Job's continual care and concern for the salvation of his children as demonstrated by his continual offering of sacrifices allows Gregory to make a link with Christ whose incarnation is an offering for humanity's purification.[53] Job's being especially marked out by God as a man unlike any other because of his holiness of life also foreshadows, for Gregory, Christ's uniqueness in having both a human and

---

[46] For passages on the Church as the body of Christ confined to issues of church order and spiritual gifts see *Moralia*, 19.14.22 and 28.10.23.

[47] Gregory the Great, *Moralia*, 23.1.3.

[48] Gregory the Great, *Moralia*, 35.16.36.

[49] Gregory the Great, *Moralia*, 35.14.24 and 35.16.41.

[50] Gregory the Great, *Moralia*, Preface.10.20.

[51] Gregory the Great, *Moralia*, 35.20.47. See also 35.12.22.

[52] Gregory the Great, *Moralia*, Preface.6.14.

[53] Gregory the Great, *Moralia*, 1.24.32. See also 2.23.42, wherein Gregory outlines Job's description as a servant of God as typical of Christ's coming to earth as a servant in the incarnation.

a divine nature.[54] Christ's humility in life for the purpose of redemption is pointed out, according to Gregory, by God's acknowledgment that Job was a man who feared God and forsook evil.[55] Christ's manner of life in avoiding all sin and his triumph over the temptation of Satan is demonstrated by Job's refusal to sin in the midst of his trial.[56]

Job also prophesies of the passion of Christ. This is generally affirmed by Gregory in several places as the logical fulfillment typified by the various sufferings of Christ in mind and in body that find their ultimate fulfillment in Christ's suffering and death.[57] Just as Satan had not spared anything that was Job's afflicting him in his property, his progeny, and his person so also did he attack the redeemer causing him great suffering and tormenting him in manifold ways. Christ suffered through the pain inflicted upon his own body, through his rejection by the Jewish people, and through the faithlessness of his own apostles when they forsook him at the end. This latter sorrow was compounded by the fact that these followers had been regenerated in his love but were still unwilling to follow him into his suffering; preferring instead to deny any affiliation with him or with his ministry.[58]

But Job also foretells the continuing interaction of Christ with his Church. Job directly prophesied that Christ who had been derided by his enemies, crowned with thorns, spat upon, and crucified would be resurrected from the dead and herald the end of death for all humanity.[59] Even though his apostles had forsaken him during his passion, they returned to him after the resurrection and were confirmed in their faith. Then, Christ sent them to spread his gospel to the Gentiles. Job's birth, described by him as destitute and unclothed, Gregory takes as a prefiguring of the spreading of the Gospel to the Gentiles who had not had the law or the covenants but despite their ill birth had now been adopted into the kingdom.[60] Job's intercession for his children is a type that prefigures Christ's continual intercession for us as the mediator between God and humanity.[61] Finally, the judgment of Christ in the last day is foretold by Job's imprecations of evil. Job looks forward to the day of the final recompensing wherein the reprobate will be condemned and the righteous rewarded as it should be according to justice in contrast with this present life in which the righteous suffer and the evil prosper.[62]

Job serves not only as a type of Christ but also as a type of the Church.

---

[54] Gregory the Great, *Moralia*, 2.23.42.
[55] Gregory the Great, *Moralia*, 1.13.17.
[56] Gregory the Great, *Moralia*, 13.30.34.
[57] Gregory the Great, *Moralia*, Preface.6.14; Preface 7.16; 17.1.1; and 23.1.2-3.
[58] Gregory the Great, *Moralia*, 6.1.1
[59] Gregory the Great, *Moralia*, 14.54.67.
[60] Gregory the Great, *Moralia*, 2.35.59.
[61] Gregory the Great, *Moralia*, 1.24.32.
[62] Gregory the Great, *Moralia*, 17.2.2.

Gregory's consistent identification of Christ as the head of the Church or, less frequently, Christ as the bride-groom serves to make this connection a simple one. The connection may be simple to make but it is more difficult to tease out the nuances of such a relationship. Gregory outlines his method in words reminiscent of Origen and hearkening back to the rules of Tyconius expressed in Augustine. It is for the reader to interpret the text of Job with careful discernment in order to determine how Job is a figure of one or the other or even both in differing degrees.[63]

Gregory's identification of Job as a type of the Church rests in his theological understanding of the lives of saints as examples for the faithful. The saints are like the stars in the sky which guide Christians on their path to God. As they follow these stars by living their lives in imitation of the saints, they will assume a likeness to the saints in the particular virtues for which they are known. The lives of the saints are gifts of divine providence and teach the elect that their present lives are transitory and only look forward to the perfection of the eternal life which is to come. The saints herald this perfection in their own bodies and show the members of the Church what they lack in addition to what they will become in the eternal state if they are able to live up to their example. Job holds a privileged place in this pantheon of higher beings who have received the manifold grace of God and have been marked by him as examples for those in the Church to follow. But more than examples, the very virtues of the saints look forward to the merits of Christ and their works and words prefigure and prophesy his appearance in the flesh.[64]

The trial of Job was very important for Job's serving as a type of the Church and one who was to be emulated by the faithful. Gregory assures his readers that Job had virtues before his testing. But for Gregory, the mere presence of virtues does not make one an example. These virtues must be tried and true. If they are not tested then they lack proof. A doubter could say, together with Satan, that the virtues were merely present in the life of Job because God had made a hedge around him. But more than that, Job's experience of suffering gave an opportunity to demonstrate his righteousness to the world. Doubtless, had he not undergone such tribulations the world would never have heard of him and the glory of God's grace in his life which were his virtues would not have been known. Instead, God saw fit to allow him to be stricken by Satan and to be tested under the scourge to prove God's grace and Job's virtue so that they would both emerge victorious and the Church would gain an example.[65]

The particular virtue which Job demonstrated to the faithful was of course his patience.[66] Christians should respond to suffering just as Job did. They must

---

[63] Gregory the Great, *Moralia*, Preface. 6.14. See also 17.1.1 which speaks of this discernment as an aspect of scriptural interpretation.

[64] Gregory the Great, *Moralia*, Preface. 6.13-14.

[65] Gregory the Great, *Moralia*, 3.3.3.

[66] Gregory the Great, *Moralia*, 3.3.3. See also Preface. 6.13.

endure their suffering patiently; never striking out against the judge because of a sure faith in his justice but always examining themselves inwardly for the cause of the fault and following this act of *discretio* with penitence.

Just as Christ suffered to save humanity, humans suffer in their own bodies so that they may attain this salvation. Pain can be salvific because God has so ordered it to drive the Christian to discretion and penitence. The sins of the elect are covered by the disciplining of the body to develop virtue and perform good works.[67] This inward discipline is often forced upon them by outward discipline. In other words, Christians suffer external ills so that they may inflict their own punishment upon themselves in the interior. This punishment is penitence and it too serves to cover the sins of the elect. The sins of Christians are cleansed by weeping and lamenting makes them spiritually rich.[68] They must realize that they can never meet the perfect example of God and will inevitably fall into sin by falling short of his example. This is true even of Job. Even though Gregory strives throughout his work to argue that Job's suffering was not because of sin he cannot help but turn aside for a brief time from this well-worn argument to show how Job himself is a picture of the penitence of the Christian. Suffering exists partly so that the godly may be brought to self-knowledge and self-judgment. Job's acknowledgment of his own inherent sinfulness before the vision of God in Job 40 allows Gregory to demonstrate Job's own failure in this regard and at the same time to set him up as an example to be followed by the penitent.[69]

The reason a Christian could respond to pain in this way is because of the way in which Job demonstrates, as a type of the Church, the perspective that members of the Church should have when they find themselves in similar circumstances. Suffering allows the Christian to regain the proper perspective that was lost in the fall. With the sin of the original parents humanity lost its spiritual eyes and unable to contemplate eternity, became enslaved by this world. Instead of considering what they have lost humans turn to the goods of this world seeking to fill the void that can only be filled by God in eternity. But the focus that humanity places upon this world is broken by the experience of pain. Pain naturally forces the person to look at the larger questions of existence that transcend the present and inquire into eternity. It is only when Christians find that the things exterior to them are nothing that they can move on to the solidity of inward things. God often brings the elect to this realization through the pain of this present life.[70]

Job is also a type of the Church when he suffers rebuke at the hands of his wife and his friends. The Church is afflicted by the presence of certain ones remaining inside it which are either not truly part of the body of Christ or are

---

[67] Gregory the Great, *Moralia*, 32.2.2.
[68] Gregory the Great, *Moralia*, 20.14.36.
[69] Gregory the Great, *Moralia*, 32.3.4. See also 1.25.35.
[70] Gregory the Great, *Moralia*, 1.25.34.

puerile and misled in their faith. The hypocrites and the immature afflict the Church through their words of rebuke and through their evil activities that in turn cause the Church to be slandered. Just as Job's counselors spoke against him and slandered his name and life, the lives of unholy persons in the Church do grave damage to its reputation.[71]

Job's wife who tempted him to curse God so that he could die represents, for Gregory, the carnal in the Church. These members cause a greater sense of suffering in the elect because their words are unexpected, coming from one so close. Such things are expected from those outside but when they are launched by those inside the Church the sting of the blow is heightened.[72] Job's friends also reveal themselves to be inner enemies. They come to him in order to give solace but only intensify his suffering. In the same way, the heretics afflict the Church while they think that they are doing good. Though they seek to defend God they only offend him. Job's responses to his friends typify the way that the Church must respond to the heretics by preaching against them and teaching true doctrine against their creed of corrupt doctrines.[73]

Although both groups inflict suffering upon the Church, it suffers them in its midst in the hope that they will mature or return to the true faith. Even though the presence of such among the body invites calumny against it, the Church hopes for confession and penitence and is willing to suffer in the present for their future reconciliation. The Church may indeed return suffering for suffering in placing such individuals under censure but the hope is that through their pain they might return and the pain of the Church in enduring their presence will be rewarded.[74]

Gregory likens the Christian's suffering here to the suffering of Christ in one of four ways. Suffering is one of the things which inextricably binds the Christian to Christ. The very suffering of the elect in this life is first of all an imitation of the suffering which Christ endured for them. As Christ suffered during his incarnation and death, the Christian suffers now. The Christian suffers as Christ suffered by imitating his passion. The fact that Christ actually saw beforehand and even ordained his own punishment at the hands of wicked humanity for their benefit before his incarnation reproves humanity for its own inconstancy under the scourge.[75] If Christ who was very God was persecuted what else could the Church expect but to be likewise persecuted.[76] Christ left his labors in the flesh to his followers as an example and their suffering is an imitation of his passion.[77] The suffering that the Christian experiences serves to

---

[71] Gregory the Great, *Moralia*, 14.25.29.

[72] Gregory the Great, *Moralia*, Preface.6.14.

[73] Gregory the Great, *Moralia*, Preface.6.15.

[74] Gregory the Great, *Moralia*, Preface.8.17-18.

[75] Gregory the Great, *Moralia*, 29.19.36.

[76] The scriptural background to this concept is no doubt John 15:18-20.

[77] Gregory the Great, *Moralia*, 31.18.33. See also 17.7.9; and 29.30.65.

unite the believer to Christ who suffered in his first advent.

This connection of suffering between Christ and the elect is further strengthened by Gregory's argument that as the Church suffers now, Christ continues to suffer. Since Christ is the head of the Church it follows that he experiences the suffering of his own body. Therefore, when the Church falls into tribulation Christ is present with it and suffers as well. Christ continues the suffering he began in his flesh at his incarnation and passion with the painful experiences of his Church now. Quoting Colossians 1:24, Gregory argues that just as Satan strove against Christ in his earthly ministry the tempter even now harasses Christ's body through the Church. Christ received wounds in all the members of his body on the cross and this punishment continues today in the Church so that it may fill out what is lacking in the afflictions of Christ.[78] More than just an organic image of unity Gregory seeks to establish this connection as one of love. Christ loves his Church by continuing to take its pain upon himself while the Church is willing to suffer for Christ as it rejoices in the glory of his resurrection and mediation.[79] In this image Gregory finds a contemplative spiral of mutual love and self-sacrifice for the benefit of the other which unites the two ever closer in mystical union.

This love brought on by the mutual suffering of Christ and the Church together with the spiritual benefits of such suffering serves as the basis for Gregory's understanding of the joy of Christ at the suffering of Christians. As Christians suffer, Christ rejoices because he knows that this suffering will drive his children away from a corrupt love of the world and temporal things and drive them into his loving arms. The desire of the faithful is to be remade in the image of Christ's holiness. Thus, they look forward to their death and their coming eternal bliss in which they will ever be with the Lord. Now however, they embrace suffering as a preparation for the eternal life and add to these sufferings their own chastening in penance. Because of these things, Christ laughs for joy at the pain of the elect.[80]

The suffering that unites the Church with its head will give way in the last day to glory. As Christ is glorified because of his suffering, the Church will be glorified. Following the example of Christ, each member of the elect is overwhelmed with calamity in this life and is both reviled and held contemptible by those outside the Church. But, "in the eyes of the hidden judge he is bright with virtues, and full of luster from the merits of his life".[81] The elect are already showing forth the goodness of the redeemer through the character of their lives for it is his grace which has so endowed them.[82] They

---

[78] Gregory the Great, *Moralia*, 6.1.1.

[79] Gregory the Great, *Moralia*, 3.13.25.

[80] Gregory the Great, *Moralia*, 9.27.42-43.

[81] Gregory the Great, *Moralia*, 10.30.51. "Sed tamen ante occulti iudicis oculos virtutibus emicat, vitae meritis coruscat."

[82] Gregory the Great, *Moralia*, 10.18.34.

are connected even now by their suffering and by their virtues but they will be joined with him in glory and power at the return of the judge. The glory of the elect is now hidden because the "power of lost sinners towers high" but in the day of judgment the pride of the wicked will be broken and the humility of the elect will be exalted.[83]

In the last day Christ will give judgment to the poor who are now oppressed because they will come with him to judge their oppressors.[84] Just as Christ is the "despised lamp" who will break out in the last judgment so also is the Church. Christ is glorified in the last day because of the suffering that he endured for the benefit of humanity. The Church is glorified in the last day for the suffering it endured for him whether this suffering was endured from others or was self-inflicted out of love for him.

> For the "appointed time" for "the despised lamp" is the predestined day of final judgment, wherein it is shown how each one of the righteous, who is now contemned, shines bright in greatness of power. For then they come as judges with God, who now are judged unjustly for God's sake. Then their light shines over so much the wider space, the more cruelly the persecutor's hand confines and fetters them now. Then it will be made clear to the eyes of the wicked, that they were supported by heavenly power, who forsook all earthly things of their own free will...for whosoever being urged by the incitement of divine love, has forsaken all that he possessed here, shall doubtless attain there to the height of judicial power; that he may then come as judge in company with the judge, who now by consideration of the judgment chastens himself with voluntary poverty.[85]

Gregory's Christology serves to link his themes of pain and eschatology in the *Moralia* through his understanding of the relationship between Christ and his Church. Gregory's discourse on the Christian's use of pain in the spiritual life is likewise derived in consequence of his Christology and is applied in this text through the use of Job as a type of Christ. The Church and Christ are united into one flesh with Christ serving as the "head of the body." His expression seems to move beyond allegory to a real sense of mystical, if not almost organic, unity. The Church and Christ are united in their suffering for the Church suffers in imitation of its head. This experience of pain is understood by

---

[83] Gregory the Great, *Moralia*, 12.10.13.

[84] Gregory the Great, *Moralia*, 26.27.49.

[85] Gregory the Great, *Moralia*, 10.31.52. "Statutum quippe contemptae lampadis tempus est extremi iudicii praedestinatus dies, quo iustus quisque qui nunc despicitur, quanta potestate fulgeat demonstratur. Tunc enim cum Deo iudices veniunt, qui nunc pro Deo iniuste iudicantur. Tunc eorum lux tanto latius emicat, quanto eos nunc manus persequentium durius angustat. Tunc reproborum oculis patescet quod caelesti potestate subnixi sunt qui terrena omnia sponte reliquerunt...quia quisquis, stimulo divini amoris excitatus, hic possessa reliquerit, illic procul dubio culmen iudiciariae potestatis obtinebit, ut simul tunc iudex cum iudice veniat qui nunc consideratione iudicii sese spontanea paupertate castigat."

Gregory to be salvific. Christ suffered for our salvation and the Church suffers to apply the merits of this salvation. The Church expresses its love for its redeemer by inflicting the pain of penance upon itself and Christ's love is demonstrated in his joy at the Christian's spiritual progress through pain and suffering. But the final thrust of the unity which Gregory describes is found in the last judgment. Christ's glory will be manifested in the last day. The Father has honored him with glory and given him the task of judging the world because of his humble suffering during his first advent. By virtue of its union with Christ, the Church also will be glorified in the last judgment when it comes together with him to judge the world.

Interiority and Exteriority

The concepts of interiority and exteriority as they have developed in Gregorian study will serve as a helpful way for us to outline the connection between the use of pain in the spiritual life and the last judgment in light of Gregory's Christology. I will show that Dagens' approach to these concepts in Gregory's conceptualization of the spiritual life, and Bélanger's use of them in outlining Gregory's Christology can be reconciled. In fact Gregory's application of interiority and exteriority in Christ serves as the bridge that outlines the concepts of interiority and exteriority within salvation history. It is only in the last day, and at the last judgment that humanity will once again find the interiority that was lost during the fall. Interiority is gained through diminishing the exteriority of this life. As humans experience pain in this life it forces them to turn inward and this is the beginning of conversion. At the last judgment, the process of interiorization will be completed by the internal judge who initiates the beatific vision.

Paul Aubin opened a new chapter in the discussion of Gregory's spiritual thought with his discussion of interiority and exteriority in Gregory the Great's *Moralia*.[86] His review of almost 2,500 Gregorian uses of terms which denote this concept in the *Moralia* has helped to outline not only how pervasive is this concept in his writings but how it informs his theological expression. Most important for our investigation is his observation that there is an interaction between the processes of interiorization and exteriorization. He argues that in the places where the two concepts are opposed there appears to be either a contrast of ideas for comparison or of proportional evolution or influence.[87] As humans turn toward the exterior they turn away from the interior and vice versa. What is important for us to note is the connection or the relationship between the two.

Starting from Aubin's precise and technical arrangement, Claude Dagens

---

[86] Paul Aubin, "Intériorité et extériorité dans les *Moralia in Job* de saint Grégoire le grand", *Recherches de science religieuse* 62 (1974), 117-166.
[87] Aubin, "Intériorité et extériorité", 122.

has placed these concepts in a broader outline of Gregory's thought.[88] He outlines the way in which interiority and exteriority move together in a dance of contrast and complementarity. He demonstrates the way that this concept enters into Gregory's reflections upon the mixed life, his understanding of the Christian life, and even his exegesis. Thus, he argues that, for Gregory, interiority and exteriority form a consistent "structure" upon which hangs his spiritual doctrine.[89] Most helpful for our discussion is his outline of interiority and exteriority in the bounds of salvation history where he sees the fall of humanity as a loss of interiority and salvation being a return to this interiority.[90]

The contrast between the interior and the exterior in Gregory's thought finds resonance in Carole Straw's structural analysis of Gregory's use of contrast and complementarity and she makes full use of the opportunity to defend her thesis. This concept serves as the backdrop in at least three different contexts within her work. First, she notes the war between the body and the soul.[91] The exteriority of the body weighs down the interiority of the soul and the two are constantly at odds. She sees in the horizontal movement from exterior to interior also a vertical movement from the lower body to the higher soul. But Straw's analysis seems to lack nuance. The war between the body and the soul is indeed present in Gregory but her identification of the exterior with the flesh and sin in this case is only part of the story.[92] She makes Gregory to be too much of an Origenist. Dagens has argued convincingly that "flesh" for Gregory is not simply the desires of concupiscence. Gregory does make use of Paul's concept of the inner and outer man discussed by Ambrose and Augustine but he adds his own spiritual and moral flavor to the concept of the flesh. It is not simply sin but that aspect of humanity which has been opened up to mutability by the fall. As such it can include flesh and spirit. Likewise, "the 'spirit' is not simply that which is opposed to the flesh, but that which, in humanity, aspires to contemplate God".[93] Dagens also demonstrates that Gregory's emphasis in discussing the war between the flesh and the spirit lies not in the evil of the flesh but on human weakness and divine power.[94] It is humanity's spiritual weakness that is aided by God's power in granting grace that leads to spiritual progress and interior growth.[95]

Straw also develops the concepts of interiority and exteriority in the context

---

[88] Dagens, *Grégoire*, 133-240.

[89] Dagens, *Grégoire*, 134.

[90] Dagens, *Grégoire*, 173-176.

[91] Straw, *Gregory, Perfection*, 38-46.

[92] For an interesting quotation from Gregory that seems to deny this premise of a strict dichotomy see *Moralia*, 5.34.61 in which Gregory argues that corruption reaches also to the soul of fallen humanity.

[93] Dagens, *Grégoire*, 186. "l'esprit n'est pas simplement ce qui s'oppose à la chair, mais ce qui, en l'homme, aspire à contempler Dieu."

[94] Dagens, *Grégoire*, 187.

[95] Dagens, *Grégoire*, 188.

of her discussion on human mutability.[96] This section proves less problematic. Since the fall humanity has lost the constancy with which it was endowed at creation and suffers from the catastrophic effects of mutability. This mutability serves to separate humanity even further from God. Even more, humanity has lost a vision of itself. The exteriority brought upon humanity after the fall has blinded it to the interiority of both the vision of God and the vision of itself.[97]

She also brings up interiority and exteriority in her discussion of *discretio* in Gregory's writings.[98] Here, she outlines Gregory's understanding of living the spiritual life in a temporal world. She emphasizes in this place the interconnection of body and soul.[99] As the exterior (body) decreases the interior (soul) increases. Building upon the realization of Aubin she outlines how both adversity and prosperity can be either a good or an evil depending upon how they are used by the individual. If humans allow suffering to turn them inward then they will increase their interiority by the means of exterior events. If however, their experience of prosperity roots them in the exterior experience they will not grow in the interior life.[100] Gregory's answer for this situation is *discretio*.[101] Straw outlines how discretion builds *constantia mentis*. Each person is called to maintain a proper perspective that is firmly rooted outside the mutability of this world in the constancy of the interior life.[102]

Rodrigue Bélanger has moved beyond all of these in positing that the themes of interiority and exteriority in Gregory can be helpful in elucidating not only Gregory's spirituality but also his theology.[103] Bélanger outlines the exterior and interior movements in Gregory's appreciation of the incarnation of Christ. Gregory's anthropology is underscored by interiority and exteriority. If Christ is to be the mediator between God and humanity this concept must also be involved in Gregory's Christology. Christ's becoming human is the Word (logos) becoming flesh. In that one instant what is interior (the Word) becomes exterior (flesh) so that humanity, lost in its own exteriority, can both see and apply the benefits of an interior life. Christ's incarnation is in a very real sense an exterior beatific vision or at least a means to that vision.

---

[96] Straw, *Gregory, Perfection*, 107-127.

[97] Straw, *Gregory, Perfection*, 113-116. On *discretio* in Gregory see also Rodrigue Bélanger, "*Discretionis lineam bene tendere* (Mor. 28,29): la règle d'un juste exercice de la vertu selon Grégoire le Grand," *Studia Patristica* 28 (1993), 15-23.

[98] Straw, *Gregory, Perfection*, 236-256.

[99] Straw, *Gregory, Perfection*, 237.

[100] Straw, *Gregory, Perfection*, 239-243. See also her "'Adversitas' et 'prosperitas': une illustration du motif structurel de la complémentarité," in Jacques Fontaine, Robert Gillet and Stan Pellistrandi (eds.), *Grégoire le Grand* (Paris 1986), 277-288.

[101] Straw, *Gregory, Perfection*, 252-255.

[102] Straw, *Gregory, Perfection*, 247-248.

[103] Rodrigue Bélanger, "La dialectique Parole-Chair dans la christologie de Grégoire le Grand," in John C. Cavadini (ed.), *Gregory the Great: A Symposium* (Notre Dame 1995), 82-93.

The work of these authors has done much to outline how Gregory's spirituality influences his theology through his use of the concepts of exteriority and interiority. They have each, in their respective works, pointed out the intricacies of the relationship and established the connection between the two. In inverse proportion they affect one another. But how does this relate to the experience of pain? Still yet, is there an eschatological ramification to these concepts? To answer these questions, we must look to Gregory himself.

Gregory's perspective of interiority and exteriority is colored by a long line of philosophic traditions. Most notably the Stoic tradition is outlined in the *constantia mentis* as Carole Straw has so eloquently pointed out.[104] The Stoic tradition called for an equilibrium of the soul in the midst of physical and spiritual turmoil. The connection of the body and the soul is underscored in such a system because the philosophers realized the ability of one to influence the other. Yet, this influence must always be kept in the proper perspective and all fluctuations should be kept to a minimum. Nevertheless, Gregory moved beyond the Stoics in his argument that the goal of the contemplative was not *apatheia*.[105] Humanity was instead meant to feel physical and spiritual adversity so that it might turn to the cultivation of the interior. Pain (or prosperity) was to be used and to be used it had to be felt. Like them, however, Gregory did emphasize the importance of perspective and for him the appropriate perspective became the eternal state. One's life in this world is only a way to the higher reality which would be inaugurated at Christ's second coming and judgment.

This higher reality also points back to an earlier philosophical tradition. Gregory worked from within a Neoplatonic world-view in which the things that were experienced in this life via the senses were less real than the underlying spiritual reality.[106] Not only were they less real but they were potentially illusory and misleading. The only sure source, and for that matter the only proper goal, of knowledge was this underlying spiritual reality. The Neoplatonic understanding of a spiritual hierarchy is the basis for Gregory's understanding of the beneficial impact of pain upon the soul. As one experiences pain, the outer senses are stripped away and the inner realities emerge. As pain forces the flesh to descend, the spirit is allowed to ascend to the realm of the really real. Thus, Gregory's thematic development of

---

[104] Straw, *Gregory, Perfection*, 237-238. See also 75-76.

[105] Straw, *Gregory, Perfection*, 240.

[106] Susan E. Schreiner, "The Role of Perception in Gregory's *Moralia in Job*," *Studia Patristica* 28 (1993) 87-95. See especially 88-89 and 91. See also Straw, *Gregory, Perfection*, 75-76. Schreiner calls "perception" in Gregory what I have chosen to call "perspective". Though the two terms are quite similar "perception" seems to fit well with Schreiner's emphasis upon Gregory's experience of pain whereas I believe "perspective" is the more appropriate term for my purposes because it underscores the underlying reality of the coming judgment for Gregory which becomes the basis for the way in which Gregory argues that adversity should be "perceived".

interiority and exteriority is filled out on a frame of spiritual ascent first erected by the Neoplatonists whose hierarchy of ascent provided Gregory with a ladder of contemplation by which the soul could mount up to God.

At creation humanity had no need for such a ladder but could have mounted up to the citadel of contemplation with an erect mind of itself.[107] This inner contemplation was lost in the fall of the original parents. Every part of the human is now touched by corruption. This fall was a movement from the interior to the exterior. Instead of maintaining this inner contemplation of mind, humanity instead chose a life of exteriority, following the flesh instead of the mind.[108] Now humanity has been enslaved by the flesh and trapped in exteriority. It has lost its power of contemplation.[109] The interior joys of the secret place of the Spirit have been closed to humans for in their sin they have lost the eyes of their mind.[110] In giving up the erect seat of the interior, humanity has lost its position of constancy and has been caught up in a slippery mutability.[111]

Original sin brings a loss of divine knowledge because humanity's contemplative abilities have been destroyed but humanity has also lost the knowledge of itself. Because humans are composed of both physical and spiritual realities (body and soul) and they turned away from the spiritual reality in an act of sin toward the exterior, they no longer even posses accurate knowledge of the spiritual aspect of themselves.[112] Unlike the angels who maintain their internal and external knowledge through their contemplation of God, humans have been cast out from God's presence and their mind has been darkened. Because of their turning to exteriority through indulging their flesh in sin they are no longer able to know anything spiritually and only have recourse to external knowledge.[113] Yet the very senses of the body when afflicted by pain and shown the perfect image of Christ can become a throughroad to true spiritual knowledge.[114]

In order for humans to regain such knowledge it had to be revealed to them. For this reason God sent his son into the world. Knowledge of God and the knowledge of self are intricately connected on the spiritual plane and Gregory argues in Neoplatonic fashion that the two are parallel.[115] In fact, knowledge of self becomes the means to the knowledge of God for it is only when humans realize the blindness of their condition that they can then begin to realize their

---

[107] Gregory the Great, *Moralia*, 9.10.12.
[108] Gregory the Great, *Moralia*, 24.4.7.
[109] Gregory the Great, *Moralia*, 9.33.50.
[110] Gregory the Great, *Moralia*, 9.13.20.
[111] Gregory the Great, *Moralia*, 8.6.8.
[112] Gregory the Great, *Moralia*, 20.14.37. See also Straw, *Gregory, Perfection*, 115ff.
[113] Gregory the Great, *Moralia*, 2.3.3.
[114] Gregory the Great, *Moralia*, 5.34.61.
[115] Dagens, *Grégoire*, 178.

very need for contemplating God.[116] Because of this loss of self-knowledge Gregory argues that humanity is enabled to see what it has lost through enduring the pain of this present life.[117]

This is of course why Christ came; to show humans the reality of their miserable condition of exteriority and the blessings of inner contemplation which they had lost through sin. This movement on the part of Christ was also bound to the concept of interiority and exteriority for "he whom man had forsaken within [*intus*], having assumed a fleshly nature, came forth God without [*foris*]; and when he presented himself outwardly [*exterius*], he restored man who was cast forth without [*foras*], to the interior [*interiora*] life".[118] In a wonderful juxtaposition of opposites Christ is exteriorized so that humanity may once again be interiorized. Here we see the inverse proportion of which Aubin speaks at work.[119] Christ as God is wholly interior yet in the incarnation that which is invisible is made visible, the interior is exteriorized by Christ's assumption of a human nature.[120] This works to the benefit of humans because on account of sin they had lost their created interiority and been captivated by the exteriority of the flesh. They could no longer contemplate the interior but were forced to rely upon the exterior for all knowledge. For this reason the spiritual truth, became physical in that Christ took on flesh. In the flesh he could be seen and contemplated and show humans what they had lost. Seeing what they had lost provided the self-knowledge necessary for reacquainting themselves with the initial purpose of their creation which was the contemplation of God.[121] Christ shows humans a picture of what they were created to be, demonstrating what they have lost and providing an example of how they should live. At the same time Christ's interiority (divine nature) shines through his exteriority (human nature, here identified by Gregory as the flesh) in that he is the express image of the Father and shows them, in a way which they could comprehend, the character of the Father.[122]

The same interiority and exteriority is also manifested in the passion of Christ. We have seen how Gregory has connected interiority with the divine nature of Christ and exteriority with his human nature. Christ's flesh allowed him to die so that humanity might benefit but in order to show the acceptance of his sacrifice, he was raised on the third day in a demonstration of the fact

---

[116] Dagens, *Grégoire*, 177. See also Aubin, "Interiorité et exteriorité", 135-138.

[117] Gregory the Great, *Moralia*, 7.2.2.

[118] Gregory the Great, *Moralia*, 7.2.2. "Sed is quem **intus** homo reliquerat assumpta carne, **foris** apparuit Deus; cumque se **exterius** praebuit, expulsum **foras** hominem ad **interiora** revocavit..." (emphasis mine). See Belanger, "Dialectique Parole-Chair", 89; and Aubin, "Intériorité et extériorité", 133, to whom I am indebted for pointing out this passage.

[119] Aubin, "Intériorité et extériorité", 122.

[120] Aubin, "Intériorité et extériorité," 156.

[121] Gregory the Great, *Moralia*, 8.10.19. See also 8.19.35.

[122] Gregory the Great, *Moralia*, 5.35.64. See also 27.40.67.

that the exterior sacrifice of Christ had strengthened the interior nature of humanity. Humanity, by virtue of Christ's exterior death had been awakened to spiritual knowledge and the interior light of hope for a future vision of God was kindled.

> Our Redeemer, in his human nature, was subjected both to the powers of the Gentiles, and to the tongues of the Jews by dying, but in the power of his divine nature he overcame them by rising again. By which same resurrection what else is brought to pass than that our weakness is strengthened to conceive hope of the life hereafter?[123]

Christ's death and resurrection is the ultimate victory of interiority over exteriority. "The death of Christ is in fact a defeat of Satan, whose attacks against his interiority have totally failed; it is the victory of interiority in humanity: a total victory, because the attacks of the enemy have not even shaken the human interiority of Christ, whose soul is *interius inhaerens* in its divinity".[124] Gregory understands the passion of Christ as the battle between Christ and Satan over humanity. Satan's choice to smite the body of Christ prevented him from further striking the elect. In Christ's death, humans are freed from Satan's claim to authority over them.[125] In the image of a large fish being caught upon a hook, Christ is described as God's bait. The human nature of Christ, upon which Satan was allowed to strike, concealed within it the hook which was his divinity and by his divinity he conquered Satan and the elect were allowed to escape Satan's clutches through the wound left in the mouth of the great fish by the hook of the divine nature of Christ.[126] Christ's exterior death provided both exterior and interior liberation for humanity for humans could now have hope in the resurrection of their own flesh and could once again feel the joys of inner contemplation. (Notice the terms of interiority and exteriority in the following quotation.)

> When the Lord for our salvation gave himself up to the hands of Satan's members, what else did he, but let loose that Satan's hand to rage against himself,

---

[123] Gregory the Great, *Moralia*, 6.20.35. "...quia videlicet Redemptor noster et vires gentilium, et linguas Iudaeorum moriendo ex humanitate pertulit sed ex divinitatis suae potentia resurgendo superavit. Qua videlicet resurrectione quid aliud agitur, nisi ut ad spem vitae subsequentis infirmitas nostra roboretur?" One should be careful to note in this quotation the emphasis placed upon human weakness and divine power mentioned above and emphasized by Dagens, *Grégoire*, 187.

[124] Aubin, "Intériorité et extériorité", 133. "La mort du Christ est en effet une défaite de Satan, dont les attaques contre son intériorité ont totalement échoue; c'est la victoire de l'intériorité dans l'humanité: victoire totale, car les attaques de l'Ennemi n'ont pas même ébranlé l'intériorité humaine du Christ, dont l'âme est **interius inhaerens** à la divinité." (emphasis mine).

[125] Gregory the Great, *Moralia*, 3.16.31.

[126] Gregory the Great, *Moralia*, 33.7.14 and 33.12.22.

that by the very act whereby he himself outwardly [*exterius*] fell low, he might set us free both outwardly [*exterius*] and inwardly [*interius*].[127]

The concepts of interiority and exteriority are also at work during the coming second advent of Christ. In the first advent of his incarnation, his humanity served the purpose of veiling his divinity from unbelievers but at the second coming his divinity will be revealed to all. The Christ who was once despised because of the exterior flesh will be glorified at the last judgment.[128]

In the last judgment the lamp that was despised will be glorified and in this glorification all sinners will view in exterior splendor the interior divinity that they refused to see in the exteriority of his incarnation for in his second coming it will not be his humility but the brightness of his majesty that will be displayed.[129] This interiority and exteriority is also to be manifested in his body, the Church at the last judgment. During this time the wheat will be separated from the chaff. The interior (elect) and exterior (hypocrites and heretics) of the church will be marked out. The true nature of all persons within and without the Church will be displayed for all to see. It may be possible in times of peace for persons to present themselves as something in the Church that they are not in reality. But God does not judge by the exterior as does humanity, he judges by the interior and according to his own divine decrees.[130]

Gregory also uses the same illustration of the wheat and chaff to mark out the condemnation of those outside the Church in the last judgment. Those who have struck out at the Church and sought to harm it either by words or by deeds will be recompensed for their animosity. Evil deeds sometimes go unpunished in the present life but they will no doubt be mercilessly punished in the final judgment of separation. As they were unafraid to outwardly despise the Church their sentence will be outwardly proclaimed from the interior decrees of God. Gregory describes this judgment in the image of inhalation and exhalation which likewise speaks to his concept of interiority and exteriority.

> God then is said to 'breath' in recompensing vengeance, in that from occasions without [*ab exterioribus*] he conceives the purpose of judgment within [*introrsus*] him, and from the internal [*interno*] purpose sends forth the sentence without [*extrorsus*]. When God 'breathes' as it were, somewhat is drawn in [*introrsus*] from things without [*ab exterioribus*], when he sees our evil ways without [*foras*], and ordains judgment within [*intus*]. And again as if by God 'breathing,' the breath is sent forth [*extrorsus*] from within [*ab interioribus*], when from the

---

[127] Gregory the Great, *Moralia*, 3.16.29. "Cum ergo se pro nostra redemptione Dominus membrorum satanae manibus tradidit, quid aliud quam eiusdem satanae manum in se saevire permisit; ut unde ipse **exterius** occumberet, inde nos **exterius interiusque** liberaret?" (emphasis mine).

[128] Gregory the Great, *Moralia*, 10.31.53.

[129] Gregory the Great, *Moralia*, 20.3.10.

[130] Gregory the Great, *Moralia*, 25.10.26-7 and 29.6.11.

internal [*interno*] conception of the purpose, the outward [*exterius*] decree of condemnation is delivered.[131]

Christ's movement from divine interiority to the exteriority of the flesh in his incarnation establishes an inverse model of humanity's ascent back to God. Humanity must move from the exterior entrapment of the flesh to the interior realm of contemplation. Interiority and exteriority in humanity are connected just as they are connected in Christ and they move and flow in unison. Unlike Christ however, whose exteriority remained perfectly rooted in the interiority of his divine nature, the effects of the fall on humanity led to a mutability which set the external aspect of humanity over the internal. The application of Christ's salvation is all about reversing this condition and this is done through the use of the exterior. As the interior life is strengthened the exterior flesh is abased and vice versa. The things that benefit one do harm to the other. Because of this God strikes humans on the exterior to motivate them to internal growth, for just as soft treatment benefits the body at the expense of the soul, hard dealing benefits the soul to the detriment of the body.[132] This is why God so often uses pain and fear to drive humanity toward the first steps of conversion.

Conversion is the beginning of the movement from exteriority to interiority. This occurs chiefly in two ways, either by the experience of pain or by the fear of the judgment. God often stimulates the interiority of humanity by the pain of exteriority. The exterior things of this world are turned by God into scourges which afflict humanity's own exteriority. By this Christians realize their own mutability and look for the constancy of the interior so that the breach between humanity and God might be mended.[133]

Of course this affliction on the exterior also brings affliction on the interior. "He afflicts his elect outwardly [*exterius*], that they be quickened with inner [*interius*] life in that he for this reason applies stripes without [*foras*], in order that he might heal the wounds of sin within [*intus*]".[134] The exterior wounding affects the interior in that Christ, in the first stage of conversion, through external pain "inflicts wounds within [*intus*], in that he strikes the hardness of

---

[131] Gregory the Great, *Moralia*, 5.18.37. "Flare ergo Deus in vindictae retributione dicitur quia **ab exterioribus** causis **introrsus** iudicii consilium concipit, et **ab interno** consilio **extrorsus** sententiam emittit. Quasi flante Deo, **ab exterioribus** aliquid **introrsus** trahitur quando **foras** mala nostra conspicit, et **intus** iudicium disponit. Et rursum quasi flante Deo, **ab interioribus** spiritus **extrorsus** emittitur, quando **ab interno** conceptu consilii, **exterius** iudicium damnationis infertur." (emphasis mine). See also 34.5.10.

[132] Gregory the Great, *Moralia*, 10.24.42.

[133] Gregory the Great, *Moralia*, 3.9.15.

[134] Gregory the Great, *Moralia*, 6.25.42. "Vulnerando ergo ad salutem revocat cum electos suos affligit **exterius**, ut **interius** vivant...quia idcirco **foras** verbera admovet ut **intus** vulnera delictorum curet." (emphasis mine).

the heart with the desire of himself".[135] By external affliction the elect are wounded by the desire of his love.

The elect are also moved in the interior by fear. The exterior forces placed upon the body in affliction are the source of healing for the elect and they are healed by this wounding because through it they are "pierced with the dart of his dread" and "he recalls [them] to a right sense".[136] As humans fear the exteriority of the judgment God wins access to the interior of their hearts.[137] The fear of God's judgment opens the soul to the grace of God and this fear serves at the beginning of conversion as the first step in the ascent to greater interiority. Humanity is moved by God's grace through fear. Because of the fall humans hold God in contempt and are incapable of viewing him in the interior. Once God's grace has opened their minds and they do get their first glimpse of his holiness and glory they are frightened by the knowledge of themselves that results. They fear God because they see in themselves the sin that is not in God. Because of this they fear his judgment but God converts this fear to love through his interior grace. Through this grace humanity's hatred of God is slowly transformed through charity to love.[138]

Both the experience of pain and the fear of the exterior judgment of God lead humanity to its first steps of conversion. In both cases the ascent of the soul is explained in similar ways. What binds the two together is the concept of interiority and exteriority and the image of Christ as judge. God judges humans now with scourges and affliction in the exterior so that he may open a path for them to interiority. The fact that he will one day judge perfectly all that is done also opens their minds to interiority for this knowledge of exterior judgment calls them to consider themselves in light of God's holiness. The vision brings fear but God will use this fear to increase their interiority and to lead them further into the contemplation of interior love.

The process of interiorization continues for the elect in this life. The exteriority of the flesh is a constant traveling companion and it must be continually afflicted by God's scourge and by penance so that the mind might be lifted up to higher things.[139] The only sure way to keep down the exteriority of the flesh is to continue to promote the interior by contemplation.[140] Even though exteriority remains in the flesh and it continues to war against the spirit, Christians can make a profitable use of the remnants of exteriority by allowing them to promote their humility and lead their interior advancement. If the spirit

---

[135] Gregory the Great, *Moralia*, 6.25.42. "...**intus** vulnera infligit, quia mentis nostrae duritiam suo desiderio percutit..." (emphasis mine).
[136] Gregory the Great, *Moralia*, 6.25.42. "...quia terroris sui iaculo transfixos ad sensum nos rectitudinis revocat."
[137] Gregory the Great, *Moralia*, 19.7.13.
[138] Gregory the Great, *Moralia*, 22.20.48.
[139] Gregory the Great, *Moralia*, 6.8.15.
[140] Gregory the Great, *Moralia*, 10.8.13 and 10.10.17.

lifted them up without the temptation of the flesh they would no doubt fall into pride. The elect are however enabled to withstand these temptations of the flesh by their own interior advancement. Gregory argues that the soul needs both exteriority and interiority to continue to advance in the contemplation of God. The key is a Stoic concept of balance wherein each aspect of the person accomplishes its purpose within the divine plan.

> Thus by high appointment we se in the interior [*interiori*] advancement what we receive, in the exterior [*exteriori*] shortcoming what we are, and by a strange method it is brought to pass that a man should neither be lifted up on the ground of virtue, nor despair on the ground of temptation, because while the spirit draws, and the flesh draws back, by the exactest regulating of the interior [*interni*] judgment, the soul is balanced in a kind of mean above the things below, and below the things above.[141]

The balance of interiority and exteriority will vanish at the last judgment. The end of the world brings the perfection of interiority and the perfection of exteriority. All humans will receive there the reward merited by their life. Those that sought interiority will be rewarded. The love that found a place in their hearts by the grace of God will find the beloved for following the judgment the elect will live in the vision of the light which enlightened them. At that time they will no longer be bound by exteriority. The virtues it increased in them in this present life will not then be needed, the vision of God will be enough.[142]

Those however that sought the exterior and refused to be enlightened by the scourges of God and the fear of his judgment will be terribly judged. They refused to see themselves clearly in this present life but there it will become known. They will remember how they lived their lives in the gratification of the exterior flesh to the detriment of the interior. They will see that their exteriority is incompatible with the divine interiority.[143] "Who then can adequately estimate how exceeding great will be the confusion of the wicked then, when both the judge eternal is discerned without (*foris*), and sin is set in review

---

[141] Gregory the Great, *Moralia*, 19.6.12. "Sicque magno ordine cognoscimus in **interiori** profectu quid accipimus, in **exteriori** defectu quid sumus. Et miro modo agitur, ut nec de virtute quisquam extolli debeat, nec de temptatione desperet, quia dum spiritus trahit et caro retrahit, subtilissimo iudicii **interni** moderamine, infra summa et supra infima in quodam medio anima libratur." (emphasis mine). This entire passage is one of the finest examples of interiority and exteriority in Gregory's understanding of the Christian life and warrants further study in itself.

[142] Gregory the Great, *Moralia*, 35.17.44.

[143] Aubin, "Intériorité et extériorité", 140. Aubin describes this final visitation at the last judgment as a "total exteriorization".

before their eyes within (*intus*)?"[144] The exteriority of the reprobate will finally lead them to a moment of clear interiority but it will be a terrible vision of judgment just before they are cast into outer darkness.[145]

Gregory's use of interiority and exteriority demonstrates the way in which the person of Christ unites his understanding of the human experience of pain and his emphasis upon eschatology. For the purpose of humanity's salvation Christ came into the world. The divine which was interior took on exteriority by assuming flesh at the incarnation. His movement from interiority to exteriority enlightens the human mind and allows humanity to move from exteriority to interiority. Both pain and the fear of the judgment can lead one into interiority but they do so only through the exterior. At the same time this movement is seen as the grace of Christ who is now judging his elect so that there will be no need for them to be judged in the future. The image that lies behind the movement of interiority in humanity is that of Christ as judge. Humans can view this image now in fear so that love may be the result or they may look upon this image now in contempt and later in fear, experiencing a final clear vision of interiority before their eternal suffering.

intus iudex

One of the principle areas of expression for Gregory's concepts of interiority and exteriority lies in his expression of the inner judge. As a title this refers exclusively to Christ but it also demonstrates the interior contemplation that the Christian is called to apply. Christ is the judge of the interior but Christians are to judge themselves in their interior. Their judgment of themselves participates and in some cases supplants the judgment of the judge. In this way the judgement of the interior is part and parcel of the final judgment and betrays an eschatological dimension. The judging of one's self also comes to bear in the Christian's experience of pain. Pain leads the elect to return to their interior and they then follow this pain with their own judgment of penance upon themselves once the reason for the scourging has been discovered. This practice of judging themselves prepares the elect for their subsequent judging of the world together with Christ on the last day. The process of interiorization starts with Christ the inner judge and ends with him as well connecting his scourges with the pain of penance and demonstrating an eschatological expectation of the inner judge appearing on the last day.

According to Aubin this concept of interiority is the second most common in the *Moralia* following the interiority and exteriority of the Church.[146] As a title,

---

[144] Gregory the Great, *Moralia*, 8.53.90. "Quis igitur digne penset iniquorum confusio quanta tunc erit, quando et **foris** aeternus iudex cernitur et **intus** ante oculos culpa versatur?" (emphasis mine). See also Aubin, "Intériorité et extériorité", 140.

[145] Gregory the Great, *Moralia*, 25.9.22.

[146] Aubin, "Intériorité et extériorité", 126.

(*internus iudex, intimus iudex, internus arbiter,* and *intimus arbiter*) it only refers to God and more specifically to Christ.[147] Gregory himself identifies the judge as the Father's "only begotten Son, our redeemer" in discussing the relationship between the human and divine natures of Christ.[148] The terms *iudex* and *arbiter* are never qualified by terms of exteriority but instead serve to demonstrate the divinity of Christ and his divine right to judge humanity.[149]

The title of "inner judge" outlines the exteriority and interiority of the divine immanence and transcendence. The transcendent God has become immanent through the incarnation. As human, Christ experiences all things in exteriority but as divine he is both "within and without all things" (*intra omnia...extra omnia*).[150] Christ is the interior judge because he perceives all things including the human mind and soul, seeing them as they truly are and not simply as they appear on the exterior. Christ is immanent and transcendent in that even though he presides over all things as creator he presides especially as judge in the inner seat of judgment in the mind of humanity.[151]

When the elect approach the "secret recesses of their own heart" they are entering into the "secret chamber of the judge".[152] From here, Christ judges the inmost thoughts and intentions of the human heart with a strict and exacting scrutiny. This means that the interior judge will condemn even the one who had a desire to sin but did not have the means in this life in the same way that he will judge those who had the means and accomplished the act.[153] It is the intention as much as the action that is culpable. This does not mean that the outward deeds of humanity are not judged however, because the one who sits in the heart to judge sees all things, including our works.[154] When the inner judge discovers such things in humans he responds in judgment often turning those things which were used for the purpose of sin against the sinner. "The strict judge in comprehending all things, penetrates the subterfuges of wickedness in a marvelous way; and in ordering for the best, condemns the same by its own devices".[155]

Christ's role as the inner judge demonstrates his divine authority to rule and exercise dominion. The transcendence of God is shown by his immanent activity among humanity. His judgment at the incarnation, in the present life

---

[147] Aubin, "Intériorité et extériorité", 126.

[148] Gregory the Great, *Moralia*, 33.7.14. "unigeniti Filii sui Redemptor nostri."

[149] Aubin, "Intériorité et extériorité", 127.

[150] Gregory the Great, *Moralia*, 2.20.38. Gregory makes similar concepts regarding the immanence and trancendence of the Father in 2.12.20. See also Aubin, "Intériorité et extériorité", 127.

[151] See Michael Frickel, *Deus totus ubique simul.* (Freiburg 1956), 124-126.

[152] Gregory the Great, *Moralia*, 25.7.13.

[153] Gregory the Great, *Moralia*, 20.56.65.

[154] Aubin, "Intériorité et extériorité", 128.

[155] Gregory the Great, *Moralia*, 9.26.40. "Districtus iudex, cuncta comphehendens, occulta malitiae mirabiliter penetrat, et suis hanc invenionibus bene ordinans damnat."

and at the last judgment is rooted in this authority. Perhaps more importantly it was by this authority that in the mystery of the divine decrees he elected certain souls to receive salvation. The judge mixes mercy and justice in all of his actions and this is nowhere more greatly emphasized than by the actions of the judge in election. "Compassion so carries on the mystery of the divine work, that anger still attends it, in order that the secret judge may look favorably on and ransom some, and pass over and ruin others."[156]

There is also an eschatological focus to the interiority and the exteriority of Christ's role as the inner judge. On the last day he will be manifested to the eyes of all who are to be judged. The glory of the one who was unjustly judged during his life on earth will shine on the exterior but he will take his place of judgment in the interior. Those judged will be terrified by his appearance outside them but they will also be terrified by his judgment within. For in their hearts they will find that their own consciences will bind them over and agree in accusation with the judge against them. All their sins will pass before the eyes of their interior and they will be tortured by the justness of their own judgment.[157]

The pain that Christians undergo in this life; that pain which moves them to interiority is the work of the interior judge. The external pains that they experience drive them inward where the internal judge chastises them for their sin. But this chastisement is connected to the final judgment as well. Christians are condemned here and now for their failings but this is only part of his judicious domain. The culmination of the judgment that occurs now is the last judgment and the two are connected in the image of the interior judge. Each person must use the judgment against them now to prevent their being judged again on the last day. "The fierce wrath of the internal judge goes over, his terrors still do cut us off, in that we already suffer one evil by condemnation, and still dread another from everlasting vengeance".[158]

Aubin is right in noting that the title "*internus iudex*" is used only of God and specifically of Christ. The action of judging the interior is not however, confined only to him. In fact, all Christians are called to judge themselves on the interior. This judgment of the interior has been linked by Dagens to Gregory's concept of contemplation. The process of interiorization involves contemplation and this contemplation must begin with one's self. Only after the elect have truly come to know themselves can they truly come to know God.[159]

---

[156] Gregory the Great, *Moralia*, 29.2.4. "...divini operis mysterium sic misericordia peragat, ut tamen et ira comitetur, quatenus occultus arbiter alios respiciens redimat, alios deserens perdat..."

[157] Gregory the Great, *Moralia*, 7.32.47.

[158] Gregory the Great, *Moralia*, 7.6.6. "Interni quippe iudicis postquam irae pertranseunt etiam terrores conturbant, quia iam aliud de damnatione patimur, et adhuc aliud de aeterna ultione formidamus."

[159] Dagens, *Grégoire*, 176-178.

This movement is also the first of the two stage process of conversion mentioned by Straw.[160] When sinners are awakened to fear beneath the external scourges of God they must move to the inner courtroom of their mind and try themselves there upon God's scales.

> As sinners reel under God's mysterious wrath, they should "retire to the hidden recesses of their hearts" and consider the "eyelids" of God's judgment (Ps. 10:5). Examining their own consciences, they ponder their deeds; already feeling God's stinging rebuke, they imagine his secret judgment. What sins known and unknown can account for this wrath of God? What evil committed, what good omitted warrants his scourging? In the courtroom of the mind, the inner scales of the human heart serve as counterparts to the external scales [*lanx*] that God holds above man, dispensing his "scourges" as he deems fitting...While God holds his scales of cosmic justice, the sinner, in the bright light of the interior, weighs his own actions carefully on "scales of discretion," "scales of the heart," and "scales of scrutiny."[161]

Job becomes the pattern for all Christians in the way in which he judges himself on the interior. Even as Job was despised by his friends without he was seated "within upon the throne of judgment" and pronounced a sentence against himself.[162] Job sifted his heart to determine if he was scourged for any sin that he had committed. Even though he was incapable of discerning any sin he still agreed with God in his judgment because he knew that God's judgment could never be unjust. By agreeing with God's judgment in this way he associated himself with God's judgment and "set up himself against himself".[163] Job's desire in judging himself was to clear himself from any debt of sin that might be a reason for the trials which he was undergoing. He knew his own weakness and his own ignorance. Instead of denouncing the scourges he embraced them trusting in the justice of the divine judge without relying on his own righteousness.[164]

The righteous are zealous to judge themselves and all their interior with careful attention because they know that they are seen by the judge and that all their sinful thoughts and deeds will be punished.[165] Christ has entered into their hearts and as they follow him within so does repentance.[166] As they move to the interior of their heart they see the inner judge already there before them and

---

[160] Straw, *Gregory, Perfection*, 214-215.

[161] Straw, *Gregory, Perfection*, 215.

[162] Gregory the Great, *Moralia*, 7.23.27.

[163] Gregory the Great, *Moralia*, 32.4.5.

[164] Gregory the Great, *Moralia*, 9.19.30. "Libet intueri vir sanctus quanta se subtilitate diiudicat, ne quid in illo divina iudicia reprehendant. Infirmitatem namque suam intuens ait: Quantas ego sum qui respondeam ei, et loquar verbis meis cum eo? De iustitiae suae meritis non confidens, sed ad solam se spem postulationis conferens."

[165] Gregory the Great, *Moralia*, 21.4.8.

[166] Gregory the Great, *Moralia*, 27.19.39.

work to search out their sin before he works his judgment. They judge themselves with suspicion because they know that now they can judge themselves in his presence and this will be much better than being judged by him on the last day.[167] The process of inner judging in the elect begins with contemplation. As the soul contemplates the perfection of the inner judge in the heart it sees also its own guilt and by comparison pronounces its own sentence against itself.[168] But if the process begins in contemplation it must end in compunction. Compunction is set up in the heart as a kind of "machine" that continually sifts and reexamines all actions and motives and continually checks its categories of "good" and "evil" against the perfect pattern of Christ the judge through prayer.[169]

Gregory's understanding of God's justice in judging makes the claim that God will only judge sin once. If Christians are judged now for a particular sin, either by him or by themselves there will be no judgment for that sin in the last judgment.[170] Because the elect know this they turn back to the inner chamber of their hearts and present themselves before the judgment of his interior majesty. They refuse to remain secure and are "troubled before the presence of the judge".[171]

Their fear of the judge drives them to interior reflection.[172] The fact that sin is only punished once is why it is so unsettling for the elect when they cannot discern the reason that God might be smiting them. If Christians can only discover the sin that brought on the scourge they can punish it themselves and avoid further rebuke. Gregory counsels the person thus afflicted to turn within and pray for enlightenment. This seeking is an attempt to agree with the justice of the judge in smiting the sin so that the judge may be appeased and the Christian may grow in grace through penance.[173]

There are of course other reasons for turning to the interior as well. Perhaps the most important reason for this judging of the interior is to gain the self-knowledge necessary for contemplation. Gregory outlines in an important passage the way in which inner contemplation and reflection guide the Christian to self-knowledge and can continue to serve as a meditative medium. When the elect turn inward to the heart they are able, indeed are urged, to consider four separate questions.

For there are four modes in which the mind of a righteous man is strongly affected by compunction: when he either calls to mind his own sins, and considers WHERE HE HATH BEEN; or when fearing the sentence of God's judgments,

---

[167] Gregory the Great, *Moralia*, 25.8.13.
[168] Gregory the Great, *Moralia*, 5.33.60.
[169] Gregory the Great, *Moralia*, 1.34.47.
[170] Gregory the Great, *Moralia*, 11.35.48-11.36.49.
[171] Gregory the Great, *Moralia*, 16.40.50.
[172] Gregory the Great, *Moralia*, 16.40.50.
[173] Gregory the Great, *Moralia*, 9.45.69

and examining his own self, he thinks WHERE HE SHALL BE; or when, carefully observing the evils of this present life, he reflects with sorrow WHERE HE IS; or when he contemplates the blessings of his heavenly country, and, because he does not as yet enjoy them, beholds with regret WHERE HE IS NOT.[174]

All four of these questions lead to four different means and four different ends but the object is always the self. In this reflection we see how the pain that one is undergoing now is the result of past sin. This moral emphasis is however connected to an eschatological focus that culminates either in the judgment of God or in the beatific vision. What one does in contemplation and how one responds will determine the outcome of the pain that is experienced in this life. Standing as a backdrop to this contemplation is the image of Christ the judge who sees and judges sin but also reveals the Father. In a real sense Christ becomes a mirror; as the elect see their reflection he shows them their shortcomings, but if they look more deeply into the glass he will show them the Father.[175]

Contemplation begins on the interior with the knowledge of the self but this cannot occur without at least a "taste of the blessings of the eternal country".[176] The image then moves in reverse from the heavenly country where contemplation is eternal to the very moment of the beginning in which one discovers that the reason for creation was contemplation. Then it moves ahead to the evil results of the fall. Humanity has become corrupted and has been cut off from its source. Humanity was created for one end but earned another end through sin.[177] The call is for the Christian to respond to this self revelation with a focus on attaining what was lost through sin. Only through a new commitment to rebirth and recreation in the interior can humanity hope to regain the proper perspective.[178] And only in this way will the Christian find security against the judgment, consolation amid the present evils of the world, and the hope for future goods.[179]

---

[174] Gregory the Great, *Moralia*, 23.21.41. "Quattuor quippe sunt qualitates quibus iusti viri anima in compunctione vehementer afficitur, cum aut malorum suorum reminiscitur, considerans ubi fuit; aut iudiciorum Dei sententiam metuens et secum quaerens, cogitat ubi erit aut cum mala vitae praesentis sollerter attendens, maerens considerat ubi est, aut cum bona supernae patriae contemplatur, quae quia necdum adipiscitur, lugens conspicit ubi non est."

[175] The image of a mirror (*speculum*) occurs in the *Moralia* as early as 2.1.1. and fits in well with Gregory's emphasis upon contemplation. Excerpts of some practical sections from the *Moralia* even circulated throughout the medieval period under the title *Speculum*. See Gregory the Great, *Moralia*, Preface.3.

[176] Gregory the Great, *Moralia*, Preface 23.21.41.

[177] Gregory the Great, *Moralia*, Preface 23.21.42.

[178] Gregory the Great, *Moralia*, 23.21.41.

[179] Gregory the Great, *Moralia*, 31.27.54.

This contemplation by means of judging the interior is also connected to the exterior. It is a means for Christians to judge their advances and merits. It provides a schema for them to understand the proper perspective of all that goes on in the present world. By turning inward they realize that this present life is merely a way and not a place. They are only sojourners. It is in the future life that they will experience the true reality of God's presence but they can taste that now through contemplation. Having said that, this focus on interiority is not unconcerned with the present world. In the mind, Christians must weigh their works and their motives. Still more, this judging of the heart becomes an impetus toward good works and all that is done for others can be presented to God in the interior. All that is done for others the elect may "sacrifice in honor of the judge of the interior upon the altar of (their) hearts".[180]

The *Moralia* is a moral commentary meant to guide Christians in their spiritual lives. Gregory's addresses to monks came from the heart of a pastor who desired to see spiritual growth in his brothers. Steeped in the monastic tradition, Gregory found recourse in the practice of contemplation and developed this spiritual exercise as a chain that bound the sinner to the judge. Gregory implores all Christians to find God by turning within themselves before it is too late. Once within, Christians are commanded to judge themselves and to pronounce sentence upon themselves through penitence. Gregory argues that for the moment they may judge themselves but at the last judgment the opportunity of judging will be past and that power will have passed to the strict and exacting judge.[181]

The Christians' judgment of themselves is not a passive process. It is more than a simple noetic grasping of sin and depravity. It is also active. Christians judge themselves on the interior by recognizing and by punishing their sin. Their sins are punished through penance. Penance is the second step in the process of conversion mentioned by Straw.[182] Penance is a punishment of the Christian's own sin discovered in the interiority of the heart. When pain is inflicted the penitent is purified. "The very pain of penitence makes it a punishment, a cure, a discipline, and, above all, a sacrifice reconciling man to God".[183]

Compunction punishes the Christian on the interior and penance on the exterior. Gregory unites both body and soul in this fashion arguing that both bodily and spiritual pain work to cleanse sin.[184] The process of judging one's self involves the whole being. The soul, the mind, the body, and the emotions are all called to bear witness against the self. The accused is also the accuser

---

[180] Gregory the Great, *Moralia*, 8.47.79. "Hoc ad honorem intimi iudicis in ara cordis immolemus."

[181] Gregory the Great, *Moralia*, 25.7.14.

[182] Straw, *Gregory, Perfection*, 114.

[183] Straw, *Gregory, Perfection*, 219.

[184] Gregory the Great, *Moralia*, 23.21.40.

and the executor.

> And, in this secret chamber of inward judgment, constrained by the sentence of
> their own conscience, they chasten with penitence, that which they have
> committed through pride. For they there count over whatever comes against, and
> assails them. There do they crowd before their eyes everything they should weep
> for. There do they behold whatever can be searched out by the wrath of the severe
> judge. There do they suffer as many punishments as they are afraid of suffering.
> And, in the sentence thus conceived in the mind there is present every agency
> which is needed for the fuller punishment of those convicted by it. For the
> conscience accuses, reason judges, fear binds and pain tortures.[185]

In the interior, the sadness demonstrated over sins intercedes for the Christian
before the merciful judge[186] and these sins are cleansed by weeping.[187]

Penance is the process wherein Christians are continually bound to their
redeemer. It serves to strengthen the bond by reminding them of their sins and
the grace of God in conversion. It shames them by pointing out the way that
they have repaid the grace of God with continued sin. The fact that Christians
are smitten without by Christ and agreement is made within their hearts further
unites them to Christ by reminding them that the grace of God is bountiful in
expression and does not abandon the sinner even when it is slighted.[188]
Although conversion has taken place, redemption is still in process. Christians
are after all still bound in this mortal and corruptible body and until such a time
as they are released from the body or the body has been completely renewed
penance will continue to be necessary.[189] As Christians turn inward and punish
their sins they are released from their corrupted bond to the physicality of this
world and the idolatrous love for it is replaced by the love of the redeemer.[190]
All these things are learned and relearned by sinners until they are convicted of
sin and committed to continued spiritual advancement through penance.[191]

God always punishes sin. This will occur either now or at the last judgment.
This is most often done in this present life through the visitation of external

---

[185] Gregory the Great, *Moralia*, 25.7.13. "Atque in hoc secreto interioris iudicii, ipsa
mentis suae exsecutione constricti, paenitendo feriunt quod superbiendo commiserunt.
Ibi namque adversum se quicquid se impugnat, enumerant; ibi ante oculos suos omne
quod defleant coaceruant; ibi quicquid per iram districti iudicis decerni possit intuentur;
ibi tot patiuntur supplicia, quot pati timent; nec deest in hoc iudicio mente concepto
omne ministerium, quod punire reos suos plenius debeat. Nam conscientia accusat, ratio
iudicat, timor ligat, dolor excruciat."
[186] Gregory the Great, *Moralia*, 10.18.34.
[187] Gregory the Great, *Moralia*, 20.14.36.
[188] Gregory the Great, *Moralia*, 8.22.38
[189] Gregory the Great, *Moralia*, 9.37.43.
[190] Gregory the Great, *Moralia*, 20.14.36. In contrast see Gregory's discussion of the
unconverted and their relationship to temporal objects in 20.14.37.
[191] Gregory the Great, *Moralia*, 8.22.38

afflictions. But God has provided Christians with another way of judging. They can judge themselves and thereby do away with any need for him to judge.[192] If the chastisement of the elect upon themselves alters them then they can be assured that the wrath of the judge has been satisfied and there is no need to look for future pains.[193] If they are soft in smiting themselves then God will strike them harder in the future but "as he is appeased by the tears of self-correction, he alone obtains a hiding place from his face, who after the commission of a sin hides himself from him now in penance".[194]

We can see that the Christian's judgment of self on the interior actually takes the place of and participates in the judgment of Christ. If this penance forestalls the wrath of the judge it prevents the penitent from being judged at the last judgment.[195] The present evils that Christians inflict upon themselves assure them of future goods.[196] The image of the judge sets fear in the hearts of all humanity. But for the Christian who can encounter the judge in the interior, the image is one not only of judgment but also of mercy. If sinners are willing to present themselves as guilty before him at the judgment seat of their own hearts, they will find mercy before the eternal judge as long as they are not merciful as their own judge.

The association of the elect's judgment of themselves with the judgment of Christ on the last day is further strengthened by Gregory's understanding that what Christians suffer willingly on the interior by means of compunction and penance is what they are afraid of suffering on the last day.[197] The opportunity for Christians to hide themselves and their sins from the judge through self-judging and penance is a grace that has been granted to humans but it will not always be available to them. On the last day when the judge himself comes he will judge instead of the person.[198] Thus, the Christian's self-judging, though not identical with that of the judge on the last day, carries the same weight and accomplishes the same purpose in the life of the believer. In fact, it is the judge's presence in the heart of the believer that guarantees this identification. The judge of the interior heart of the Christian is the same as the judge of the final inquest and this practice of self-judgment is equivalent to his own. Even during this present life the judge is at work with both mercy and justice casting some out to outward punishments but leading others to inward ones.[199] The judge judges both but those that are led to inward punishment judge themselves

---

[192] Gregory the Great, *Moralia*, 9.34.54.

[193] Gregory the Great, *Moralia*, 9.45.68.

[194] Gregory the Great, *Moralia*, 4.15.27-4.15.28. "Sed quia correctionis nostrae fletibus placatur, solus ab illo locum fugae invenit, qui post perpetratam culpam nunc se ei in paenitentia abscondit."

[195] Gregory the Great, *Moralia*, 4.19.35-4.19.36.

[196] Gregory the Great, *Moralia*, 31.27.54.

[197] Gregory the Great, *Moralia*, 25.7.13.

[198] Gregory the Great, *Moralia*, 25.7.14.

[199] Gregory the Great, *Moralia*, 25.8.19.

as well and through their penance their judgment of themselves is subsumed under his divine direction and granted his divine approval.

The judgment of the Christian participates in the judgment of Christ also in its application in the exterior world. This is possible because of the connection between the judgment of the Church and that of Christ, since the Church is his body, and because of the temporal link in the advents of Christ. The kingdom was inaugerated in his first coming. The judgment that will attend his second advent is even now present. Speaking of this awareness in Gregory, Wasselynck has said that, "after the first advent of the Lord, we have entered upon the last days, we are already in judgment".[200] "Our judgment is unwound in the celestial mystery but we ought to recognize the signs in the verdict of pastors and in the voice of our conscience."[201] The eschaton has broken in upon the world at the coming of Christ and the judgment of the Church and of individual Christians participates in the last judgment that is to come. It is announced before by the words of pastors and by the judgment of the Christian in the interior before the internal judge.

The elect will be better judges the more they are judged now in this present life.[202] In fact their judgment of themselves prepares them for the judgment of others and in both actions they participate in the righteous judgment of God. The elect are moved by fear to judge themselves so that they will not be judged. The fear does not last though because they are moved by the Holy Spirit and receive the grace of consolation which ceases their love for outward things and by chastening their sins inflames a love for heavenly things.[203] Their terror before the judge of the interior gives them authority to rule over others as their lives are amended.

> Lo! The terror of the converted is turned into power; because while they punish their sins by penance, they ascend up even to the exercise of judgment; so as to receive this power from God, which before they used themselves to fear at his hands. For they in truth become judges, who feared greatly the judgment of heaven; and they now begin to remit the sins of others, who had before been afraid that their own would be retained.[204]

---

[200] R. Wasselynck, "La voix d'un père de L'Église: L'orientation eschatologique de la vie chretienne d'après saint Grégoire le Grand." in *Assemblées du Seigneur* series 1, volume 2 (Bruges 1962), 66-80, 70. "Depuis le premier avènement du Seigneur, nous sommes entrés dans les derniers temps, nous sommes aujourd'hui en jugement."
[201] Wasselynck, "La voix d'un père", 70. "Notre jugement se déroule dans le mystère céleste, mais nous devons, en reconnaître les signes dans le verdict des pasteurs et dans la voix de notre conscience."
[202] Gregory the Great, *Moralia*, 26.39.71.
[203] Gregory the Great, *Moralia*, 27.17.34.
[204] Gregory the Great, *Moralia*, 27.17.34. "Ecce conversorum terror vertitur in potestatem, quia dum mala sua paenitendo puniunt, usque ad exercendum iudicium

This spiritual judging of the Church is not always recognized by those outside the Church at the present time.[205] The holy indeed judge the world now but their power and right to judge will be made fully manifest on the last day when Christ returns to judge together with his saints.[206] Those who have been oppressed in this life will come in judgment over their oppressors.[207] They have won this right because they have surpassed the divine law in the contemplation of their hearts. They will not be judged themselves for their judgment has already occurred. Instead, they will reign and judge with Christ.[208] Their judgment will agree with Christ's divine character. There they will judge like Christ with justice and without human compassion.[209]

Thus, the elect have come full circle. They began in the presence of the internal judge and the sight was terrible. Yet as they contemplated this vision they met within themselves the enemy. By penance this enemy was destroyed and they emerged from this battle scathed yet changed for the better. They suffered many pains from the judge himself, from their own judging, and finally from the unjust judgment of those that viewed them from without the confines of the Church. Yet, through it all they were being prepared as judges who would reign together with Christ on the last day, having been recreated in the full image of the divine judge. At the last judgment, the toil of this life concludes with the full realization and manifestation of the goal of their contemplation. The elect are restored and rightfully take their places of rule beside their redeemer. Pain has guided them to their eschatological end, but now pain has ceased forever as they behold the image of the inner judge fully manifested in all his glory at the last judgment.

Conclusion

The book of Job provides a wonderful backdrop for Gregory's emphases of eschatology and the experience of pain. They are both undergirded by his Christology and are flavored by his contemplative bent. Job serves as a type of Christ and a type of the Church in such a way as to bind them both together in the pain that is experienced in this present life and in the judgment to come. Both are focused through the contemplation of Christ the inner judge. The medieval emphasis of Christ as judge finds a forerunner in Gregory's Christology and it is this image which serves to focus both his themes of the experience of pain and eschatology.

---

ascendunt; ut hoc in Deo posse accipiant, quod prius de Deo ipsi metuebant. Iudices quippe fiunt qui supernum iudicium perfecte timuerunt; et aliena iam incipiunt peccata dimmittere qui prius formidaverant ne retinerentur sua."

[205] Gregory the Great, *Moralia*, 27.17.34.

[206] Gregory the Great, *Moralia*, 27.17.34 and 9.22.33. See also 10.31.52.

[207] Gregory the Great, *Moralia*, 26.27.49.

[208] Gregory the Great, *Moralia*, 26.27.51.

[209] Gregory the Great, *Moralia*, 6.30.48.

These themes are first connected in the way that Gregory discusses the advents of Christ. He does not strongly distinguish between Christ's first and second comings but sees them both as part of the whole of salvation history. The work of Christ began in the incarnation but it will be finally completed in the eschaton. In the last judgment all things will be restored to their original created order in the divine *apokatastasis*. In both advents, Christ is active in providing both mercy and justice in that he offers grace and condemns through judgment at all times.

In the incarnation Christ came to redeem and to judge humanity. His taking on human nature allowed humans to grasp the spiritual realities they had lost in the fall. Because of the fall, humanity had lost its spiritual vision but Christ's incarnation negated this fault. In Christ humanity saw the express image of the Father. Christ became a man to redeem humanity. He also came in judgment. The ways in which individuals around him responded to his call of repentance became an indicator of the divine decrees of election. As those that rejected him turned away they demonstrated the fact that God had already rejected them. In his earthly ministry Christ demonstrated the same median between mercy and justice. He demonstrated mercy and forgiveness but was not loathe to denounce others for their hypocrisy. The culmination of his judgment begun in the incarnation lies in the last judgment. In that great and terrible day of the Lord he completes the work of election. He makes public all the wickedness of the reprobate and casts them into hell but the elect find in him a merciful savior who has hidden their sins.

Even when Gregory does appear to make a distinction in the advents of Christ, noting the humility and obedience of his first advent in contrast to his second advent when he comes with wrath and justice, the analogy serves to emphasize the judgment present in his first coming. In a pastoral call for preparation before the last judgment he notes that if individuals could not stand before Christ's judgment when he came in humility how could they expect to stand on the day when he comes in wrath.

Christ is ever the mediator interceding for his elect. In the incarnation he demonstrates the love and concern of the Father. He judges himself for the sins of humans so that he might be a propitiation for them. He shows them the way back to the Father by showing them the Father. In his life he becomes the perfect example of what humanity was created to be. As Christ suffered for the sins of his children they should expect to suffer as well.

Christ as the mediator will judge on the last day. Because of his active obedience he has won this right. The law of God was not abrogated at his incarnation but was subsumed in his person. Christ became the law written where everyone could see it. Humans will not be judged by their obedience to a written law but by their obedience or disobedience in following his example. He continues to intercede for humans as the second Adam and is the representative from humanity to God and from God to humanity. In this intercession he also bestows grace which often appears in the form of pain and punishment. He has not left his children alone but continues to guide them through the events of their earthly lives.

Through his linking of the advents of Christ, Gregory unites eschatology and pain in his Christology. Mercy and judgment are intertwined. Humanity should look for God's mercy in his judgment. The pain that confronts Christians is a grace which will allow them to grow in their inner lives of contemplation. But humanity should also look for judgment in God's mercy. Even in his incarnation, Christ demonstrated the holiness of the Father. This is evident in his sinless offering of himself as a propitiation and his continued interest in humanity through intercession. The eschatological expression of the last judgment links humanity to Christ through his mediation as the judge. He judged himself with pain in this life and continues to judge his elect so that they will not need to face the last judgment without an advocate. His suffering guarantees the possibility of redemption but the suffering of individual Christians applies the benefits of his redemption. It is only in pain, following the example of Christ's death, that the Christian can be prepared for the coming judgment.

The Pauline image of the head and the body indicates the shared nature of pain and the common end of Christ and the Church. Job himself serves as a wonderful example of this organic unity because he is both a type of Christ and a type of the Church. Gregory's typology centers in this case on the experience of pain and the eschatological end.

Job is a type of Christ throughout the revelation of his deeds and words in his trial. His care for his children typifies the love and concern shown by Christ in the incarnation. His physical and emotional turmoil prefigure that experienced by Christ in his passion. His words of imprecation over evil bespeak the final reordering of Christ in the last judgment and his ultimate sentence against the wicked. Just as Job is victorious through his trials, Christ's work in the history of salvation is a tale of God's victory over the wiles of Satan.

Job is also a type of the Church. Job's pain offered him an opportunity to demonstrate his virtues. In the same way the Church is persecuted so that it will shine in the luster of virtues on the last day. Job's display of patience moves the Church to stand firm under tribulation. If it can maintain the proper perspective of pain as Job did through discretion, it will realize the transitory nature of pain in this world when compared to the everlasting glory of the world to come. Just as Job was rebuked by his wife and his friends the Church is troubled by the presence of carnal members and hypocrites. But the Church, as Job, endures their presence hoping for the eventual reconciliation of the heretics and the conversion of the carnal.

The Church is united to Christ in an organic unity. Like Christ who suffered pain for its redemption the Church suffers to apply the fruits of this redemption in imitation of its head. The two are connected in a union of purpose and will. Both seek to see individuals brought back to the knowledge of God and to escape the judgment no matter the physical cost to themselves. As Christ suffered in his passion the Church suffers now. As the Church suffers now Christ continues to be persecuted. He feels the pain in his body and the Church fills up what is lacking in the passion of Christ. As Christians suffer, Christ rejoices because he knows that the experience of pain now works a wonderful spiritual benefit to the elect. The presence of suffering in this world means that they will not suffer in the next if they follow the humble and obedient example of Christ. Finally, the two are eschatologically connected. Christ was reviled by members of humanity in his day just as the Church continues to be reproached. However, Christ, the despised lamp, will shine forth on the day of final judgment and the Church will shine with him for they both have been granted the authority to judge based upon their humility and patient enduring of pain and tribulation in the present life.

The concepts of interiority and exteriority also bear out the importance of Gregory's operative Christology for the understanding of his emphases on pain and eschatology. Interiority has reference to the divine and to the contemplation for which humanity was created. Exteriority represents, for Gregory, the outer world, especially since the fall, and all its mutability. Aubin, Dagens, and Straw have demonstrated the importance of this concept in Gregory and the fact that they are reciprocally connected. As one advances in the interior the exterior is diminished and vice versa.

These concepts are based in the philosophical dictums of Stoicism and Neoplatonism. Gregory emphasizes the Stoic tradition of *constantia mentis* in the presence of pain. Unlike the philosophers, however, Gregory understands the goal of constancy not to be *apatheia* but contemplation. He emphasizes the importance of having the proper perspective in the midst of pain. One must remember that the pain of this life is only important inasmuch as it prepares one for the future and final judgment of Christ on the last day. With Neoplatonism he emphasizes the fact that the pain we experience because it is exterior is not the highest reality. The highest reality is the spiritual good done by such affliction. In a ladder of ascent one may move from the pain of the exterior to contemplation on the interior. The body and soul are connected.

This interiority and exteriority are demonstrated even in Christ. In the incarnation the internal God is externalized. What is invisible is made visible. Christ is externalized by taking a body so that humanity might become internalized through their vision of the divine. In the passion, the exteriority of the flesh allowed Christ to die and his human nature allowed him to serve as humanity's representative. In his death, Christ won the ultimate victory of interiority over exteriority through his defeat of Satan. Satan was tricked by the bait of Christ's fleshly exteriority so that he could be caught on the hook of interiority which was Christ's divine nature. At the last judgment interiority will be revealed in exteriority. The hidden sins of individuals will be openly condemned and the chaff will be separated from the grain for all to see.

Christ's movement from interiority to exteriority becomes an inverse model for humanity's ascent to God. Humans had fallen into exteriority by the sin of the first parents. They found themselves enslaved to sin but Christ offers a way back to interiority. Conversion is this first movement. Affliction on the exterior causes humans to turn inward just as the fear of the exterior judgment of God does. Through both external ways humans are led back to the interior. Their fear and confusion is however turned to love. Growth in the Christian life is the advancement of interiority over exteriority. As Christians advance they find themselves less attached to the external goods of this present life and discover a heightened desire for the inner spiritual truths. But this interiority must find itself once again displayed in exteriority for the contemplation of the elect is a spur toward good works. Finally, at the last judgment, interiority and exteriority will both be perfected. The elect will finally be perfectly interiorized in the beatific vision. The reprobate, however, will find themselves cast completely outside the pale of God's grace when they are thrown into outer darkness.

The active focus of contemplation is the image of the inner judge. The title refers specifically to the person of Christ. In the language of interiority and exteriority Gregory describes the immanence and transcendence of God in Christ. He has come near in the incarnation, his presence is felt within the heart, and his divine nature assures humans that in his transcendence he sees all things and the judgment of their interior will be complete and exact. The judge examines the thoughts and intentions of every individual from his secret chamber of justice in the heart. Those that in terror see the judge without on the last day will feel his terrible judgment within unless they have already judged themselves.

Christians also judge themselves on the interior. Christians try themselves before the inner judge in the courtroom of their minds. They know that they are seen by the judge and the fear that comes from this realization leads them to contemplation. In contemplation they see the holiness of the judge in stark contrast to their own sinfulness. This fear then leads to penance. God judges sin only once and if Christians judge themselves then the judge's wrath is placated. Knowledge of self in the interior promotes the knowledge of God. Pain brings the remembrance of sin and in the mirror of Christ Christians see not only their own sinfulness but the mercy and justice of the Father. The pain that is inflicted upon one's self brings purification. Compunction punishes the interior and penance punishes the exterior. The penance of Christians binds them to the redeemer in that as they agree with the inner judge in judging themselves they become disconnected from the material world around them and their love for God's grace is heightened.

The judgment of the elect is united to the judgment of Christ on the last day. Self-judgment accomplishes the same purposes as God's judgment in the lives of the elect. The judgment of the Church now is Christ's continued judgment in the world. Through the voice of the preachers and the inner voice of the conscience, God's divine decrees in election are made known. The elect are punished so that they might be better judges on the last day. Their judgment now by God works in their lives so that they may judge others. Their terror before the judge is turned into power. They suffer at the hands of their oppressors now but on the last day their oppressors will suffer at their hands. The elect however will not be judged then because they judged themselves in this life in the interior.

Pain and eschatology are united in Gregory's Christology. Christ is the judge who is coming to judge all humans unless they judge themselves first. The pain that each individual experiences is either a turning from judgment on the last day or a down payment of future suffering after the last judgment. Pain, if used to turn the believer inward, will result in an interior judgment that brings an interior reconciliation with God. The fear of Christ at the last judgment works in much the same way driving the individual to interiority. Contemplation is the way back to God for the individual but this contemplation requires an active component of judging. It is only as Christians judge themselves through the pain of compunction on the inside and the pain of penance on the outside that they are reconciled to the inner judge. Self-judgment participates in the judgment of the judge on the last day. If Christians judge themselves now they will be released from judgment then. If instead they refuse to judge themselves they have already misjudged Christ and their unjust judgment will be punished by Christ.

CHAPTER 5

The Judge and the Judged:
A Contemplative Christology

Two major themes of Gregory the Great's *Moralia in Iob* are eschatology and the experience of pain. The two seem to be disconnected but we have seen how they are connected, related, and reconciled in Gregory's Christology, especially through his image of Christ as the inner judge. Gregory was above all things a pastor and his counsel was always given for the spiritual benefit of his hearers. The monastic tradition of which he was a part drove him to express his understanding of the Christian life as a life of contemplation and service; a life of both interiority and exteriority. The exteriority of the terrible vision of the coming judge and that of the experience of pain in this life drove him to an inner seat of contemplation and in this haven of interiority Gregory found at once the image of the interior God exteriorized for the benefit of humanity by taking a human nature, together with the same Christ seated upon the throne of the interior as a judge. In Christ all things interior and exterior are brought to focus because he is the mediator between God and humanity; between this world and the next. A being of human and divine natures he encompasses all and subsumes them in his nature through his incarnation and his *apokatastasis* of all things before his throne of judgment. For Gregory, it is only against the backdrop of the salvific designs of this supreme judge of the interior that the pain of this world can be understood as it leads one hastily toward the eschatological judgment of Christ.

Gregory's eschatology has the primary focus of preparing his hearers for the coming judgment of Christ. He reads in the events of his times the "signs of the end" revealed in the Olivet Discourse. He makes use of both apocalyptic and triumphant images in the eschatological portrait which he paints. The world is swiftly coming to its end. It has grown old and awaits its final days of sickness on its deathbed. The city of Rome had fallen and was in peril once again. The natural disasters of drought, earthquakes, and tempests heralded the coming end. In dark images of apocalyptic fervor Gregory describes the end of the world and its death. But in the midst of such an apocalypse Gregory finds hope; hell for the world, but hope for the Church. The Church would triumph in the last day. Though it was presently surrounded by tribulations and hardships, God was preparing it for a great day of victory. His goals were being met in the very pain that the Church was suffering. The carnal were being cast out of the Church and the virtues of the elect were rising with the strong unguent of a holy scent even as they were crushed with persecution. The elect may suffer and be crushed on the exterior but their interior ascent to God was being sped by their pain.

The end was very near but it had not yet come. Gregory awaited a few more signs to be revealed before the last day. The Church had grown weak and not many were being gathered to it. But there was hope in new missionary endeavors and the Church longed for the last great outpouring of God's grace on the earth, when he would add the last numbers of the faithful to his Church and bring back the Jews to the true faith. Whether this would come with the appearance of the Antichrist none knew but it was sure that they were connected. Although there were many antichrists already present, the damned man of perdition, had not yet arisen to lead away so many in active perversion. With him would come the final tribulation. In the pain of this final persecution the Church would once again grow strong. As in the days of its youth it will once again bloom with the blood of martyrs and shake off its dead slumber with prayer and good works. The bride will adorn herself for the bridegroom in anxious anticipation of his return.

The imminence of the end had many practical ramifications for the Church and for its members as they awaited these final events. They were called to respond to the swift coming judge in fear and turn themselves inward in contemplation. Out of this interiority would flow virtues and good works. In the interior they would come to know themselves as sinful and they would come to know the inner judge as holy. Their gaze must lead to contrition of the heart and punishment of the body. But their fear of the judge will change to love for the giver of mercy. Fear leads to correction and correction to repentance and penance finds the hatred of the judge turned aside for the sweet mercy of the redeemer. The image of the judge offers a reason for fear but also a reason to love.

Gregory emphasizes God's sovereignty in his discussion of the millennium and the great tribulation. Gregory is no millennialist. He scorns their interpretation as too literal and too Jewish. Instead, he follows a spiritual interpretation which understands the millennium as the present reign of Christ in the Church. The kingdom has both positive and negative ramifications. In this time of preparation before the last judgment the Church finds itself entrusted with the keys to the kingdom. The Church forgives and the Church binds under the authority of Christ. Negatively, the power of Satan to rise up against the Church has been greatly curtailed. Although he still has power, he is not given free reign to try the Church without the direct permission of God who remains at all times sovereign. God will maintain his sovereignty even in the days of the final persecution and the brief terror of the Antichrist. Persecution will be open and universal but it will serve to purify the Church, accomplishing the purposes of God in preparing it for the second coming of Christ in judgment.

The last judgment is the central focus of almost all of Gregory's discussions of eschatology. The reality of the final judgment is the central motivating factor in the Christian life. Christ will be fully realized as the Son of God when he comes in the glory of his divinity. Satan will be cast down and hurled into the pit. Christ and the Church, despised in this life, will be lifted up in glory for all to see.

Christ as the judge at the last judgment is the gatekeeper who crushes the reprobate in the gate but allows the elect to enter. Those that have already participated in the judgment by judging themselves have already been judged. Those that have not judged themselves will be judged by him there. The present life is connected to the future life by the last judgment. Humans will be judged (or not judged) based upon the merits they accumulated in this life. Their use of pain will be weighed. If they allowed the pain to turn them inward they will receive his reward and become perfectly interiorized in the beatific vision of heaven. If they instead fled from pain and scorned its usefulness they will receive the due of their exterior attachment to the world in the perfection of exteriority cut off from the presence of the divine interiority.

Even in his discussion of eschatology Gregory must constantly make reference to pain and the presence of Christ as the judge. They are all connected in the life of the Christian through the interiority of contemplation. God's sovereignty assures the Christian that all of the pain of open persecution is governed by God. God rules over all things and even the persecution of his Church works his own divine ends. As pain moves the elect from their exterior attachment to this life, they fear the judge because they know his holiness and they realize their own fallen condition. All of the signs which are present portend his swift appearance. They are afraid that their works will be tried on the last day without mercy and they know that they will be found wanting in the scales of the judge. But mercy can be found in the face of the judge if Christians will only judge themselves. The pain of the last judgment and of hell can be avoided through the proper use of pain now. The judge will judge in the last day but he will only judge those things which have not already been judged.

The fact that pain exists in this world is only minimally problematic for Gregory. Instead of trying to explain it away he redefines it. This does not make the pain any less real for those undergoing it but it does make sense of how a good God could govern a world in which pain existed. He argues that God is good. If pain is sent upon humanity by a good God then the pain must in some sense be good. It is of course not a good in itself but a good because of what can come out of it or better what God can do with it.

Job is the perfect example of the use of pain in the Christian life for Gregory. His name means "grieving" and Gregory argues that his pain foreshadows that of Christ. Job becomes a type of the suffering archetype and both serve as examples to the faithful. Grace is bound to suffering. The body is the nexus between the spiritual and the physical worlds. Pain inflicts harm upon the body so that it might be felt in the soul. It is thus a pedagogical tool which leads to enlightenment. As Christians feel the pain of the exterior they turn inward to behold themselves and the holy judge. The elect may fear the pain but they fear the judge more and embrace the pain as Job did. It is a sign of favor to try their virtues and just as with Job, God enters into the fray with them.

Even though pain is used by God it did not originate with him. Gregory understands that pain came from the fall of humanity. Pain is the result of sin. Pain exists because the body now seeks to rule over the mind in contrast to the order established by God at creation. Humanity was created in the image and likeness of God to contemplate him. In innocence and purity it walked with him and beheld his face exercising dominion over all other created things. But the original parents soon sought to enhance their likeness to God in the wrong way. Instead of pursuing a likeness to God in holiness they sought a likeness in power and their pride was their downfall.

The sin of Adam and Eve becomes for Gregory a template of all sin. Satan tempted the body (Eve) and the mind (Adam) succumbed. Sin is the body ruling over the mind. In the fall humanity lost its likeness to God. It was no longer innocent or holy. Still worse humans lost the eyes of their mind. They were no longer capable of contemplating God in his holiness as they were created to do. Instead they were enslaved to the earth from which they were created; living in bondage to the material world of the body.

Sin brought with it guilt and corruption. Humans who were created immortal and immutable now became both mortal and mutable. Their mortality brought with it physical pain and death. Their mutability brought various physical infirmities and annoyances. The created order was set against humanity. All of the divine order had been upset. Humanity's position was no longer secure. Still worse the body had revolted against the mind and an open war raged against humanity on all fronts. This war brings pain to all individuals as a punishment for the sins of the original parents. Nevertheless through and over this pain God remains sovereign and Christ is still the judge who mixes mercy with judgment. The upheaval of the divine order did great harm but God's power is still to be felt in the world. His power is felt through pain. In a remarkable turn of events God uses this pain not simply as punishment but as a pedagogical tool. Just as humanity fell into sin by the body, God has made the source of sin its cure, for the pain that has so characterized the life of humanity after the fall is also used by God as a medicine.

Gregory differentiates between two kinds of pain depending upon whether they are experienced in the body or in the mind (or the soul). External or material pain is that which is experienced in the body. This includes things such as physical illness as well as natural disasters which affect the body such as flood and drought. Gregory also places demonic and satanic oppression in this category. Although they at times enter upon the mind they find their root in external things. Satan is able to rule in the mind of individuals only because of their attachment to material things. Gregory understands this pain to include what many would call blessings. The one who has a great store of wealth might be considered to be blessed but these goods cause such evils in the life of an individual that being attached too closely to them is actually pain because too often those individuals with so many goods are so overly concerned with keeping and adding to them that they are worn out with exhaustion and have no time or desire for spiritual things. Humans are also oppressed in the body by others. There are those who would steal from them and deprive them of their property; or worse, murder them and deprive them of their life. Gregory argues however that the most burdensome of all these physical evils and pain is the mutability that has passed upon humanity because of the fall. Each day humanity suffers from it. No sooner has a child taken breath in this world than he or she slowly begins to approach the end of all mutable things. Sickness and death await all persons and it is only through a constant and laborious effort that the body is ill maintained against all the enemies bent upon its destruction.

Pain is also felt upon the interior of humanity. The mind suffers the grief of the fall as well as the body. Basic to all interior pain is corruption. Under the blows of punishment for sin the mind no longer seeks to contemplate God but being enslaved to the flesh seeks how it can add to the delight of the flesh. It hearkens to the exterior and not to the interior. The joyful existence for which humanity was created has been replaced with the exile of slavery. The mind has lost its vision of God. Humanity can no longer look within to find him nor does it desire to do so without the grace of God. The mind now drags down the soul just like the body. Temptations arise from within and without. Even though not all sins of the mind can effectively be carried out the individual is just as culpable for having desired them.

Pain is an inescapable part of the fall. It is the punishment for sin but it can also be the cure. God's use of pain is tied to his divine election. Pain is always either the smiting of the judge or the discipline of a father. If it is the smiting of the judge it is simply the foretaste of greater pain which is to come at the last judgment. If, however, it is the discipline of a father it is a means out of the exterior slavery of humankind and the grace of conversion. God's mercy and justice are mixed together in the experience of pain. Neither can exist without the other.

For the reprobate, pain is always punitive. The just judge always judges sin. When the reprobate experience pain in this life and fail to respond in repentance they are actually meriting greater punishment in the future. God judges those more harshly who have had more opportunity to repent. Yet in this life it occasionally appears that the evil person goes unpunished for wickedness. This is also a punishment from God. Evils that go unpunished here will be more harshly punished by the judge when he appears at the last judgment.

For the elect there are many more types of pain. They also experience punitive pain. They are punished for their sins as well. The elect however respond very differently from the reprobate. Instead of striking out against the scourge they use the scourge as a means to grace. God inflicts pain upon his elect in order to turn them from their wickedness and to instill a desire for contemplation once again upon their corrupted minds. Their pain is the beginning of conversion. Pain is also prohibitive for the elect. Sin is a slippery slope which leads down a sure path to destruction. God however puts stops in this way for his elect. Even if they do not fear to sin against God they may at least fear the pain of his judgment upon their sin. As the lash is felt the desire to sin is often decreased as the level of pain from sin increases. Pain also serves the purpose of increasing the love and desire of the elect for God. This works in two ways. First, God sometimes distances himself from them so that they will be drawn by their love more fiercely. In an image of unrequited love, the soul desires to have God and its distance from him increases its pain. Second, the pain that is experienced upon the exterior reminds the elect that this world is not a habitation but merely a road to their final destination. As they suffer on the outside they achieve a proper perspective on the inside. External pain is not really real for it will give way at the last judgment to the love of Christ the judge and the beatific vision. Pain also serves to aid believers on their way through increasing their merits. Just as Job's merits were increased by his suffering so also are the merits of the elect. Gregory argues that the smell of a rose is not released unless it is crushed; that of incense is not spread abroad unless it is burned. The pain that Christians experience in this life allows them to demonstrate the virtues that God's grace has produced in their lives. The pain of others also works in this regard for it allows the Christian to meet the needs of others in compassion and works of mercy.

Pain for Gregory plays an indispensable role in salvation. This is based in the example of Christ. The image of the suffering Christ is the basis for Gregory's soteriology. In the incarnation Christ suffered by being made weak. He was opened up through his human nature to the same pain and adversities of this life that all humans experience. This weakness allows him to become one with humanity and serve as their mediator. His life and ministry allowed him to sympathize with the full scope of human pain. But most importantly for Gregory the human nature of Christ allowed him to die. It was through his weakness that Christ was able to win the victory over Satan and negate his right of authority over humanity. In the accommodation of the incarnation the flesh of Christ allows humanity to see God. The spiritual senses given to humanity at creation have fallen under corruption so Christ's work reveals the Father to humanity through the external senses. Christ's pain is the guarantee that the

Christian's pain is redemptive because the message of the resurrection heralds the acceptance of Christ's pain and sacrifice on behalf of humanity before the Father.

Just as pain is the basis for the redemption worked by Christ it is also the basis of the Christian's advance in the spiritual life. Gregory demonstrates how pain is active in the three primary stages of salvation; conversion, sanctification, and final sanctification. Pain is the source and the impetus for the ongoing ascent to God in the life of the Christian. Humanity is led to conversion by pain either through the fear of the judgment of Christ or by external pain. In reality the two are the same. The elect are afraid that their painful punishment now may be a foreshadowing of the pain of the final judgment of Christ. Pain awakens their spiritual senses by afflicting the exterior body. As they are pressed without they turn within for solace. If they find in their interior the image of the judge they fall in fear, trembling with their guilt and offer a full confession of their sins.

Pain is also active in sanctification. Pain strikes the exterior so that the interior can be healed. It leads to contemplation. By demonstrating the faults and the weakness of the corrupt state of the elect it breeds humility. Grace is borne by pain and through the contemplation of the judge in the interior the grace works other virtues as well. Love and service of others is established and strengthened by the process. As Christians experience pain themselves and accept it in a creative or redemptive way they become more compassionate as they view the pain of others.

The death of the elect is the passage of the soul to the perfection of final sanctification. It is the last pain that must be overcome, the last debt humanity has to pay and in it the last vestige of human depravity is laid aside. The fear of death is linked to salvation because this fear is based on the dread of appearing at the last judgment. In this final test Christians are frightened by the holiness of the judge they have come to know in the interior of their heart. They realize their own depravity and fear that perhaps some small sin has escaped their notice and their judgment. If it has not been judged by them they are sure that it will be judged by Christ. But the fear and the sorrow which precede judgment are followed by joy. The mutability that passed upon humanity at the fall is changed to constancy at the sight of the merciful judge.

We see then in Gregory how pain is a constant accompaniment to the spiritual life. Christ provides an example for the elect in the pain and sorrow of his incarnation, ministry, and death. Pain makes the elect aware of their need for conversion by demonstrating their poverty. It drives them on in holiness by forcing them to inner contemplation. It provides an opportunity for growth in humility and patience while at the same time providing an opportunity for charity and good works. Finally, it brings them to continually reflect upon their life and to maintain an attitude of penance so that they can greet the coming judge as redeemer instead of condemner. Pain is, for Gregory, the constant motivating force behind the entire salvation experience from conversion to sanctification to the final judgment and his spiritual understanding of its nature and purpose is rooted in the two advents of Christ; in his incarnation and death and in his judging on the last day.

Gregory does not make a strong distinction between the two advents of Christ. In fact he sees them almost as one act in the course of salvation history. The incarnation, earthly ministry, and death of Christ are telescoped into his judgment at the end of the world. The work of Christ to redeem humanity began in the incarnation but it is not completed until the final *apokatastasis* of the eschaton. Even in the time between the two advents Christ continues his work as the mediator between God and humanity offering mercy and judgment. The mercy and judgment of Christ begin with the divine decrees of election but they continue through his incarnation and reach their final fulfillment in the last judgment which makes public both the wickedness of the reprobate and the glory of the elect.

The distinction that Gregory does make in the two advents has to do with the distinctive tenor of Christ's method. The incarnation may be characterized by his mercy and the second advent may be characterized by his judgment but the two cannot be so easily separated. Christ may have come in humility and obedience in his first advent but his coming was not without judgment. As he condemned those who brought before him the woman caught in adultery, none could stand before the mildness of his reproach. When he was approached by those who wished to arrest him in the garden he simply announced his identity and they fell to the ground before him. If God's judgment in his first advent of humility could not be withstood how can anyone stand in the last judgment when he comes in wrath? The judgment of Christ's first advent was the wrath of the dove but that of the second will be the wrath of a king who was scorned, now crowned in glory. The pain and suffering which Christ endured in his first advent won for him from the Father the right to judge in his second. Pain and judgment are connected in Christ. They are also connected in humanity.

Christ's role as mediator between God and humanity demonstrates the connection between pain and judgment. The *kenosis* of his incarnation reveals the love of the Father but also the need for judgment. Christ came to earth to suffer for the benefit of humanity. He judged himself as a propitiation so that humanity would not need to be judged on the last day. He intercedes for the faithful having experienced their pain in his own human nature. In his loving acceptance of suffering for others and in his humility he shows humanity the way back to the Father. His life is an example for all the elect. If Christ willingly suffered and even ordained his own suffering how much more should Christians embrace the pain which God sends into their lives and accept it as an opportunity for spiritual growth. The law was not abrogated in Christ but subsumed by him. In his earthly life he became the law for humanity and humans will be judged according to their success in following his example.

Gregory's Christology links the experience of pain and the judgment of Christ by uniting the two advents of Christ. Instead of seeing the incarnation as wholly merciful and the judgment as wholly concerned with the justice of God, Gregory prefers to see both mercy and judgment in both advents. They are intertwined and cannot be separated. One cannot have God's mercy without his justice. Christ judged himself with pain for the benefit of humanity and through pain humans are guaranteed that they will be prepared for the last judgment. If they are judged now and are changed no judgment will await them at the second coming of Christ. His role as a mediator assures them that they will find in the judge an advocate of mercy and not a judge of justice.

Gregory's use of the Pauline image of the Church as the body of Christ also serves to unite the themes of pain and the last judgment. Pain is always salvific in the lives of the elect. The union between the Church and Christ is a union of purpose and will. The Church accomplishes the will of Christ on earth and Christ feels the pain of the Church as it suffers on earth. Job is demonstrated to be both a type of Christ and a type of the Church. He offers the prototype of the redemptive nature of suffering.

Christ suffered to win redemption for each person and each person applies the fruit of this redemption through suffering. Pain drives Christians to discretion and to penitence. It develops virtue and spurs them on to good works. Christians suffer now as Christ suffered before them. In their pain they live in humble imitation of the suffering servant. Christ continues to suffer as the Church is persecuted in this world. The two are united in an organic bond that allows the Church to fill out what is lacking in the suffering of Christ. Yet as Christ feels the pain of the Church in the present he rejoices because he knows that it benefits its members, turning them away from the world and toward the contemplation of the Father. Just as Christ was despised in this world the Church is despised as well. But as Christ is revealed in power and glory as the just judge at the consummation of all things the Church will also be glorified. Through the humility of each in their obedience in undergoing pain they become shining lamps at the end and judge all of those who judged them unjustly in this life.

Gregory's understanding of the complex interplay between interiority and exteriority also helps us to understand the way in which his Christology outlines, informs, and connects his themes of pain and eschatology. Interiority and exteriority may perhaps best be described as manners or aspects of living. Interiority is marked by care and concern for interior and spiritual matters while exteriority is characterized by an attachment to the outer world of materiality. The two are inversely proportional. As one ascends the other descends. Humanity has fallen into exteriority through sin but the way of the Christian lies in an ever increasing interiority of detachment from this world and desire for God.

Gregory's thought in this matter is influenced by Neoplatonism and Stoicism. With the Stoics he emphasizes the constancy of the mind in the midst of pain and trials. He calls Christians to maintain a proper perspective and to do this they must turn to the interior. It is only through contemplating the blessings of the eternal state and the justness of the judge that pain can be understood. Physical pain is secondary and if one undergoes it to attain a spiritual ascent it is well worth the trouble. With the Neoplatonists he argues that the external world is not what is ultimately real. The spiritual realm is the basis for the external and as such it is the true reality. The soul and the body are connected and if pain strikes the body, the soul ascends in correspondence to the fall of the body. The way back to God is a way of ever decreasing attachment to the external world and an ever growing internal desire for God.

The fall of humanity into sin was a fall into exteriority. Humanity was enslaved by the weight of the flesh. In losing the eyes of the mind humans could not make use of the interiority of contemplation. In the fall they lost the knowledge of God and they lost the knowledge of themselves. But the two are connected on the spiritual plane by contemplation and on the physical plane in the person of Christ. Christ's incarnation is a move from interiority to exteriority. In him the divine interiority is made visible. Christ therefore provided a means to interiority through his own exteriority. In his passion, his flesh allowed him to die and in his death he won the ultimate victory over exteriority. Satan was fooled into attacking his exteriority which he found weak but he was caught upon the inner hook of Christ's divine nature. In the judgment, the interiority which was the fall of Satan will also be the fall of all that rejected him. In a movement back to interiority Christ will be revealed on the exterior as he is in the interior. His divinity will be revealed for all to see in the fullness of his glory.

Christ's incarnation becomes an inverse model for all humans. As he moved from interiority to exteriority he revealed to them the possibility of their move from exteriority to interiority. Conversion begins either with the exteriority of pain or the fear of the judge. From this exteriority Christians move within their own hearts to contemplate themselves and God. The knowledge of both is granted through grace when one turns to the interior. As contemplation continues this fear is turned to love. Pain and the threat of judgment continue to lead the Christian into spiritual growth. The more Christians become detached from the exteriority of this world the more they are attached to God. At the last judgment interiority and exteriority will both find their ultimate fulfillment. The reprobate will be completely exteriorized as they succumb to the judgment of God and are cast outside his divine presence. The elect however, who have sought interiority will be made perfect through their unhampered contemplation in the beatific vision. In the *Moralia* Gregory gives Christ the title of the "inner judge". This image emphasizes the immanence and the transcendence of the Son of God. As God, he is always above all things but as the mediator of God and humanity he is also within all things. This means that the judge of the interior is able to examine the thoughts and intentions of each individual in the court of their heart. Even in the last day of judgment Christ's role as the inner judge takes precedence because as sinners are terrified by the appearance of the judge without they feel the judgment of the judge within.

Although Christ is the "inner judge" Christians have been given the opportunity to judge themselves before his presence in their own interior. By weighing themselves on God's scales of justice they agree with him in their own judgment. God judges sin only once and if Christians will inflict the pains of inner compunction and external penance upon themselves, they will escape the pain of Christ's judgment on the last day. The pain of penitence brings purification. It binds Christians in order to redeem them. The pain of penance on the exterior squelches the fallen bent of humanity toward material things. As the idols of the exterior are torn down by penance the true God and judge of the interior shines all the brighter. Through judging themselves Christians learn to judge. Their hard won expertise in self judgment will serve them well on the last day when they come with Christ to judge those that oppressed them.

Christ's judgment on the last day and the judgment of the elect on the interior are united together as one and the same judgment. They both serve the same purpose of bringing the one judged back to God through inner contemplation and reflection upon the judge. The pain of self judgment mitigates the pain of Christ's last judgment. The Church judges the world even now in the same judgment as Christ through the words of its preachers and in the conscience of the elect. Christ has given the keys of the kingdom to the Church and what they forgive he forgives and what they bind he will bind. The more the members of the Church are judged now the better judges they will be when they come to judge with him on the last day.

Pain is judgment and the pain of judgment has its roots in Christ who judged himself so that humanity might not be judged. Sin brought pain but this pain has been turned into redemption. Christ came and died to show humanity the Father and to reveal his love. The Church suffers to show the Father to the world. Its pain drives it ever deeper in the knowledge of the judge and ever higher in its contemplation of God.

The coming judgment at the end of the world is the focal point of Gregory's eschatology and Christ stands at the center as the judge. The final judgment is the completion of the mercy and judgment of God begun in election, manifested in the incarnation, and fulfilled in the last judgment. The end will be terrible for the world but it will prove to be a triumph for the Church. The bride will join the bridegroom in celebration of his return and the Church will receive its reward for faithful service when each member of the elect joins him to reign and judge the world.

Gregory's spirituality is that of a contemplative looking for Christ and finding him in the pain of this world. The judge who punishes is also the God who saves and he does so often through the very pain of human existence. The pain of the elect unites them to Christ in following the example of the judge who judged himself and suffered pain for their redemption. Christ revealed the inner truth of his divinity by the suffering of his external humanity. If Christians follow his example they can find the interiority they lost in sin through the pain of the exterior. As they judge themselves their union with the inner judge nears its completion for the pain of their penance leads them to him. And on the last day their glory will be the reward for their humility and suffering as they judge the world together with the judge who they so often consulted in the interior of their own hearts.

Gregory's emphases of the experience of pain and eschatology found in his *Moralia in Iob* find their connection in his Christology. Gregory's Christ is always the suffering servant and always the just judge of the final reckoning; dealing out both mercy and justice throughout the course of salvation history. The threat of his return brings fear and joy, terror and exultation but the pain of this life will find its final solace in the contemplative union of the self-judged sinner and the inner judge of salvation. In this contemplative union with Christ the pain of this life will make sense and in the last judgment the great mystery of the divine purpose will be revealed.

Bibliography

Primary Sources

Corpus Christianorum. Series Latina. 162C vols. Turnhout: Brepols, 1953-

Corpus Scriptorum Ecclesiasticorum Latinorum. 95C vols. Vindobonae: Hoelder-Pinchler-Temsky, 1866-.

Migne, J. P. *Patrologia cursus completus*. Series Latina. 221 vols. Paris: Migne, 1857-66.

Monumenta Germaniae Historica. Societas Aperiendis Fontibus Rerum Germanicarum Medii Aevi et al. Berlin: Apud Weidmannos, 1826-

Thiel, Andreas, ed. *Epistolae Romanorum pontificum genuinae*. Brunsburg: E. Peter, 1868.

Individual Works

Ambrose. *De bono mortis. Patristic Studies* 100. ed. W. T. Wiesner. Washington D.C.: Catholic University of America Press, 1970.

— *Epistulae. CSEL* 82; 1, 2, 3, 4. ed. Otto Faller.

— *Expositiones in Luc.* ed. Giuseppe Coppa. Rome: Città nuova, 1978.

Augustine. *Contra Faustum. CSEL* 25, 251-797. ed. J. Zycha

— *De catechizandis rudibus. CCSL* 46, 121-78. ed. J. B. Bauer.

— De civitate Dei contra paganos. *CCSL* 47-48. ed. B. Dombart and A. Kalb.

— *De genesi contra Manichaeos. PL* 34, cols.173-220.

— *De trinitate. CCSL* 50, 50A. ed. W. J. Mountain.

— *Enarrationes in Psalmorum. CCSL* 38-40. ed. E. Dekkers and J. Fraipont.

— *Epistulae. CSEL* 34,1; 34,2; 44; 57; 58. ed. A. Goldbacher.

— *Sermones. PL* 38-9.

Cyprian. *Ad Demetrianum.* ed. Ezio Gallicet. Torino: Società editrice internazionale, 1976.

Gregorii Turonensis. *Historia Francorum, MGH*. eds. W. Arndt and Bruno Krusch. In *Scriptorum rerum Merovingicarum*, vol. 1, pt. 1.

Gregory the Great. *Ad Leandrum.* in *S. Gregorii Magni: Moralia in Iob, CCSL* 143. ed. Marcus Adriaen.

— *Dialogi de vita et miraculis patrum Italicorum.* ed. U. Moricca. Rome: Fonti per la storia d'Italia, 1924.

— *Dialogorum Libri IV, PL* 77, cols. 149-430.

— *In Registrum Gregorii Magni studia critica 11.* ed. Dag Norberg. Uppsala: Lundequistska Bokhandeln, 1939.

— *Moralia in Iob, Libri I-X, CCSL* 143. ed. Marcus Adriaen.

— *Moralia in Iob, Libri XI-XXII, CCSL* 143A. ed. Marcus Adriaen.

— *Moralia in Iob, Libri XXII-XXXV, CCSL* 143B. ed. Marcus Adriaen.

— *Registrum Epistolarum, MGH.* ed. Paulus Ewals and Ludovicus M. Hartmann. In
    Epistolarum, vols. 1 and 2.
— *XL Homiliarum in Evangelia. CCSL* 141. ed. Raymond Étaix.
Hippolytus. *In Danielem.* ed. G. Nathanael Bonwetsch. Berlin: Akademie Verlag, 2000.
Jerome. *Commentariorum in Danielem prophetem libri. CCSL* 75A. ed. F. Glorie.
— *Commentariorum in Hiezechielem. CCSL* 75. ed. F. Glorie.
— *Epistulae. CSEL* 54. ed. I. Hillberg.
— *In Isaiam. CCSL* 73,73A. ed. M. Adriaen.
— *In Sophiam. CCSL* 72, 247-361. ed. M. Adriaen.
Joanne Diacono. *Sancti Gregorii Magni Vita, PL* 75, cols. 59-242. *Liber Pontificalis.*
    Text, introduction, and commentary by L. Duchesne. 3 vols. Paris: E. De Boccard,
    1955-7.
Lactantius. *Institutiones. SC* 204-5, 326, 337, 377. ed. Pierre Monat.
Orientius. *Commonitorium.* ed. Carmelo Rapisarda. Catania: Centro di studi sull' antico
    Christienesmo (Università di Catania), 1960.
Origen. *Commentariorum in Matthaeum.* ed. Hermann J. Vogt. Stuttgart: J. V.
    Hiersemann, 1983-93.
— *De principiis.* Die Ggriechischen christlichen Schriftsteller 22. ed. P. Kotschau.
— *Homiliae in Genesim. SC* 7. ed. Louis Doutreleau.
Orosius. *Historiarum adversus paganos.* 3 vol. ed. Marc-Pierre Arrand-Lindet. Paris:
    Belles Lettres, 1990-1.
Paulo Diacono. *Pauli Historia Langobardorum, MGH.* eds. L. Bethamm and G. Waitz.
    In *Scriptores rerum Langobardicarum et Italicarum Saec. VI-IX,* 12-187.
— *Sancti Gregorii Magni Vita, PL* 75, vol. 42-60.
Peter Chrysologus. *Sermones. CCSL* 24, etc. ed. Alexandre Olivar.
Philo Judaeus. *Legum allegoriae.* In *Opera Quae Supersunt.* 7 vol. ed. Leopold Cohn
    Paulus Wedland. Berlin: W. de Gruyter, 1962-3.
— *Quaestiones et solutiones in Genesin.* In *L'ancienne version latine des Questions sur
    la genèse de Philon d'Alexandrie.* 2 vol. ed. Françoise Petit. Berlin: Akademie
    Verlag, 1973.
Procopius. *De bello Persico.* 2 vol. eds. Jakob Haury and Gerhard Wirth. In *Procopius
    Caesarensis Opera Omnia.* Revised edition. Monachii: K. G. Saur, 2001.

Translations

The Earliest Life of Gregory the Great: By an Anonymous Monk of Whitby. trans.
    Bertram Colgrave. Lawrence, KS: The University of Kansas Press, 1968.
Gregory the Great. *The Book of Pastoral Rule and Selected Epistles of Gregory the
    Great.* trans. James Barmby. In vol. 12: *A Select Library of Nicene and Post-Nicene
    Fathers of the Christian Church.* Second Series. eds. Philip Schaff and Henry Wace.
    Grand Rapids: Eerdman's, 1979.
— *S. Grégoire le Grand: Commentaire moral du Livre de Iob (Moralia).* trans. René
    Wasselynck and Philipp Delhaye. Namur: Editions du Soleil Levant, 1964.
— "Gregory the Great: The Commentary on Job (Selections), *Early Medieval Theology.*
    trans. G. E. McCracken in collaboration with Allen Cabaniss. In vol. 9: The Library
    of Christian Classics. London: SCM Press, Ltd., 1957.
— *Saint Gregory the Great: Dialogues.* trans. Odo John Zimmerman. In vol. 39: The

Fathers of the Church. eds. Roy Joseph Deferrari et al. New York: Fathers of the Church, Inc., 1959.

— *Grégoire le Grand: Dialogues.* Vol. 1 ed. Adalbertde Vogüé. In nos. 251, 260, 265: *Sources Chrétiennes.* Founded by H. de Lubac and J. Daniélou. Paris: Les Editions du Cerf, 1978-80.

— *Grégoire le Grand: Morales sur Iob.* First Part, Books 1-2. Revised and corrected second edition. trans. André de Gaudermaris with introduction and notes by Robert Gillet. In no. 32 bis: *Sources Chrétiennes.* Founded by H. de Lubac and J. Daniélou. Paris: Les Editions du Cerf, 1975.

— *Grégoire le Grand: Morales sur Iob.* Third Part, Books 11-16. trans. Aristide Bocognano. In nos. 212 and 221: *Sources Chrétiennes.* Founded by H. de Lubac and J. Daniélou. Paris: Editions du Cerf, 1974-5.

— *Moralia I-II (Passi scelti).* ed. Bonifacio Borghini. Ancona: Editions Paoline, 1965.

— *Morals on the Book of Job, by S. Gregory the Great.* In vols. 18, 21, 23, 31: *A Library of Fathers of the Holy Catholic Church.* 46 vols. Trans. Members of the English Church. Oxford: John Henry Parker, 1838-85.

— *Gregory the Great: Forty Gospel Homilies.* trans. David Hurst. Kalamazoo, MI: Cistercian Publications, 1990.

— *Pope Saint Gregory the Great: Parables of the Gospel.* trans. Nora Burke. Chicago: Scepter, 1960.

— *Selected Epistles of Gregory the Great.* trans. James Barmby. In vol. 13: *A Select Library of Nicene and Post-Nicene Fathers of the Christian Church.* Second Series. eds. Philip Schaff and Henry Wave. Grand Rapids: Eerdmans, 1956.

Secondary Sources

Altaner, Berthold. *Patrology.* Translated by Hilda C. Graef. London: Nelson, 1960.

Astell, Ann W. "Translating Job as female: (Gregory's Moralia in Iob and Chaucer's Patient." In *Translation Theory and Practice in the Middle Ages,* ed. Jeanette Beer, 59-69. Kalamazoo, MI: Western Michigan University Press, 1997.

Atwell, R. R. "From Augustine to Gregory the Great: An Evaluation of the Emergence of the Doctrine of Purgatory," *Journal of Ecclesiastical History* 38 (1987): 173-86.

Aubin, P. "Intériorité et extériorité dans les Moralia in Job de saint Grégoire le Grand." *Recherches de science religieuse* 62 (1974): 117-66.

Baasten, Matthew. *Pride according to Gregory the Great: A Study of the Moralia.* Studies in the Bible and Early Christianity 7. Lewiston: Edwin Mellon Press, 1986.

Barmby, J. *Gregory the Great.* London: Society for Promoting Christian Knowledge, 1908.

Battifol, Pierre. *Saint Gregory the Great.* Translated by John L. Stoddard. New York: Benziger Brothers, 1929.

Bauer, Leonardo. "De Christo Vivificatore Sancti Gregorii Magni Doctrina." Ph.D. diss., Seminarii Sanctae Mariae ad Lacum, 1938.

Bélanger, Rodrigue. "Discritionis lineam bene tendere (Mor. 28,29): la règle d'un juste exercice de la vertu selon Grégoire le Grand." *Studia patristica* 28 (1993): 15-23.

— "La dialectique Parole-Chair dans la christologie de Grégoire le Grand." In *Gregory the Great: A Symposium,* ed. John C. Cavadini, 82-93. Notre Dame, IN: University of Notre Dame Press, 1995.

Benkart, P. "Die Missionsidee Gregors des Grossen in Theorie und Praxis." Ph.D. diss., University of Leipzig, 1946.

Bertolini, Ottorino. "I Papi e le missioni fino alla meta del secolo VIII." *Settimane* 14 (1967): 327-63.

Bloomfield, M. W. "The Origin of the Concept of the Seven Cardinal Sins." *Harvard Theological Review* 34 (1941): 121-8.

Boglioni, Pierre. "Miracle et nature chez Grégoire le Grand." *Cahiers d'études médiévales* (Montréal: Bellarmin, 1974), I, 11-102.

Bonomo, C. "Chiesa, Corpo di Cristo secondo S. Gregorio Magno." Ph.D. diss., Université de la Propagande (Rome), 1961.

Bower, Archibald. *The History of the Popes to A.D. 1758*. 3 vols. Philadelphia: Griffin & Simon, 1844.

Braga, Gabriella. "Moralia in Iob: Epitomi dei secoli VII-X e loro evoluzione." In *Grégoire le Grand*. eds. Jacques Fontaine, Robert Gillet and Stan Pellistrandi, 561-8. Paris: Éditions du centre national de la recherche scientifique, 1986.

Brechter, Heinrich Suso. *Die Quellen zur Angelsachsenmission Gregors des Grossen*. Munich: Aschendorff, 1941.

Brouwer, Christian. "Egalite et pouvoir dans les Morales de Grégoire le Grand." *Recherches Augustiniennes* 27 (1994): 97-129.

Brown, Peter. "The Rise and Function of the Holy Man in Late Antiquity." *Journal of Roman Studies* 61 (1971): 80-101.

— *Religion and Society in the Age of Saint Augustine*. 1st ed. New York: Harper & Row, 1972.

Bury, J. B. *History of the Later Roman Empire*. London: Macmillan, 1923.

Busenbarrick, M. C. "The Missionary Spirit of Gregory the Great as evidenced by His Interest in the Angles." Ph.D. diss., Creighton University, 1952.

Butterworth, R. ed. *Hippolytus of Rome: Contra Noetum*. London: Heythrop College (University of London), 1977.

Calati, B. "S. Greogrio Magno e la Bibbia." *Bibbia e Spiritualitá* (1967): 121-78.

— "S. Gregorio maestro di formazione spirituale." *Seminarium* 2 (1969): 245-68.

Calligaris, G. "San Gregorio Magno e le paure del prossimo finimondo nel medio evo." In *Atti della R. Accademia delle scinze di Torino*, 31, 4 (1895-6), 264-86.

Carluccio, Gerard G. *The Seven Steps to Spiritual Perfection according to Gregory the Great*. Ottawa: University of Ottawa Press, 1949.

Catry, Patrick. "Epreuves du juste et mystére de Dieu. Le commentaire littéral du 'Livre de Job' par saint Grégoire le Grand." *Revue des études augustiniennes* 18 (1972): 124-44.

— "Lire l'Ecriture selon saint Grégoire le Grand." *Collectanea Cisterciensia* 34 (1972): 177-201.

— "Amour du monde et amour de Dieu chez saint Grégoire le Grand." *Studia monastica* 15 (1973): 253-75.

— "Cómo leer la Escritura según S. Gregorio Magno." *Cuadernos Monasticos* 11 (1976): 309-32.

— *Parole de Dieu, Amour et Esprit-Saint chez Saint Grégoire le Grand*. Vie monastique 17. Bégrolles-en-Mauges: Abbaye de Bellefontaine, 1984.

Cazier, Pierre. "Analogies entre l'encycopédie chrétienne des Moralia et l'inseignment du Grammaticus: L'exemple du l'angélogie." In *Grégoire le Grand*, eds. Jacques Fontaines, Robert Gillet and Stan Pellistrandi, 419-28. Paris: Éditions du centre national de la recherche scientifique, 1986.

Chadwick, Henry. *The Early Church.* New York: Penguin Books, 1967.

Chadwick, O. "Gregory of Tours and Gregory the Great." *Journal of Theological Studies* 50 (1949): 38-49.

Chazottes, Charles. *Grégoire le Grand.* Paris: Editions Ouvriéres, 1958.

Clausier, Edouard. *Saint Grégoire le Grand, pape et docteur de l'Eglise; sa vie, son pontificat, ses oeuvre, son temps, 540-604.* Paris: Berche et Tralin, 1887.

Colish, Marcia L. *The Stoic Tradition from Antiquity to the Early Middle Ages.* Leiden: E. J. Brill, 1990, II, 252-66.

Courcelle, Pierre. "St. Grégoire le Grand á l'école de Juvénal." *Studie materiali di storia della religioni* 38 (1967): 97-117.

— *Late Latin Writers and their Greek Sources.* Cambridge, MA: Harvard University Press, 1969.

Crouzel, Henri. *Theologie de l'image de Dieu chez Origene.* Aubier: Éditions Montaigne, 1955.

Dagens, Claude. "Grégoire le Grand et la culture, de la sapientia huius mundi á la docta ignorantia." *Revue des études augustiniennes* 14 (1968): 17-26.

— "La Conversion de St. Grégoire le Grand." *Revue des études augustiniennes* 15 (1969): 149-62.

— "La fin des temps et l'église selon saint Grégoire le Grand." *Recherches de science religieuse* 58 (1970): 273-88.

— "Grégoire le Grand et le ministére de la parole." In *Forma futuri. Studi in onore del Cardinae Michele Pellegrino,* 1054-73. Torino: Bottega d'Erasmo, 1975.

— "L'Eglise universelle et le monde oriental chez saint Grégoire le GGrand." *Istina* 20 (1975): 457-75.

— *Saint Grégoire le Grand: culture et expérience chrétiennes.* Paris: Études Augustiniennes, 1977.

— "Saint Gregory the Great between the East and the West: Historical Crises and Universalism of the Faith." *Communio* 18 (1991): 356-64.

Daley, B. *Eschatologie in der Schrift und Patristik.* Freiburg: Herder, 1986.

— The *Hope of the Early Church: A Handbook of Patristic Eschatology.* Cambridge: Cambridge University Press, 1991.

Deanesly, Margaret. *A History of the Medieval Church 590-1500.* 7th ed. London: Methuen & Co., 1951.

Delehaye, H. "St. Grégoire le Grand dans l'Hagiographie Grecque." *Analecta bollandiana* 23 (1904): 449-64.

Delahaye, Ph. "La Morale de saint Grégoire." *L'Ami du clergé* 69 (1959): 97-109.

Doignon, Jean. "'Blessure d'affliction' et 'blessure d'amour' (Moralia, 6,25,42): une jonction de thèmes de la spiritualité patristique de Cyprien à Augustin." *In Grégoire le Grand.* eds. Jacques Fontaine, Robert Gillet and Stan Pellistrandi, 297-304. Paris: Éditions du centre national de la recherche scientifique, 1986.

Doucet, Marc. "Pédagogie et théologie dans la Vie de saint Benoît par saint Grégoire le Grand," *Collectionae Cisterciensis* 38 (1976): 158-73.

Duckett, Eleanor Shipley. *The Gateway to the Middle Ages.* New York: Macmillan Company, 1938.

Dudden, F. Homes. *Gregory the Great: His Place in History and Thought.* 2 vols. London: Longmans, Green and Co., 1905.

Edwards, Otis Carl, Jr. "Preaching in the Thought of Gregory the Great," *Homiletics* 18

(1993): 5-8.

Evans, G. R. *The Thought of Gregory the Great.* Cambridge, Cambridge University Press, 1986.

Fèvre, V. *Étude des Morales de saint Grégoire le Grand sur Job.* Paris: J. B. Gros et Donnaud, 1858.

Fonash, I. *The Doctrine of Eternal Punishment in the Writings of Saint Gregory the Great.* Studies in Sacred Theology, Series II. 66. Washington: Catholic University of America Press, 1952.

Fontaine, J. "L'expérience spirtuelle chez Grégoire le Grand. Reflexions sur une thésé récente." *Revue d'histoire de la spiritualité* 53 (1976): 141-56.

— "Augustin, Grégoire et Isidore: esquisse d'une recherche sur le style des Moralia in Iob." In *Grégoire le Grand.* eds. Jacques Fontaine, Robert Gillet and Stan Pellistrandi, 499-510. Paris: Éditions du centre national de la recherche scientifique, 1986.

Frank, S. "Actio und contemplatio bei Gregors dem Grossen." *Trierer Theologische Zeitschrift* 78 (1969): 283-95.

Frickel, Michael. *Deus totus ubique simul.* Freiburg: Verlag Herder, 1956.

Gardiner, Eileen. *Visions of Heaven and Hell before Dante.* New York: Italica Press, 1989.

Gastaldelli, Ferruccio. "Il meccanism psicologico del peccato nei Moralia in Iob di san Gregorio Magno." *Salesianum* 27 (1965): 563-605.

— "Prospettive sul peccato in San Gregorio Magno." *Salesianum* 28 (1966): 65-94.

— "Teologia e retorica in San Gregorio Magno. Il ritratto nei <<Moralia in Iob>>. *Salesianum* 29 (1967): 269-99.

Gillet, Robert. "Introduction: Saint Grégoire le grand et l'oeuvre des <<Morales>> sur Job." In *Grégoire le grand: Morales sur Job.* trans, André de Gaudemaris. Vol. 32. *Source Chrétienne.* eds., Henri de Lubac, J. Danielou and C. Mondésert. Paris: Les Éditions du Cerf, 1950.

Godding, Robert. *Bibliografia di Gregorio Magno (1890/1989). Opere di Gregorio Magno, complementi/I.* Rome: Città Nuova Editrice, 1990.

Harnack, Adolph von. *History of Dogma.* Translated from the 3rd German ed. by Neil Buchanan. 7 vols. New York: Russell and Russell, 1958.

Hartke, Werner. *Römische Kinderkaiser.* Berlin: Akademie Verlag, 1950.

Hauber, Rose Marie. "The Late Latin Vocabulary of the Moralia of St. Gregory the Great." Ph. D. diss., The Catholic University of America, 1938.

Hempelmann, L. Dean. "The Concept of Ministry in Gregory the Great." Ph. D. diss., Saint Louis University, 1984.

Hill, Nikolaus. "Die Eschatologie Gregors des Grossen," Ph.D. diss., University of Freiburg im Breisgau, 1941.

Hobbel, Arne J. "The Imago Dei in the Writings of Origen." *Studia Patristica* 21 (1987): 301-7.

Jones, A. H. M. *The Later Roman Empire, 284-602.* 3 vols. Oxford: Oxford University Press, 1964.

Judic, Bruno. "L'angelologie de Grégoire le Grand chez Raban Maur." *Studia Patristica* 23 (1989): 245-9.

Katz, S. "Gregory the Great and the Jews." *Jewish Quarterly Review* 24 (1933-34): 113-36.

Koch, H. *Cyprianische Untersuchungen.* Bonn: A. Marcus and E. Weber, 1926.

Krautheimer, R. *Rome: Profile of a City, 312-1308*. Princeton, NJ: Princeton University Press, 1980.

Laporte, Jean. "Gregory the Great as a Theologian of Suffering." *The Patristic and Byzantine Review* 1 (1982): 22-9.

— "Une théologie systématique chez Grégoire?" In *Grégoire le Grand*. eds. Jacques Fontaine, Robert Gillet and Stan Pellistrandi, 235-44. Paris: Éditions du centre national de la recherche scientifique, 1986.

Lebon, J. "Le Prétendu Docetisme de la Christologie de s. Grégoire le Grand." *Recherches de Théologie ancienne et médiévale* 1 (1929): 177-201.

Leclercq, J. "From Gregory the Great to St. Bernard." *Cambridge History of the Bible*. Cambridge: Cambridge University Press, 1969, II, 183-97.

LeGoff, Jacques. *The Birth of Purgatory*. Trans. by Arthur Goldhammer. Chicago: University of Chicago Press, 1984.

Limone, O. "La vita di Gregorio Magno dell' anonimo di Whitby." *Studi medievali* 19 (1978): 37-67.

Llewellyn, Peter. "The Roman Church in the Seventh Century: The Legacy of Gregory the Great." *Journal of Ecclesiastical History* 25 (1974): 363-80.

Loi, V. "La problema storico-letteraria su Ippolito di Roma." *Richerche su Ippolito: Studi Ephemeridis 'Augustinianum'* 13 (1977): 9-16.

— "L'identità letteraria di Ippolito di Roma." *Richerche su Ippolito: Studi Ephemeridis 'Augustinianum'* 13 (1977): 67-88.

Louis, F. "Saint Grégoire le Grand et la Bible." *Chronique de Landevennec* 30 (1982), 68-72.

— "Saint Grégoire le Grand et la Bible." *Chronique de Landevennec* 31 (1983): 95-9.

Lubac, Henri de. *Exégése Médiévale*. 3 vols. Paris: Aubier, 1959-61.

— "Gregory the Great and a Papal Missionary Strategy." *Studies in Church History* 6 (1970): 29-38.

Luneau, A. *L'Histoire du salut chez le Pères de l'église. La Doctrine des âges du monde*. Paris: Beauchesne et ses fils, 1964.

McClain, J. P. *The Doctrine of Heaven in the Writings of Saint Gregory the Great*. Studies in Sacred Theology. Series II. 95. Washington D.C: Catholic University of America Press, 1956.

McCready, William D. *Signs of Sanctity: Miracles in the Thought of Gregory the Great*, Studies and Texts 91. Toronto: Pontifical Institute of Mediaeval Studies, 1989.

McGinn, Bernard. "Contemplation in Gregory the Great." In *Gregory the Great: A Symposium*, ed. John C. Cavadini, 146-67. Notre Dame, IN: University of Notre Dame Press, 1995.

McLeod, Frederick G. *The Image of God in the Antiochene Tradition*. Washington D.C: Catholic University of America Press, 1999.

McNally, Robert E. "Gregory the Great (590-604) and his Declining World." *Archivum historiae pontificiae* 16 (1978): 7-26.

Mann, Horace K. *The Lives of the Popes in the Early Middle Ages*. 2nd ed. Vol. 1, Part 1: *The Popes under the Lombard Rule: St. Gregory I (the Great) to Leo III, 590-795*. St. Louis: B. Herder, 1925.

Manselli, Raoul. "L'escatologismo de Gregorio Magno," In *Atti del I Congresso internazionale di studi longobardi*, 383-7. Spoleto: Presso l'accademia Spoletina, 1952.

— "L'escatologia di Gregorio Magno." *Ricerche di Storia religiosa* 1 (1954): 72-83.

— "Gregorio Magno e la Bibbia," *Settimane* 10 (1963): 67-101.

— *Gregorio Magno*. Torino: Giappichelli, 1967.

Markus, R. A. "Gregory the Great and a Papal Missionary Strategy." In *Studies in Church History*, 6: 29-38, ed. G. J. Cuming. Cambridge, MA: University Press, 1970.

— *From Augustine to Gregory the Great: History and Christianity in Late Antiquity.* London: Variorum Reprints, 1983.

— "The Jew as a Hermeneutic Device: The Inner Life of a Gregorian Topos." In *Gregory the Great: A Symposium*, ed. John C. Cavadini, 1-15. Notre Dame, IN: University of Notre Dame Press, 1995.

— *Gregory the Great and His World*. Cambridge: University Press, 1997.

— "Exegesis and Spirituality in the Writings of Gregory the Great." In *Forms of Devotion: Conversion, Worship, Spirituality and Asceticism*. ed. Everett Ferguson, New York: Garland Publishing, 1999.

Marrou, Henri. "Saint Grégoire le Grand." *La Vie spirituelle* 69 (1943): 442-55.

Mazzarino, Santo. *The End of the Ancient World*. Translated by George Holmes. New York: Knopf, 1966.

Meyvaert, Paul. "Diversity Within Unity, A Gregorian Theme." *The Heythrop Journal* 4 (1963): 141-62.

— "Gregory the Great and the Theme of Authority." *Spode House Review* 3 (1966): 3-12.

— *Benedict, Gregory, Bede and Others*. London: Variorum Reprints, 1977.

— "Uncovering a Lost Work of Gregory the Great: Fragments of the Early Commentary on Job." *Traditio* 50 (1995): 55-74.

— "A Letter of Pelagius II Composed by Gregory the Great," In *Gregory the Great: A Symposium*, ed. J. C. Cavadini, 94-116. Notre Dame, IN: University of Notre Dame Press, 1996.

Mommsen, T. E. "St. Augustine and the Christian Idea of Progress: The Background to the City of God." In *City of God: A Collection of Critical Essays*. ed. Dorothy Donnely, 353-73. New York: Peter Lang, 1995.

Moreschini, Claudio. "Gregorio Magno e le eresie." In *Grégoire le Grand*. eds. Jacques Fontaine, Robert Gillet and Stan Pellistrandi, 337-46. Paris: Éditions du centre national de la recherche scientifique, 1986.

Moretus, Henri. "Les Deux anciennes Vies de S. Grégoire le Grand." *Analecta bollandiana* 26 (1907): 66-72.

Mortimor, Robert. *The Origins of Private Penance in the Western Church*. Oxford: Clarendon Press, 1939.

Nardi, C. "Gregorio Magno interprete di Apocolisse 20." In *Gregorio Magno e il suo tempo*. Vol. 2, *Questioni letterarie e dottrinali*, 267-83. Rome: Institutum Patristicum Augustinianum, 1991.

O'Donnell, Anne M. "Cicero, Gregory the Great, and Thomas More: Three Dialogues of Comfort." In *Miscellanea Moreana*. eds. Clare M. Murphy, Henri Gibaud and Mario A. DiCesare, 169-97. Binghamton, NY: Medieval and Rennaisance Texts and Studies, 1989.

O'Donnell, James Francis. "The Vocabulary of the Letters of St. Gregory the Great." Ph.D. diss., The Catholic University of America, 1934.

O'Donnell, James J. "The Holiness of Gregory." In *Gregory the Great: A Symposium*, ed. John C. Cavadini, 62-81. Notre Dame, IN: University of Notre Dame Press, 1995.

Paronetto, V. "Gregorio Magno e la cultura classica." *Studium* 74 (1978): 665-80.

Penco, G. "La dottrina dei sensi spirituali in Gregorio Magno." *Benedictina* 17 (1970): 161-201.

— "San Gregorio e la theologia dell'imagine." *Benedictina* 18 (1971): 32-45.

Petersen, Joan M. *The Dialogues of Gregory the Great in their Late Antique Cutlural Background. Studies and Texts* 69. Toronto: Pontifical Institute of Mediaeval Studies, 1984.

— "The Biblical and Monastic Roots of the Spirituality of Pope Gregory the Great." In *Monastic Studies.* ed. Judith Loades, 31-41. Bangor, Wales: Headstart History, 1991.

Pietri, Charles and Luce Pietri. "Eglise universelle et respublica christiana selon Grégoire le Grand." In *Memoriam sanctorum venerantes.* ed. Victor Saxer, 647-65. Rome: Pontifical Institutum Archaelogicae Christianae, 1992.

Poschmann, Bernhard. *Penance and the Anointing of the Sick.* Translated by Francis Courtney. New York: Herder and Herder, 1964.

Richards, Jeffrey. *The Popes and the Papacy in the Early Middle Ages 476-752.* London: Routledge & Keegan Paul, 1979.

— *Consul of God: The Life and Times of Gregory the Great.* London: Routledge & Keegan Paul, 1980.

Riché, Pierre. *Education and Culture in the Barbarian West, Sixth through Eighth Centuries.* Columbia: University of South Carolina Press, 1976.

Rivière, J. "Rôle du démon au jugement particulier chez les Pères." *Revue des sciences religieuses* 4 (1924): 43-64.

— "Mort et démon chez le Pères," *Revue des sciences religieuses* 10 (1930): 577-621.

Rosario, P. "Il pensiero escatologico di san Gregorio Magno nelle Omilie sui Vangeli." In *Il Sangue della Redenzione* 62 (1976): 75-92.

Rouche, Michel. "Grégoire le Grand face à la situation économique de son temps." In *Grégoire le Grand.* eds., Jacques Fontaine, Robert Gillet and Stan Pellistrandi, 41-58. Paris: Éditions du centre national de la recherche scientifique, 1986.

Rousseau, O. "La Typologie augustiniene de l'Hexaemeron et la théologie du temps." In *Festgabe Joseph Lortz,* eds. E. Iserloh and P. Manns, 47-58. Baden-Baden: B. Grimm, 1958.

Rush, Alfred C. "An Echo of Christian Antiquity in St. Gregory the Great: Death a Struggle with the Devil." *Traditio* 3 (1945): 369-80.

— "Spiritual Martyrdom in St. Gregory the Great." *Theological Studies* 23 (1962): 569-89.

Savon, Hervé. "L'Antéchrist dans l'oeuvre de Grégoire le Grand." In *Grégoire le Grand,* eds. Jacques Fontaine, Robert Gillet and Stan Pellistrandi, 389-405. Paris: Éditions du centre national de la recherche scientifique, 1986.

Schreiner, Susan. E. "'Where shall Wisdom be found?': Gregory's Interpretation of Job." *The American Benedictine Review* 39 (1988): 321-42.

— "The Role of Perception in Gregory's Morali in Job." *Studia Patristica* 28 (1993): 87-95.

Schuster, I. "Il Titolo di 'servus Dei' nell'epistolario di S. Gregorio Magno." *La Scuola cattolica* 15 (1945): 137-8.

Schwank, Hans. *Gregor der Grosse als Prediger.* Hannover-Linden: R. Petersen, 1934.

Schwarte, Karl-Heinz. *Die Vorgeschichte der augustinischen Weltaltlehre.* Bonn: Habelt, 1966.

Serrano, L. "La Obra 'Morales de San Gregorio' en la literatura hispanogoda." *Revista de archivos, bibliotecas y museos* 24 (1911): 482-97.

Simonetti, M. "A modo di conclusione: una ipotesi di lavoro." *Richerche di Ippolito: Studi Ephemeridis 'Augustinianum'* 13 (1977): 151-6.

Siniscalco, Paolo. "La età del mondo in Gregorio Magno." In *Grégoire le Grand*. eds. Jacques Fontaine, Robert Gillet and Stan Pellistrandi, 377-88. Paris: Éditions du centre national de la recherche scientifique, 1986.

Smalley, Beryl. *The Study of the Bible in the Middle Ages*. New York: Philosophical Library, 1952.

Spanneut, Michel. *Le Stoïcisme des Pères de l'église*. Paris: Éditions du Seuil, 1957.

— "La patience, martyre au quotidien: la fortun d'une sentence de saint Grégoire le Grand." *Studia Patristica* 23 (1989): 186-96.

Straw, Carole Ellen. "'Sweet Tortures' and 'Delectable Pains': The Grammar of Complementarity in the Works of Gregory the Great." Ph.D. diss., University of California, Berkeley, 1979.

— "'Adversitas' et 'prosperitas': une illustration du motif structurel de la complémentarité." In *Grégoire le Grand*. eds. Jacques Fontaine, Robert Gillet and Stan Pellistrandi, 277-88. Paris: Éditions du centre national de la recherche scientifique, 1986.

— *Gregory the Great: Perfection in Imperfection*. Berkeley: University of California Press, 1988.

— "Purity and Death." In *Gregory the Great: A Symposium*, ed. John C. Cavadini, 16-37. Notre Dame, IN: University of Notre Dame Press, 1995.

— *Gregory the Great*. vol. 4, *Authors of the Middle Ages*, ed. Patrick J. Geary, no. 12. Brookfield, VT: Ashgate Publishers, 1996.

Squire, Aelred K. "Light in Gregory the Great and in the Islamic Tradition." *Studia Patristica* 23 (1989): 197-202.

— "A Note on Friendship in Gregory the Great." *Studia Patristica* 28 (1993): 106-11.

Sullivan, R. E. "The Papacy and Missionary Activity in the Early Middle Ages." *Mediaeval Studies* 17 (1955): 46-106.

Synan, Edward A. *The Popes and the Jews in the Middle Ages*. Preface by John M. Oesterreicher. New York: Macmillan, 1965.

Tamassia, N. "La formul 'appropinquante fine mundi' nei documenti del medio evo." *Scritti di storio giuridica*, II. Padova, 1967, 97-105.

Thomson, R. W. *The Teaching of St. Gregory. An Early Armenian Catechism*. Cambridge, MA: Harvard University Press, 1970.

Tihon, P. "Fins dernières (Méditation des)." *Dictionnaire de spiritualité*, V. Paris, 1964. Coll. 362-4: 'Influene d'Augustin et de Grégoire le Grand.'

Ullmann, Walter. *A Short History of the Papacy in the Middle Ages*. London: Methuen & Co., 1972.

Vailhé, S. "Le Titre de Patriarche Oecuménique avant St. Grégoire le Grand." *Échos d'Orient* 11 (1908): 65-70.

Valori, Aldo. *Gregorio Magno*. Torino: Societá editrice internazionale, 1955.

Verhelst, D. "La préhistoire des conceptions d'Adson concernant l'Antichrist." *Recherches de théologie ancienne et médiévale* 40 (1973): 52-103.

Vogel, Cyrile. "Deux consequences de 'eschatologie gregorienne': La multipication des messes privées et les moines-prêtres." In *Grégoire le Grand*, eds., Jacques Fontaine, Robert Gillet and Stan Pellistrandi, 267-76. Paris: Éditions du centre national de la recherche scientifique, 1984.

Wallace-Hadrill, J. M. *The Barbarian West A.D. 400-1000*. New York: Harper &

Brothers, 1962.

Wasselynck, H. "La part des Moralia in Iob de san Grégoire le Grand dans le Miscellanea victorins." *Melange de Science religieuse* 10 (1953): 287-94.

— "La voix dún Père de l'Église. L'orientation eschatologique de la vie chrétienne d'apres S. Grégoire le Grand." In *Assemblées du Seigneur*, I ser., 2, 66-80. Bruges: Biblica, 1962.

— "Les compilations des Moralia in Iob du VII au XII siecle." *Recherches de Théologie ancienne et médiévale* 29 (1962): 5-32.

— "Les Moralia in Iob dans les ouvrages de morale du Haut Moyen Age latin." *Recherches de Théologie ancienne et médiévale* 31 (1964): 5-13.

Weber, L. *Hauptfragen der Moraltheologie Gregors des Grossen. Ein Bild altchristlichen.* Lebensführung, Paradosis 1. Fribourg en Suisse: Paulusdruckerei, 1947.

Wilkins, Walter J. "'Submitting the Neck of Your Mind': Gregory the Great and Women of Power." *Catholic Historical Review* 77 (1991): 583-94.

Zancan, P. *Floro e Livio.* Padua: Casa editrice dott. A. Milani, 1942.

Zimdars-Swartz, Sandra. "A Confluence of Imagery: Exegesis and Christology according to Gregory the Great." In *Grégoire le Grand*, eds. Jacques Fontaine, Robert Gillet and Stan Pellistrandi, 327-35. Paris: Éditions du centre national de la recherche scientifique, 1986.

Zinn, Grover A. "Sound, Silence and Word in the Spirituality of Gregory the Great," In *Grégoire le Grand*, eds., Jacques Fontaine, Robert Gillet and Stan Pellistrandi, 367-75. Paris: Éditions du centre national de la recherche scientifique, 1986.

— "Exegesis and Spirituality in the Writings of Gregory the Great." In *Gregory the Great: A Symposium*, ed. John C. Cavadini, 168-80. Notre Dame, IN: University of Notre Dame Press, 1995.

Index

Studies in Christian History and Thought
(All titles uniform with this volume)
Dates in bold are of projected publication

David Bebbington
Holiness in Nineteenth-Century England

David Bebbington stresses the relationship of movements of spirituality to changes in their cultural setting, especially the legacies of the Enlightenment and Romanticism. He shows that these broad shifts in ideological mood had a profound effect on the ways in which piety was conceptualized and practised. Holiness was intimately bound up with the spirit of the age.

2000 / 0-85364-981-2 / viii + 98pp

J. William Black
Reformation Pastors
Richard Baxter and the Ideal of the Reformed Pastor

This work examines Richard Baxter's *Gildas Salvianus, The Reformed Pastor* (1656) and explores each aspect of his pastoral strategy in light of his own concern for 'reformation' and in the broader context of Edwardian, Elizabethan and early Stuart pastoral ideals and practice.

2003 / 1-84227-190-3 / xxii + 308pp

James Bruce
Prophecy, Miracles, Angels, *and* Heavenly Light?
The Eschatology, Pneumatology and Missiology of Adomnán's Life of Columba

This book surveys approaches to the marvellous in hagiography, providing the first critique of Plummer's hypothesis of Irish saga origin. It then analyses the uniquely systematized phenomena in the *Life of Columba* from Adomnán's seventh-century theological perspective, identifying the coming of the eschatological Kingdom as the key to understanding.

2004 / 1-84227-227-6 / xviii + 286pp

Colin J. Bulley
The Priesthood of Some Believers
Developments from the General to the Special Priesthood in the Christian Literature of the First Three Centuries

The first in-depth treatment of early Christian texts on the priesthood of all believers shows that the developing priesthood of the ordained related closely to the division between laity and clergy and had deleterious effects on the practice of the general priesthood.

2000 / 1-84227-034-6 / xii + 336pp

Anthony R. Cross (ed.)
Ecumenism and History
Studies in Honour of John H.Y. Briggs
This collection of essays examines the inter-relationships between the two fields in which Professor Briggs has contributed so much: history—particularly Baptist and Nonconformist—and the ecumenical movement. With contributions from colleagues and former research students from Britain, Europe and North America, *Ecumenism and History* provides wide-ranging studies in important aspects of Christian history, theology and ecumenical studies.
2002 / 1-84227-135-0 / xx + 362pp

Maggi Dawn
Confessions of an Inquiring Spirit
Form as Constitutive of Meaning in S.T. Coleridge's Theological Writing
This study of Coleridge's *Confessions* focuses on its confessional, epistolary and fragmentary form, suggesting that attention to these features significantly affects its interpretation. Bringing a close study of these three literary forms, the author suggests ways in which they nuance the text with particular understandings of the Trinity, and of a kenotic christology. Some parallels are drawn between Romantic and postmodern dilemmas concerning the authority of the biblical text.
2006 / 1-84227-255-1 / approx. 224 pp

Ruth Gouldbourne
The Flesh and the Feminine
Gender and Theology in the Writings of Caspar Schwenckfeld
Caspar Schwenckfeld and his movement exemplify one of the radical communities of the sixteenth century. Challenging theological and liturgical norms, they also found themselves challenging social and particularly gender assumptions. In this book, the issues of the relationship between radical theology and the understanding of gender are considered.
2005 / 1-84227-048-6 / approx. 304pp

Crawford Gribben
Puritan Millennialism
Literature and Theology, 1550–1682
Puritan Millennialism surveys the growth, impact and eventual decline of puritan millennialism throughout England, Scotland and Ireland, arguing that it was much more diverse than has frequently been suggested. This Paternoster edition is revised and extended from the original 2000 text.
2007 / 1-84227-372-8 / approx. 320pp

Galen K. Johnson
Prisoner of Conscience
John Bunyan on Self, Community and Christian Faith
This is an interdisciplinary study of John Bunyan's understanding of conscience across his autobiographical, theological and fictional writings, investigating whether conscience always deserves fidelity, and how Bunyan's view of conscience affects his relationship both to modern Western individualism and historic Christianity.

2003 / 1-84227-223-3 / xvi + 236pp

R.T. Kendall
Calvin and English Calvinism to 1649
The author's thesis is that those who formed the Westminster Confession of Faith, which is regarded as Calvinism, in fact departed from John Calvin on two points: (1) the extent of the atonement and (2) the ground of assurance of salvation.

1997 / 0-85364-827-1 / xii + 264pp

Timothy Larsen
Friends of Religious Equality
Nonconformist Politics in Mid-Victorian England
During the middle decades of the nineteenth century the English Nonconformist community developed a coherent political philosophy of its own, of which a central tenet was the principle of religious equality (in contrast to the stereotype of Evangelical Dissenters). The Dissenting community fought for the civil rights of Roman Catholics, non-Christians and even atheists on an issue of principle which had its flowering in the enthusiastic and undivided support which Nonconformity gave to the campaign for Jewish emancipation. This reissued study examines the political efforts and ideas of English Nonconformists during the period, covering the whole range of national issues raised, from state education to the Crimean War. It offers a case study of a theologically conservative group defending religious pluralism in the civic sphere, showing that the concept of religious equality was a grand vision at the centre of the political philosophy of the Dissenters.

2007 / 1-84227-402-3 / x + 300pp

Byung-Ho Moon
Christ the Mediator of the Law
Calvin's Christological Understanding of the Law as the Rule of Living and Life-Giving

This book explores the coherence between Christology and soteriology in Calvin's theology of the law, examining its intellectual origins and his position on the concept and extent of Christ's mediation of the law. A comparative study between Calvin and contemporary Reformers—Luther, Bucer, Melancthon and Bullinger—and his opponent Michael Servetus is made for the purpose of pointing out the unique feature of Calvin's Christological understanding of the law.

2005 / 1-84227-318-3 / approx. 370pp

John Eifion Morgan-Wynne
Holy Spirit and Religious Experience in Christian Writings, c.AD 90–200
This study examines how far Christians in the third to fifth generations (c.AD 90–200) attributed their sense of encounter with the divine presence, their sense of illumination in the truth or guidance in decision-making, and their sense of ethical empowerment to the activity of the Holy Spirit in their lives.

2005 / 1-84227-319-1 / approx. 350pp

James I. Packer
The Redemption and Restoration of Man in the Thought of Richard Baxter
James I. Packer provides a full and sympathetic exposition of Richard Baxter's doctrine of humanity, created and fallen; its redemption by Christ Jesus; and its restoration in the image of God through the obedience of faith by the power of the Holy Spirit.

2002 / 1-84227-147-4 / 432pp

Andrew Partington,
Church and State
The Contribution of the Church of England Bishops to the House of Lords
during the Thatcher Years

In *Church and State*, Andrew Partington argues that the contribution of the Church of England bishops to the House of Lords during the Thatcher years was overwhelmingly critical of the government; failed to have a significant influence in the public realm; was inefficient, being undertaken by a minority of those eligible to sit on the Bench of Bishops; and was insufficiently moral and spiritual in its content to be distinctive. On the basis of this, and the likely reduction of the number of places available for Church of England bishops in a fully reformed Second Chamber, the author argues for an evolution in the Church of England's approach to the service of its bishops in the House of Lords. He proposes the Church of England works to overcome the genuine obstacles which hinder busy diocesan bishops from contributing to the debates of the House of Lords and to its life more informally.
2005 / 1-84227-334-5 / approx. 324pp

Michael Pasquarello III
God's Ploughman
Hugh Latimer: A 'Preaching Life' (1490–1555)

This construction of a 'preaching life' situates Hugh Latimer within the larger religious, political and intellectual world of late medieval England. Neither biography, intellectual history, nor analysis of discrete sermon texts, this book is a work of homiletic history which draws from the details of Latimer's milieu to construct an interpretive framework for the preaching performances that formed the core of his identity as a religious reformer. Its goal is to illumine the practical wisdom embodied in the content, form and style of Latimer's preaching, and to recapture a sense of its overarching purpose, movement, and transforming force during the reform of sixteenth-century England.
2006 / 1-84227-336-1 / approx. 250pp

Alan P.F. Sell
Enlightenment, Ecumenism, Evangel
Theological Themes and Thinkers 1550–2000

This book consists of papers in which such interlocking topics as the Enlightenment, the problem of authority, the development of doctrine, spirituality, ecumenism, theological method and the heart of the gospel are discussed. Issues of significance to the church at large are explored with special reference to writers from the Reformed and Dissenting traditions.
2005 / 1-84227-330-2 / xviii + 422pp

Alan P.F. Sell
Hinterland Theology
Some Reformed and Dissenting Adjustments
Many books have been written on theology's 'giants' and significant trends, but what of those lesser-known writers who adjusted to them? In this book some hinterland theologians of the British Reformed and Dissenting traditions, who followed in the wake of toleration, the Evangelical Revival, the rise of modern biblical criticism and Karl Barth, are allowed to have their say. They include Thomas Ridgley, Ralph Wardlaw, T.V. Tymms and N.H.G. Robinson.
2006 / 1-84227-331-0 / approx. 350pp

Alan P.F. Sell and Anthony R. Cross (eds)
Protestant Nonconformity in the Twentieth Century
In this collection of essays scholars representative of a number of Nonconformist traditions reflect thematically on Nonconformists' life and witness during the twentieth century. Among the subjects reviewed are biblical studies, theology, worship, evangelism and spirituality, and ecumenism. Over and above its immediate interest, this collection provides a marker to future scholars and others wishing to know how some of their forebears assessed Nonconformity's contribution to a variety of fields during the century leading up to Christianity's third millennium.
2003 / 1-84227-221-7 / x + 398pp

Mark Smith
Religion in Industrial Society
Oldham and Saddleworth 1740–1865
This book analyses the way British churches sought to meet the challenge of industrialization and urbanization during the period 1740–1865. Working from a case-study of Oldham and Saddleworth, Mark Smith challenges the received view that the Anglican Church in the eighteenth century was characterized by complacency and inertia, and reveals Anglicanism's vigorous and creative response to the new conditions. He reassesses the significance of the centrally directed church reforms of the mid-nineteenth century, and emphasizes the importance of local energy and enthusiasm. Charting the growth of denominational pluralism in Oldham and Saddleworth, Dr Smith compares the strengths and weaknesses of the various Anglican and Nonconformist approaches to promoting church growth. He also demonstrates the extent to which all the churches participated in a common culture shaped by the influence of evangelicalism, and shows that active co-operation between the churches rather than denominational conflict dominated. This revised and updated edition of Dr Smith's challenging and original study makes an important contribution both to the social history of religion and to urban studies.
2006 / 1-84227-335-3 / approx. 300pp

Martin Sutherland
Peace, Toleration and Decay
The Ecclesiology of Later Stuart Dissent
This fresh analysis brings to light the complexity and fragility of the later Stuart Nonconformist consensus. Recent findings on wider seventeenth-century thought are incorporated into a new picture of the dynamics of Dissent and the roots of evangelicalism.
2003 / 1-84227-152-0 / xxii + 216pp

G. Michael Thomas
The Extent of the Atonement
A Dilemma for Reformed Theology from Calvin to the Consensus
A study of the way Reformed theology addressed the question, 'Did Christ die for all, or for the elect only?', commencing with John Calvin, and including debates with Lutheranism, the Synod of Dort and the teaching of Moïse Amyraut.
1997 / 0-85364-828-X / x + 278pp

David M. Thompson
Baptism, Church and Society in Britain from the Evangelical Revival to
Baptism, Eucharist and Ministry
The theology and practice of baptism have not received the attention they deserve. How important is faith? What does baptismal regeneration mean? Is baptism a bond of unity between Christians? This book discusses the theology of baptism and popular belief and practice in England and Wales from the Evangelical Revival to the publication of the World Council of Churches' consensus statement on *Baptism, Eucharist and Ministry* (1982).
2005 / 1-84227-393-0 / approx. 224pp

Mark D. Thompson
A Sure Ground on Which to Stand
The Relation of Authority and Interpretive Method of Luther's Approach to Scripture
The best interpreter of Luther is Luther himself. Unfortunately many modern studies have superimposed contemporary agendas upon this sixteenth-century Reformer's writings. This fresh study examines Luther's own words to find an explanation for his robust confidence in the Scriptures, a confidence that generated the famous 'stand' at Worms in 1521.
2004 / 1-84227-145-8 / xvi + 322pp

Carl R. Trueman and R.S. Clark (eds)
Protestant Scholasticism
Essays in Reassessment
Traditionally Protestant theology, between Luther's early reforming career and the dawn of the Enlightenment, has been seen in terms of decline and fall into the wastelands of rationalism and scholastic speculation. In this volume a number of scholars question such an interpretation. The editors argue that the development of post-Reformation Protestantism can only be understood when a proper historical model of doctrinal change is adopted. This historical concern underlies the subsequent studies of theologians such as Calvin, Beza, Olevian, Baxter, and the two Turrentini. The result is a significantly different reading of the development of Protestant Orthodoxy, one which both challenges the older scholarly interpretations and clichés about the relationship of Protestantism to, among other things, scholasticism and rationalism, and which demonstrates the fruitfulness of the new, historical approach.
1999 / 0-85364-853-0 / xx + 344pp

Shawn D. Wright
Our Sovereign Refuge
The Pastoral Theology of Theodore Beza
Our Sovereign Refuge is a study of the pastoral theology of the Protestant reformer who inherited the mantle of leadership in the Reformed church from John Calvin. Countering a common view of Beza as supremely a 'scholastic' theologian who deviated from Calvin's biblical focus, Wright uncovers a new portrait. He was not a cold and rigid academic theologian obsessed with probing the eternal decrees of God. Rather, by placing him in his pastoral context and by noting his concerns in his pastoral and biblical treatises, Wright shows that Beza was fundamentally a committed Christian who was troubled by the vicissitudes of life in the second half of the sixteenth century. He believed that the biblical truth of the supreme sovereignty of God alone could support Christians on their earthly pilgrimage to heaven. This pastoral and personal portrait forms the heart of Wright's argument.
2004 / 1-84227-252-7 / xviii + 308pp

Paternoster:
thinking faith

Paternoster
9 Holdom Avenue,
Bletchley,
Milton Keynes MK1 1QR,
United Kingdom
Web: www.authenticmedia.co.uk/paternoster

July 2005